QUR'ANIC SCIENCES

AN INTRODUCTION TO

QUR'ANIC SCIENCES

('ULŪM AL-QUR'AN)

Abbas Jaffer

Masuma Jaffer

With foreword by

Mohammad Saeed Bahmanpour

British Library Cataloguing-in-Publication Data

A catalogue record for this book is available from the British Library.

ISBN 1-904063-30-6 (pbk)

This edition first published in 2009

Published by

ICAS Press

133 High Road, Willesden, London NW10 2SW.

www.islamic-college.ac.uk

CONTENTS

Foreword ix

Preface xiii

CHAPTER 1: The Qur'anic Sciences 1

1.1 - Definitions and Scope of Study 2
1.2 - Major Works in the Qur'anic Sciences 4

CHAPTER 2: The Qur'an 9

2.1 - The Status of the Qur'an 9
2.2 - The Language of the Qur'an 10
2.3 - Etymology of "Qur'an" 11
2.4 - The Names of the Qur'an 12
2.5 - Divisions of the Text of the Qur'an and their Significance 15
2.6 - The Verses of Prostration 17
2.7 - "Foreign" Words in the Qur'an 17

CHAPTER 3: Revelation (*Waḥy*) 20

3.1 - Revelation in Qur'anic Terminology 22
3.2 - Definition of *Waḥy* and *Ilhām* 26
3.3 - The Difference Between *Waḥy* and *Ilhām* 27
3.4 - *Waḥy* as Mentioned in the Qur'an 28
3.5 - *Waḥy* and the Prophets of God 31
3.6 - Some Myths About Revelation 36

CHAPTER 4: The Revelation of the Qur'an 44

4.1 - The Beginning of the Revelation 45
4.2 - The Beginning of the Divine Commission (*Al-Bi'tha*) 45
4.3 - Reconciliation Between the Dates of the Divine Commission (*Al-Bi'tha*) and the Night of Decree (*Laylat al-Qadr*) 46
4.4 - The Stages of Revelation 53
4.5 - The Benefits of Gradual Revelation 55

CHAPTER 5: Occasions of Revelation: *Asbāb al-Nuzūl* 62

5.1 - Meaning of *Asbāb al-Nuzūl* 63
5.2 - The Difference Between the Terms, "Occasion of Revelation" (*Sabab al-Nuzūl*) and "Reason For

Revelation" (*Sha'n al-Nuzūl*) 63
5.3 - Types of Occasions of Revelation 64
5.4 - The Importance of Knowing the Occasion of Revelation of a Verse 67
5.5 - The Universal and Eternal Application of Verses That Had a Particular Occasion of Revelation 67
5.6 - Examples of When the Knowledge of the Occasion of Revelation has Helped in the Understanding of Verses 69
5.7 - Reliability of *Asbāb al-Nuzūl* 71

CHAPTER 6: Verses and Chapters of the Qur'an **75**

6.1 - Verses of the Qur'an (*Āya* pl. *Āyāt*) 75
6.2 - The Present Arrangement of the Verses 77
6.3 - Chapters of the Qur'an (*Sūra* pl. *Suwar*) 78
6.4 - The Names of Chapters 79
6.5 - Classification of Chapters 80
6.6 - The Openings of Chapters 81
6.7 - The Unconnected Letters: Al-Ḥurūf al-Muqaṭṭaʿāt 84
6.8 - The First Verses of the Qur'an to be Revealed 91
6.9 - Was there an Intermission in the Revelation ? 93
6.10 - The Order of Revelation of the Chapters of the Qur'an 94
6.11 - The Last Chapter of the Qur'an to be Revealed 95
6.12 - The Last Verse of the Qur'an to be Revealed 96
6.13 - Meccan and Medinan Chapters and Verses 98

CHAPTER 7: The Compilation of the Qur'an **109**

7.1 - The Scribes of the Prophet ﷺ 112
7.2 - Recording of the Verses 113
7.3 - The Qur'an at the Time of the Prophet ﷺ 115
7.4 - The Collection at the Time of Abū Bakr 116
7.5 - The Unification of Codices by ʿUthmān 118
7.6 - Was the Order of the Chapters in the Qur'an Rearranged at the Time of ʿUthmān? 120
7.7 - The Original Script of the Qur'an and its Evolution 124
7.8 - The Qur'an in the Calligraphy of ʿUthmān Ṭāhā 130
7.9 - The Qur'an in Braille 131

CHAPTER 8: The Absence of Distortion (*Taḥrīf*) in the Qur'anic Text **134**

8.1 - Lexical and Technical Definitions of *Taḥrīf* 134
8.2 - A Critical Look at Traditions About *Taḥrīf* 139

8.3 - Evidence that the Qur'an is Free From *Taḥrīf* ... 143

CHAPTER 9: Abrogation (*Naskh*) and the Qur'an ... 147

9.1 - The Possibility of *Naskh* ... 148
9.2 - Definition of *Naskh* ... 150
9.3 - The Conditions For *Naskh* ... 152
9.4 - The Modes of *Naskh* in the Qur'an ... 153
9.5 - Abrogation in Creation (*Badā'*) ... 162
9.6 - Why is There no *Naskh* in the Post-Prophet Era? ... 164

CHAPTER 10: Definite and Indefinite Verses in the Qur'an: *Muḥkamāt* and *Mutashābihāt* ... 168

10.1 - Lexical Meanings of *Muḥkam* and *Mutashābih* ... 169
10.2 - The Term *Muḥkam* in the Qur'an. ... 170
10.3 - The Term *Mutashābih* in the Qur'an ... 170
10.4 - Qualities of the Definite and Indefinite Verses ... 172
10.5 - Indefinite Verses and How They Should be Understood ... 175
10.6 - The Danger of Following the Indefinite Verses ... 178
10.7 - The Wisdom of Having Indefinite Verses in the Qur'an ... 179
10.8 - Interpretation (*Ta'wīl*) ... 182

CHAPTER 11: The Recital of the Qur'an: *al-Qirā'a* ... 189

11.1 - The Different Groups of Readers ... 189
11.2 - Brief Details of the Seven Readers ... 192
11.3 - The Selection of the Seven Readers ... 196
11.4 - The Prerequisites for an Authentic Reading Style ... 197
11.5 - The Seven *Aḥruf* of the Qur'an ... 198
11.6 - The Science of *Tajwīd* ... 205

CHAPTER 12: The Miracle of the Qur'an *I'jāz al-Qur'an* ... 217

12.1 - The Qur'an Compared to Other Miracles ... 219
12.2 - An Overview of Works on *I'jāz* ... 220
12.3 - The Role of Miracles ... 220
12.4 - Aspects of the Miracle of the Qur'an ... 222
12.5 - The Challenge of the Qur'an ... 227
12.7 - The Hypothesis of *Sarfa* ... 228

CHAPTER 13: The Qur'an as a Literary Text ... 230

13.1 - The Style of the Qur'an ... 231

CHAPTER 14: The Qur'an in Translation ... 255

14.1 - The Challenges of Translation 255
14.2 - Challenges Particular to the Translation of the Qur'an 257
14.3 - The Early Qur'an Translations 261
14.4 - The Development of Translations in Western Languages 263
14.5 - English Translations by Muslim Scholars 274
APPENDIX 1 280
APPENDIX 2 282
APPENDIX 3 286
APPENDIX 4 288
SELECT BIBLIOGRAPHY 291
INDEX 293

FOREWORD

In the name of God, the Most Compassionate, the Most Merciful.

Sound understanding of the Qur'an requires some knowledge about general aspects of its verses before the seeker of this knowledge embarks on any attempt for exegesis (*tafsīr*), that is, explanation of the contents of the Qur'an. This general knowledge is the subject of a profound and long-lasting discipline called the "Qur'anic sciences," which developed simultaneously with the development of exegesis in the very early stages of the revelation.

The term "Qur'anic sciences" might be somewhat misleading, as it may be understood to indicate the science-related topics discussed in the Qur'an. It is reported from Abū Bakr ibn al-ʿArabī (d. 543/1148) that he believed that 77,450 different branches of science have been discussed in the Qur'an.[1] It is not certain how one is to verify this number of sciences, however, what is certain is that these are not the type of sciences that we mean here by the term "Qur'anic sciences". What we mean here are the qualities, attributes, aspects, or themes which could be attached to the Qur'an as a whole or to certain groups of its verses before discussing their contents. Hence we may include in these sciences the process of revelation, its beginning, its quality, and its duration; the collection of the Qur'an and the time it was compiled in written form; the inimitable nature of its verses; the opening and the ending of its chapters and their order and continuity; concepts which determine the type of the verse like abrogation, restrictedness, ambiguity and clarity, generality and particularity; discussions related to different modes of recitation of the Qur'an; and so forth.

As the process of revelation was brought to an end by the demise of the Prophet ﷺ, obviously some Companions stood out against others in their knowledge of the Qur'an and its exegesis. The scholars of this field agree that only ten of the Companions had reliable and scholarly knowledge of exegesis among whom four assumed the leading and uncontested position in their scholarship. These were ʿAlī b. Abī Ṭālib, Ubayy b. Kaʿb, ʿAbdullāh b. Masʿud and ʿAbdullāh b. ʿAbbās. However, it is well documented that the three latter scholars deferred to ʿAlī's superiority in all and every aspect of this field. It goes without question that the deepest concepts of exegesis and the most difficult aspects of the Qurʾanic sciences were expounded by ʿAlī as it is reported in several of his teachings and statements. The following is an example of a statement which alludes to different concepts upon which the Qurʾanic sciences were based and built during the centuries to come.

> [The Prophet ﷺ left] the Book of your Lord with you; he clarified [for you] its permissions and prohibitions, its obligations and meritorious options, its repealing verses and its repealed cases, its discretional verdicts and its decisive edicts, its particular and its general rulings, its lessons and illustrations, its qualified and unqualified [statements], its definite and indefinite verses, detailing its abbreviations and clarifying its obscurities.
>
> In it there are some verses the knowledge of which is obligatory as a covenant and others the ignorance of which is allowed for the servant. It also contains obligations which are established in the Book but its repeal is known from the *sunna*; and what is obligatory to take in the *sunna* but the leave is granted to abandon it in the Book; and what is obligatory in its time but not so in the future.[2]

Al-Hāfiẓ ibn ʿUqda (d. 333/944) has reported a whole volume from ʿAlī on Qurʾanic sciences in which he has referred to sixty different aspects of the verses of the Qurʾan in different contexts. Multiple examples are provided for each and every aspect. This existence of the book is reported through Jaʿfar al-Ṣādiq (d. 148/760) who before reporting those aspects warns his followers regarding ignorance of such knowledge saying

> He has no knowledge of the Qurʾan who cannot distinguish in the Book of God between the *abrogating* and the *abrogated* [verse], nor between *general* and *particular*, and *definite* and *indefinite*, and *permissions* and *obligations*, and Meccan [what is revealed in Mecca] and Medinan [what is revealed in Medina], and the *causes of revelation*, and the verses which refer to the knowledge of *decree* and *measure* [*qaḍāʾ* and *qadar*], and those in which there is *precedence*

> [*taqdīm*] and *deferment* [*taʾkhīr*], and what belongs to the *beginning* [*ibtidaʾ*] and belongs to the *ending* [*intihāʾ*], and *question* and *answer*, and *disjunction* [*qaṭʿ*] and *conjunction* [*waṣl*], and the general term from which an exclusion is made [*al-mustathnā minh*].[3]

It is unfortunate that despite the great knowledge of ʿAlī in this field and the huge contribution of the Prophet's ﷺ household in this regard, most books written on the topic have chosen to ignore or to diminish their role and their scholarly knowledge which helped develop and advance this science. It is therefore with great pleasure that we see that Abbas and Masuma Jaffer have taken a new approach in this field and have provided us with a textbook which has paid due attention to the contribution of the Prophet's ﷺ household and have critically analysed some concepts and areas in these sciences which have been traditionally taken for granted. This groundbreaking approach in the related literature written in the English language has added value to the well researched and beautifully presented contents of their work. Their new approach will certainly pave the way for new avenues of research in this field and will open new windows to students of this subjects which were previously neglected.

In the field of the Qurʾanic sciences written contributions can generally be divided into four categories.

1. The books which are dedicated to one particular aspect of the Qurʾanic sciences like the science of recitation, the science of abrogation, the miraculous nature of the Qurʾan, or the definite and indefinite verses.

2. The books which cover a collection of selected topics on the aforementioned sciences.

3. Contributions like *Al-Burhān* of Al-Zarkashī and *Al-Itqān* of Al-Suyūṭī, which have attempted to cover all topics of the Qurʾanic sciences.

4. Introductions to the books of exegesis in which the exegetes have

tried to give a summary of the Qur'anic sciences as a necessary prelude to their exegesis, like what we find in the introduction to *Majma' al-Bayān*.

The present book fits into the second of the four categories above. It covers the most important areas of the Qur'anic sciences and leaves out only those parts which are beyond the grasp of an average undergraduate student. The selection of the topics and the arrangement of their order are done in such a way as to make the text follow a logical sequence and to flow in a harmonious order. I am sure that students of the Qur'anic sciences will find the present book useful and that scholars will find it inspiring.

Mohammad Saeed Bahmanpour
London, 12 June 2008

NOTES

[1] Al-Zurqānī, *Manāhil al-'Irfān fī 'Ulūm al-Qur'an*, Beirut: Dār al-Kutub al-'Arabī, 1415, vol. 1, p. 16.
[2] Nahj al-Balāgha, sermon 1.
[3] Sayyid Muhsin Al-Amīn, *A'yan al-Shī'a*, Beirut: Dār al-Ta'āruf, n.d., vol. 1, p. 91.

PREFACE

In the name of God, the Most Compassionate, the Most Merciful. All Praise belongs to God, the Sustainer of the Worlds. And may His blessings flow abundantly to his last Messenger, Muhammad ﷺ and his progeny and his righteous companions.

The idea for this book came to us when we were ourselves studying *ulūm al-Qur'an,* or Qur'anic sciences, at the Islamic College in 2002. At the time, we were struck by the paucity of material available about Qur'anic sciences in English, especially texts that reflected the vast contribution of Shī'a scholars and exegetes in this field. It seemed that the authors of the existing English books on *'ulūm al-Qur'an* – such as Von Denffer and Yasir Qadhi – were unaware of, or had chosen to ignore, this rich corpus of literature in their works. At that time, we resolved to write a more balanced account, one that was representative of all the Muslim scholars who have worked in the field of Qur'anic studies and exegesis.

First and foremost we must thank God, for having given us the strength and perseverance to complete this project, much of which was completed during a sabbatical year in Qom. We would like to thank our colleagues and teachers, both at the Islamic College and in Qom, for their continuous support and helpful suggestions. A special mention is due to Dr M S Bahmanpour, for his painstaking and patient reading of the text and we are indebted to him for his valuable input to the final draft.

As always, we thank our three precious children, Shaahid Hasan, Tahira Mahdiyya and Mujtaba Husain, for their patience and indulgence while their parents debated points of *'ulūm al-Qur'an* at the oddest of moments. In the end, we would like to thank each other for what we hope the reader will find to be a fruitful collaboration.

A J & M J

London, September 2006

1

THE QUR'ANIC SCIENCES

The Prophet ﷺ presented the Qur'an as his miracle and it was the cornerstone of his mission. As a result, Muslims have always tried to adhere to its teachings and scholars have dedicated their whole lives to better understand its timeless messages.

In addition to studying the text itself, scholars have meticulously examined other aspects of this Divine book, such as the history of its compilation, the features of its composition and the details of its verses. Over time, this study has evolved into a separate branch of Qur'anic studies – known as the Qur'anic sciences, or *'ulūm al-Qur'an* – which is distinct from the exegesis, or *tafsīr*, of the Qur'an.

Being familiar with the Qur'anic sciences is an indispensable prelude to exegesis; indeed, many exegetes have begun their exegeses with a brief treatment of its main topics. However, for the English reader wishing to embark on a comprehensive study of *'ulūm al-Qur'an,* there are relatively few sources to refer to, especially those written by Muslims themselves. Some useful works are:

- *'Ulum al-Qur'an: Introduction to the Sciences of the Qur'an,* by Ahmad von Denffer, The Islamic Foundation, 1994.
- *An Introduction to the Sciences of the Qur'aan,* by Abu Ammaar Yasir Qadhi, Al-Hidaayah Publishing and Distribution, 1999.
- *An Approach to the Qur'anic Sciences,* by Mufti Muhammad Taqi Usmani, Darul Ishaat, 2000.

- *Introducing the Quran: How to Study and Understand the Quran,* by Dr Hasanuddin Ahmed, Goodword Books, 2004.

While the authors of these books have done a commendable work in presenting the salient aspects of this science to English readers, they have largely or completely ignored the enormous and important contribution of past and contemporary Shīʿa exegetes and researchers in this field, such as Ṭabrisī, Maʿrifat and Ṭabāṭabāʾī. Amongst other things, this book attempts to redress the balance, so that the reader may benefit from important material that has hitherto largely only been available in Arabic and Persian.

1.1 - DEFINITIONS AND SCOPE OF STUDY

The study of the Qur'an can be broadly divided into two aspects: a study of information about the Qur'an, and a study of the information derived from the Qur'an. When we look at Qur'anic sciences or *ʿulūm al-Qur'an,* we are concerned with the former, that is, the topics to do with information about the Qur'an. The scholars have defined these topics in different ways. For example, Zarkashī mentions 47 topics,[1] while Al-Suyūṭī lists 80.[2] In general, the subject matter covered by the discipline of *ʿulūm al-Qur'an* includes the following:

THE GENERAL DETAILS OF THE QUR'AN

- The names of the Qur'an
- The arrangement and number of chapters and verses in the Qur'an
- The unconnected letters at the beginning of some chapters (*al-ḥurūf al-muqaṭṭaʿāt*)
- The abrogated and the abrogating verses (*al-nāsikh wa al-mansūkh*)

THE HISTORY OF THE QUR'AN

- Revelation (*waḥy*) and the descent (*tanzīl*) of the Qur'an
- The occasions of revelation (*asbāb al-nuzūl*)
- The Meccan (*Makkī*) and Medinan (*Madanī*) revelations
- The period and order of the revelation of the Qur'an
- The collection and compilation of the Qur'an (*jamʿ al-Qur'an*)
- The scribes of the Qur'an
- The unification of its codices
- The orthography of the Qur'anic text

THE RECITATION OF THE QUR'AN

- The etiquette of reciting the Qur'an
- The science of pronunciation (*tajwīd*)
- The variant readings the Qur'an (*qirā'a*)
- The reasons for the variant readings
- The blessings and reward for reciting the Qur'an

THE MIRACLE OF THE QUR'AN

- The protection of the Qur'an from alteration (*taḥrīf*)
- The inimitability (*iʿjāz*) of the Qur'an
- The eloquence of the Qur'an (*balāgha*)
- Lofty and timeless concepts mentioned in the Qur'an
- Coherence and consistency in the Qur'an
- True predictions about the future contained in the Qur'an

1.2 - MAJOR WORKS IN THE QUR'ANIC SCIENCES

During the lifetime of the Prophet ﷺ, he was the focus and reference for all the information about the Qur'an. The companions learned from him, and in turn taught others. After his demise, the most able source of the commentary and knowledge of the Qur'an was ʿAlī b. Abī Ṭālib.[3] Other companions also became specialists in the field, notably ʿAbdullāh b. al-ʿAbbās.

Towards the end of the first century of hijra, Muslim scholars began to produce written works on a variety of subjects, including the Qur'an. Usually, they would write a tract on just one aspect or science of the Qur'an. In early works, exegesis (*tafsīr*), was also considered as one of the sciences of the Qur'an. Some of the early scholars who wrote on the Qur'anic sciences are mentioned in the following sub-sections.[4]

FIRST CENTURY AFTER HIJRA

Maʿrifat writes that the first person who wrote a treatise on an aspect of the Qur'anic sciences was Yaḥyā b. Yaʿmar, (d. 89/707).[5] He was a student of Abū al-Aswad al-Du'alī, and wrote a book on the art of reciting the Qur'an, which mentioned the different readings prevailing at his time. Several other works are mentioned in the texts, but none of them remain extant, including a work by Ḥasan al-Baṣrī (d. 110/728), who wrote a book describing the qualities of the verses in the Qur'an.

SECOND CENTURY

- ʿAṭā' b. Muslim al-Khurāsānī (d. 135/752) wrote the first book about the abrogated and abrogating verses.
- Abān b. Taghlab (d. 141/758) wrote on the recital and meaning of uncommon words in the Qur'an.

- Muḥammad b. Sā'ab al-Kalbī (d. 146/763) wrote the first book on the ordinances (*aḥkām*) of the Qur'an.
- Maqātil b. Sulaymān (d. 150/767) wrote the first work on the indefinite verses of the Qur'an.

THIRD CENTURY

- Yaḥyā b. Ziyād – famously known as Al-Farrā' (d. 207/822) wrote a work on the lexical meanings of words and terms used in the Qur'an.
- Abū 'Ubayda Mu'ammar b. al-Muthannā (d. 209/824) wrote the first book on the inimitable nature (*i'jāz*) of the Qur'an.
- Abū Muḥammad 'Abdallāh b. Muslim (Ibn Qutayba) (d. 276/889) wrote several treatises on various aspects of *'ulūm al-Qur'an.*
- Muḥammad b. Junaid (d. 281/903) wrote a treatise on the parables of the Qur'an.

FOURTH CENTURY

- Muḥammad b. Yazīd al-Wasiṭī (d. 309/921) wrote on the inimitable and miraculous nature of the Qur'an.
- Abū Bakr b. Abī Dāwūd al-Sajistānī (d. 321/933) wrote *"Al-Maṣāḥif",* about the codices of the Qur'an, amongst many other works.
- Muḥammad b. Ya'qūb al-Kulaynī (d. 329/940) wrote about the distinctions (*faḍā'il*) of the Qur'an.
- Abū Ja'far Aḥmad b. Muḥammad al-Naḥḥās (d. 338/949) wrote a book about the additions of vowels and other diacritical marks to the Qur'anic text.
- In his *Al-Fihrist,* Ibn al-Nadīm records that there were over 100

books available about various aspects of Qur'anic studies by the end of the fourth century.[6] These comprised approximately:

a) 45 books on exegesis (*tafsīr*)

b) over 20 books on rhetoric (*maʿānī al-Qur'an*)

c) 6 books on terminology (*lughāt al-Qur'an*)

d) more than 20 books on recitation (*qirā'a*)

e) 6 books on orthography (*al-nuqaṭ wa al-shakl li'l Qur'an*)

f) 10 books on the indefinite verses (*mutashābih al-Qur'an*)

g) 18 books on abrogation (*al-nāsikh al-Qur'an wa mansūkhahu*)

FIFTH CENTURY ONWARDS

From the fifth century onwards, there was a great proliferation of works about the Qur'an. The two most important works from this period are:

1. *Al-Burhān fī ʿUlūm al-Qur'an* by the 8th century scholar, Badr al-Dīn Muḥammad b. ʿAbdallāh b. Bahādur al-Zarkashī (d. 794/1391). He was among the prominent scholars of the eighth century. He was born in Egypt in the year 745/1344. He taught jurisprudence and issued verdicts according to the Shāfiʿī school of thought. His book discusses 47 different disciplines of Qur'anic sciences.

2. *Al-Itqān fī ʿUlūm al-Qur'an* by the 9th century scholar, Jalāl al-Dīn ʿAbd al-Raḥmān al-Suyūṭī (d. 911/1505). He was born in Egypt, in the year 849/1445. He possessed mastery over all the narrative sciences, Qur'anic commentary, and other Islamic disciplines and left behind many valuable works to his credit. Presently, this work represents one of the most comprehensive and complete treatises on Qur'anic sciences that is at the disposal of research scholars.

For a long time after *Al-Itqān*, no major work on *ʿulūm al-Qur'an* appeared. However, from the last century onwards, several important works have been written, some of which are:

- The introduction to the exegesis, *Ālā al-Raḥmān*, by Muḥammad Jawād Balāghī (d. 1352/1933). This is a well-researched work that covers the main topics of the Qur'anic sciences and dispels many false notions and criticisms about the Qur'an.

- *Manāhil al-'Irfān fī 'Ulūm al-Qur'an*, by Muḥammad 'Abd al-'Azīm al-Zarkānī. This book is the recommended textbook for the study of the Qur'anic sciences at the al-Azhar University.

- *Mabāḥith fī 'Ulūm al-Qur'an*, by Dr Subḥī al-Ṣāliḥ. This is a brief study of some important topics in the Qur'anic sciences by this Lebanese scholar.

- *Tārīkh al-Qur'an*, by Abū 'Abdallāh Zanjānī.

- *Al-Bayān fī Tafsīr al-Qur'an*, by Abū al-Qāsim al-Khū'ī. In the introduction of this incomplete exegesis, there is a useful discussion on several topics of the Qur'anic sciences by this distinguished scholar.

- *Qur'an dar Islām*, by Muḥammad Ḥusain al-Ṭabāṭabā'ī. A brief summary of the main topics of the Qur'anic sciences by the eminent exegete and philosopher, and author of the important commentary, *Al-Mīzān*.

- *Al-Tamhīd fī 'Ulūm al-Qur'an*, by Muḥammad Hādī Ma'rifat. An encyclopaedic work, spanning 7 volumes by a contemporary scholar.

- *Mūjaz 'Ulūm al-Qur'an*, by Dr Dāwūd al-'Aṭṭār.

In addition to specialist books, all the canonical collections of traditions, both Sunnī and Shī'a, also contain important material about many aspects of the Qur'anic sciences.

NOTES

[1] Badr al-Dīn Zarkashī, *Al-Burhān fī 'Ulūm al-Qur'an,* vol. 1, p. 102.
[2] Jalāl al-Dīn Al-Suyūṭī, *Al-Itqān fī 'Ulūm al-Qur'an,* vol. 1, p. 20.
[3] *Al-Itqān,* vol. 2, p. 87; *Al-Burhān,* vol. 2, p. 157.
[4] For an exhaustive account of these scholars and their works, see Muḥammad Hādī Ma'rifat, *'Ulūm-e Qur'anī,* pp. 8 - 14.
[5] *'Ulūm-e Qur'anī,* p. 8.
[6] Ibn al-Nadīm, *Al-Fihrist,* p. 52 - 59.

2

THE QUR'AN

The Noble Qur'an is the final and most comprehensive revelation from Almighty God. It was transmitted to mankind through the Prophet Muhammad ﷺ – the last of His prophets – over a period of 23 years.

The Qur'an is unique amongst the heavenly-revealed books in that it has been faithfully preserved since its revelation in the 7th century CE. For the Muslims, it represents a link between man and his Creator, a book of guidance and wisdom in the form of laws, admonitions, parables, and rational arguments. About this great bounty and blessing of mankind, God says:

﴿ يَـٰٓأَيُّهَا ٱلنَّاسُ قَدْ جَآءَتْكُم مَّوْعِظَةٌ مِّن رَّبِّكُمْ وَشِفَآءٌ لِّمَا
فِى ٱلصُّدُورِ وَهُدًى وَرَحْمَةٌ لِّلْمُؤْمِنِينَ ﴿٥٧﴾ ﴾

O mankind! There has indeed come to you an admonition from your Lord and a healing for what is in the breasts and a guidance and a mercy for the believers. (Yūnus, 10:57)

2.1 - THE STATUS OF THE QUR'AN

The lofty status of the Qur'an is evident from the multitude of narrations that mention its excellences, the merits for reciting its verses and pondering over their meaning, and the reward for teaching it to others. Some of these narrations, all from the Prophet ﷺ, are reproduced below:

1. The eminence of the Qur'an over other speech is like the eminence of God over His creatures.[1]

2. The best amongst you are those who learn the Qur'an and teach it to others.[2]

3. To the one who is intimate with the Qur'an, it will be said, "Recite, and ascend! And recite it the way you recited it in the world, because your station in the hereafter is equal to the verses you were familiar with."[3]

4. The simile of a person who has nothing of the Qur'an in his heart is that of a house that lies in ruins.[4]

5. When you desire for God to converse directly with you, recite the Qur'an.[5]

6. Whoever listens attentively when the Qur'an is recited is rewarded two-fold and every verse a person recites with care is manifested as a light that guides him on the day of judgement.[6]

2.2 - THE LANGUAGE OF THE QUR'AN

Speech and the use of language are the easiest way to communicate ideas and concepts. The use of speech is integral to man's existence, and stems from God's mercy:

﴿ ٱلرَّحْمَٰنُ ۝١ عَلَّمَ ٱلْقُرْءَانَ ۝٢ خَلَقَ ٱلْإِنسَٰنَ ۝٣ عَلَّمَهُ ٱلْبَيَانَ ۝٤ ﴾

The Beneficent. Taught the Qur'an. He created man. Taught him the mode of expression.
(Al-Raḥmān, 55:1-4)

For the purpose of guidance, the communication from God had to be in a language and words that the people could understand. Thus, each Prophet ﷺ brought the Divine message in the language of his own people:

﴿وَمَآ أَرۡسَلۡنَا مِن رَّسُولٍ إِلَّا بِلِسَانِ قَوۡمِهِۦ لِيُبَيِّنَ لَهُمۡۖ﴾

And We did not send any messenger but with the language of his people, so that he might explain to them clearly.... (Ibrāhīm, 14:4)

The Qur'an was sent down to the people of Arabia and so was revealed in plain and lucid Arabic:

﴿إِنَّآ أَنزَلۡنَٰهُ قُرۡءَٰنًا عَرَبِيّٗا لَّعَلَّكُمۡ تَعۡقِلُونَ ٢﴾

Indeed We have revealed it – an Arabic Qur'an – that you may understand. (Yūsuf, 12:2)

Its message was clear, it did not speak in riddles:

﴿قُرۡءَانًا عَرَبِيًّا غَيۡرَ ذِي عِوَجٖ لَّعَلَّهُمۡ يَتَّقُونَ ٢٨﴾

An Arabic Qur'an without any crookedness, that they may guard (against evil). (Al-Zumar, 39:28)

of course, the depth of an individual's understanding and appreciation of the Divine speech would depend on his intellectual and spiritual capacity and preparedness, as is evident from the following Qur'anic parable:

﴿أَنزَلَ مِنَ ٱلسَّمَآءِ مَآءٗ فَسَالَتۡ أَوۡدِيَةُۢ بِقَدَرِهَا﴾

He sends down water from the cloud, then watercourses flow (with water) according to their measure.... (Al-Ra'd, 13:17)

2.3 - ETYMOLOGY OF "QUR'AN"

There are several opinions about the etymology of the word "Qur'an". Ṭabarī (d. 310/922) writes that it is derived from *qara'a*, which means "to read"; as the verbal noun, Qur'an would thus mean "the reading".

Al-ʿAshʿarī (d. 324/935) said that the word Qur'an was from the root *qarana* which means "to combine" or "to associate". Thus, the Qur'an was so named because it is formed from the combination of chapters.[7]

Al-Shāfiʿī (d. 204/819) held the view that the word Qur'an, just like *Tawrāt* or *Injīl*, was a proper noun that was not derived from any word, and denoted the speech of God.[8]

Al-Farā' writes that the Qur'an derives from *qarā'in*, meaning "to resemble". Thus, it is called the Qur'an because its verses resemble one another in eloquence. (According to these three definitions, "Qur'an" is pronounced as "Quran", that is, without the *hamza*).

In the Qur'an itself, the word "Qur'an" refers to the revelation from God in the broad sense and is not always restricted to mean a book, as the following verse indicates.

﴿ وَنُنَزِّلُ مِنَ ٱلْقُرْءَانِ مَا هُوَ شِفَآءٌ وَرَحْمَةٌ لِّلْمُؤْمِنِينَ ﴾

And We reveal of the Qur'an that which is a healing and a mercy to the believers. (Al-Isrā', 17:82)

Lastly, the word "Qur'an" refers only to God's revelation to Prophet Muḥammad ﷺ.

2.4 - THE NAMES OF THE QUR'AN

The Qur'an has referred to itself by five names, which are: [9]

1. QUR'AN

This name is mentioned 58 times, and is the most common name for the Divine revelation, both in the Ḥadīth literature as well as amongst the Muslims. Examples of the usage of this name are as follows:

﴿ إِنَّهُۥ لَقُرْءَانٌ كَرِيمٌ ﴿٧٧﴾ ﴾

Indeed it is an honoured Qur'an. (Al-Wāqi'a, 56:77)

and,

﴿ فَإِذَا قَرَأْتَ ٱلْقُرْءَانَ فَٱسْتَعِذْ بِٱللَّهِ مِنَ ٱلشَّيْطَٰنِ ٱلرَّجِيمِ ﴿٩٨﴾ ﴾

So when you recite the Qur'an, seek refuge with God from the accursed Satan. (Al-Naḥl, 16:98)

2. *FURQĀN* (CRITERION)

This name is mentioned 7 times. Out of these, twice the name refers to the *Tawrāt* and the rest of the time to the Qur'an itself, for example:

﴿ تَبَارَكَ ٱلَّذِى نَزَّلَ ٱلْفُرْقَانَ عَلَىٰ عَبْدِهِۦ لِيَكُونَ لِلْعَـٰلَمِينَ نَذِيرًا ۝١ ﴾

Blessed is He Who sent down the Furqān upon His servant that he may be a warner to the nations. (Al-Furqān, 25:1)

This word is derived from *faraqa* – to distinguish or to separate. And indeed, the Qur'an is the criterion between truth and falsehood. Another meaning is the ability to discern truth and falsehood, as in the verse:

﴿ يَـٰٓأَيُّهَا ٱلَّذِينَ ءَامَنُوٓا۟ إِن تَتَّقُوا۟ ٱللَّهَ يَجْعَل لَّكُمْ فُرْقَانًا ﴾

O you who believe! If you are careful of (your duty to) God, He will grant you furqān. (Al-Anfāl, 8:29)

3. *KITĀB* (BOOK)

This name occurs approximately 250 times in the Qur'an, in most cases referring to the Qur'an itself. Examples are:

﴿ الٓمٓ ۝١ ذَٰلِكَ ٱلْكِتَـٰبُ لَا رَيْبَ ۛ فِيهِ ۛ هُدًى لِّلْمُتَّقِينَ ۝٢ ﴾

Alif Lām Mīm. This Book, there is no doubt in it, is a guide to those who guard (against evil) (Al-Baqara, 2:1-2)

and,

﴿ الٓر ۚ تِلْكَ ءَايَـٰتُ ٱلْكِتَـٰبِ وَقُرْءَانٍ مُّبِينٍ ۝١ ﴾

Alif Lām Rā. These are the verses of the Book and (of) a Qur'an that makes (things) clear. (Al-Ḥijr, 15:1)

4. *DHIKR* (REMEMBRANCE, NARRATIVE)

This name occurs 55 times in the Qur'an, and in many of these cases, it refers to the Qur'an, for example:

﴿ إِنَّا نَحْنُ نَزَّلْنَا ٱلذِّكْرَ وَإِنَّا لَهُۥ لَحَـٰفِظُونَ ۝٩ ﴾

Surely We have revealed the Reminder and We will most surely be its guardian.
(Al-Ḥijr, 15:9)

and,

﴿ وَهَـٰذَا ذِكْرٌ مُّبَارَكٌ أَنزَلْنَـٰهُ ۚ أَفَأَنتُمْ لَهُۥ مُنكِرُونَ ۝٥٠ ﴾

And this is a blessed Reminder which We have revealed; will you then deny it?
(Al-Anbiyā, 21:50)

The term refers to the fact that the Qur'an frequently reminds about man's duties and responsibilities.[10]

5. *TANZĪL* (REVELATION)

This is the verbal noun of the verb *nazzala*; the term means to send down, signifying the descent of an object from a higher place to a lower place. Zanjānī considers this as a name of the Qur'an also.[11] This name with all of its derivatives is used in the Qur'an in 146 verses.

Examples are:

﴿ وَإِنَّهُۥ لَتَنزِيلُ رَبِّ ٱلْعَـٰلَمِينَ ۝١٩٢ ﴾

And most surely this is a revelation from the Lord of the worlds. (Al-Shu'arā, 26:192)

and

﴿ تَنزِيلٌ مِّنَ ٱلرَّحْمَـٰنِ ٱلرَّحِيمِ ۝٢ ﴾

A revelation from the Beneficent, the Merciful Lord. (Fuṣṣilat, 41:2)

Al-Suyūṭī lists 55 adjectives or descriptive names of the Qur'an.[12] Some are mentioned below. All of these are derived from the verses of the Qur'an itself.

Qur'an, Kitāb, Furqān, Dhikr, Tanzīl, Karīm, Nūr, Hādī, Raḥmah,

Mubīn, Mubārak, Marfū', 'Alī, Ḥikmah, Ḥakīm, Muṭahharah, Ṣirāt, Qawl, Faṣl, Nabā , Aḥsan al-ḥadīth, Mathānī, Mutashābih, Rūḥ, Waḥy, 'Arabi, Baṣāir, Ṣuḥuf, Bayān, 'Ilm, Ḥaq, Mukarramah, 'Ajab, Tadhkirah, 'Urwat al-wuthqa, Ṣidq, 'Adl, Amr, Munādi, Bushrā, Majīd, Bashīr, Nadhīr, 'Azīz, Balāgh, Qaṣaṣ.[13]

The names and descriptions of the Qur'an highlight different facets of the Divine message.

2.5 - DIVISIONS OF THE TEXT OF THE QUR'AN AND THEIR SIGNIFICANCE

The primary division of the Qur'anic text is into verses and chapters. There are 114 chapters in the Qur'an and, depending on the method of calculation, 6,236 verses. Verses and chapters are discussed in greater length in Chapter 6.

The text of the Qur'an has also been apportioned, by the earlier scholars, into parts and sections. These divisions, mentioned below, did not exist at the time of the Prophet ﷺ, and serve no other function than to facilitate and ease the regular reading of the Qur'an.

1. PART (*JUZ'*)

Juz'[14] literally means part, or portion. The Qur'an has been divided by the Muslim scholars into 30 parts of approximately equal length for easy recitation during the 30 days of a month (especially during the month of Ramaḍān). The *juz'* is further divided into 4 parts of almost equal length. This last division is popular amongst Muslims in the Indian sub-continent.

2. PLACE OF HALTING (*MANZIL*)

For the convenience of people who wish to complete the entire recital of the Qur'an in a week, the text was divided into 7 portions of almost equal length. Each portion is known as a *ḥizb* (portion) or *manzil* (halt).

The Qur'anic scholar Ḥamza al-Zayyāt (d. 156/772) has described the details of these divisions:[15]

- First *manzil*: 4 chapters; Al-Fātiḥa (Ch. 1) to Al-Nisā' (Ch. 4);
- Second *manzil*: 5 chapters; Al-Mā'ida (Ch. 5) to Al-Tawba (Ch. 9);
- Third *manzil*: 7 chapters; Yūnus (Ch. 10) to Al-Naḥl (Ch. 16);
- Fourth *manzil*: 9 chapters; Al-Isrā' (Ch. 17) to Al-Furqān (Ch. 25);
- Fifth *manzil*: 11 chapters; Al-Shū'arā'(Ch. 26) to Yā Sīn (Ch. 36);
- Sixth *manzil*: 13 chapters; Al-Ṣāffāt (Ch, 37) to Al-Ḥujurāt (Ch. 49);
- Seventh *manzil*: 65 chapters; Qāf (Ch. 50) to Al-Nās (Ch. 114).

Thus, 4, 5, 7, 9, 11, 13, and 65 chapters are grouped together respectively.

3. SECTION (*RUKŪʿ*)

The chapters are also divided into sections or paragraphs called *rukūʿ*. Each *rukūʿ* comprises a number of verses which generally discuss one theme, and which can be conveniently recited in ritual prayer (*ṣalāt*). In fact, this division is named *rukūʿ* because after its recitation in the *ṣalāt*, one proceeds to the bowing or *rukūʿ* position.

The section breaks are indicated by the letter *ʿain* (ع) with numbers placed above it, in the body of it and below it. The number at the top indicates the number of *rukūʿ* in that specific chapter. The middle number indicates the number of verses in that *rukūʿ*. And the number at the bottom indicates the number of *rukūʿ* in that specific *juz'*. In the Indian subcontinent, the Qur'an contains 558 *rukūʿ*. The *rukūʿ* is always coterminous with a chapter, but not necessarily with the *juz'*.

2.6 - THE VERSES OF PROSTRATION

There are several verses of the Qur'an that speak about prostration. Of these verses, the recitation of four of them necessitates prostration to God by the reciter, and anyone who hears the recital. These four verses are Al-Sajda, 32:15, Fuṣṣilat; 41:38, Al-Najm, 53:62; and Al-ʿAlaq, 96:19. After the recitation of any of a further ten verses, prostration is mustaḥab, or recommended. These verses are Al-Aʿrāf, 7:206; Al-Ra'd, 13:15; Al-Naḥl, 16:50; Al-Isrā', 17:109; Maryam, 19:58; Al-Ḥajj, 22:18;[16] Al-Furqān, 25:60; Al-Naml, 27:26; Ṣād, 38:24; and Al-Inshiqāq, 84:21.

2.7 - "FOREIGN" WORDS IN THE QUR'AN

In his *Al-Itqān,* Al-Suyūṭī has a chapter entitled "foreign vocabulary", in which he lists 118 foreign words, from 11 languages other than Arabic. In some instances, he attributes a word to more than one language and sometimes he mentions that the word is foreign, but does not say where it derives from.

Typically the words designated as "foreign" are those with obscure or barren roots, or morphological features regarded as irregular and not of Arabic origin by early grammarians. Some common examples of foreign or loan-words that are commonly cited are:

FROM PERSIAN

Akwāb (cup, vessel) in 56:18; *abārīq* (goblets) also in 56:18, *istabraq* (silk brocade) in 44:53; *tannūr* (furnace) in 11:40; *sijjīl* (solidified clay;derived from *sang wa gil*) in 105:4; *surādiq* (curtains) in 18:29; *jizya* (tax) 9:29; *sirāj* (lamp) in 71:16; *firdaws* (paradise) in 23:11 etc.; *maqālīd* (treasures) in 39:63; *kāfūr* (camphor) in 76:5; *misk* (musk) in 83:26; *yāqūt* (rubies) in 55:58.

FROM HEBREW

Jahannam (Hebrew *gehenna*; a name for hell) in 2:206, etc.; *ḥiṭṭatun* (forgiveness) in 2:58; *baʿīr* (camel-load) in 12:65; *Shayṭān* (Satan) in 2:36, etc.; *manna wa salwā* (manna and quails) in 2:57.

FROM ABYSSINIAN

Arāʾik (throne) in 36:52, etc.; *awwāb* (turning to God) in 38:19, etc.; *jibt* (idols) in 4:51; *hawāriyyūn* (disciples of ʿĪsā ﷺ) in 61:14; *zarābiyy* (carpets) in 88:16; *sakar* (intoxication) in 16:67.

FROM ARAMAIC

Rabb (Lord) in 1:1, etc.; *zakāt* (alms) in 2:43, etc.; *saqar* (a name for hell) in 54:48, etc.; *ṭūbā* (bliss) in 13:29; *qisṭ* (justice) in 3:18, etc.; *malakūt* (kingdom) in 6:75, etc.; *yamm* (sea) in 7:136, etc.

FROM GREEK

Injīl (Bible) in 3:3; *Iblīs* (Satan) in 2:34, etc.; *ṣirāṭ* (road) 1:6, etc.; *zanjabīl* (a drink in heaven) in 76:17; *qisṭās* (weighing scales) in 17:35; *qalam* (pen) in 68:1; *qinṭār* (hundredweight of gold or silver) in 3:75, etc.

FROM COPTIC

Baṭāin (inner coverings) in 55:54; *rahw* (furrow) in 44:24; *safara* (scribes) in 80:15; *sayyid* (husband) in 12:25.

The important thing to realise is that every language absorbs words and concepts from other languages; and Arabic is no exception, especially given the trading nature of the Arabs, who travelled to different lands for business. Of course, if the root or origin of a particular Arabic or Qur'anic word is found in another language, it does not make that word any less Arabic as a result.

The very fact that the Arabs understood clearly the language of the Qur'an shows that these words had long been assimilated into Arabic. The Qur'an is therefore pure and clear Arabic; as it says, if this were not so, the Arabs would be the first to protest about it:

﴿وَلَوْ جَعَلْنَٰهُ قُرْءَانًا أَعْجَمِيًّا لَّقَالُوا۟ لَوْلَا فُصِّلَتْ ءَايَٰتُهُۥٓ ۖ ءَا۬عْجَمِىٌّ وَعَرَبِىٌّ﴾

And if We had made it a Qur'an in a foreign tongue, they would certainly have said: Why have not its communications been made clear? What! A foreign (tongue) and an Arab (messenger)!

(Fuṣṣilat, 41:44)

NOTES

[1] *Mīzān al-Ḥikma,* condensed edition, no. 5108.
[2] Bukhārī, *Ṣaḥīḥ,* vol. 6, bk. 61, no 545.
[3] *Mīzān al-Ḥikma,* condensed edition, no. 5170.
[4] Ibid., no. 5176.
[5] Ibid., no. 5184.
[6] Ibid., no. 5204.
[7] *Al-Itqān,* vol. 1, p. 181.
[8] *Lisān al-ʿArab,* under the entry for *qara'a*; *Al-Itqān,* vol. 1, p. 50.
[9] Ṭabrisī, "Introduction to *Tafsīr Majmaʿ al-Bayān*", vol. 1, p. 14.
[10] Ibid.
[11] Zanjānī, *Manāhil al-ʿIrfān,* vol. 1, p. 15.
[12] *Al-Itqān,* vol. 1, p. 86.
[13] See Appendix 2 for the verses that mention these names.
[14] Also called *pārā* in the Indian sub-continent
[15] See Dr Hasanuddin Ahmed, *An Introduction to the Science of the Qur'an,* Ch. 1.
[16] According to Al-Shāfiʿī, and the Shiʿa, 22:77 also.

3

REVELATION (*WAḤY*)

God has guided His creation to attain perfection through two forms of guidance. Both these forms of guidance are referred to in the Qur'an as *waḥy.* The first form, which is common to the whole of creation, is known as "intuitive guidance" (*al-hidāyat al-takwīniyya*), and is concerned with the laws of nature that govern inanimate objects and the natural instinct of animate beings. The Qur'an states:

﴿ رَبُّنَا ٱلَّذِىٓ أَعۡطَىٰ كُلَّ شَىۡءٍ خَلۡقَهُۥ ثُمَّ هَدَىٰ ﴿٥٠﴾ ﴾

Our Lord is He Who gave to everything its creation, then guided it. (Ṭā-Hā, 20:50)

Some examples of intuitive guidance, appear below, illustrating God's guidance or inspiration to inanimate objects, animals and humans.

TO THE EARTH

﴿ يَوۡمَئِذٍ تُحَدِّثُ أَخۡبَارَهَا ﴿٤﴾ بِأَنَّ رَبَّكَ أَوۡحَىٰ لَهَا ﴿٥﴾ ﴾

On that day, it [the earth] shall relate its news, because your Lord had inspired it. (Al-Zilzāl, 99:4,5)

TO THE BEE

﴿ وَأَوۡحَىٰ رَبُّكَ إِلَى ٱلنَّحۡلِ أَنِ ٱتَّخِذِى مِنَ ٱلۡجِبَالِ بُيُوتًا وَمِنَ ٱلشَّجَرِ

﴿ وَمِمَّا يَعْرِشُونَ ﴿٦٨﴾ ﴾

And your Lord revealed to the bee saying, "Make hives in the mountains and in the trees and in what they [men] build." (Al-Naḥl, 16:68)

TO MANKIND

﴿ فَأَقِمْ وَجْهَكَ لِلدِّينِ حَنِيفًا ۚ فِطْرَتَ ٱللَّهِ ٱلَّتِى فَطَرَ ٱلنَّاسَ عَلَيْهَا ﴾

Then set your face upright for religion sincerely – (this is) God's pattern in which He has made men. (Al-Rūm, 30:30)

This last verse refers to the natural instinct, or *fiṭra*, that exists in every human being, and through which he intuitively knows and comprehends certain truths.

The second form of guidance that God provides is an external form, usually through His messengers and Divine books. This guidance, which is reserved for sentient creatures, like mankind and the *jinn*, is referred to as "legislative guidance" (*al-hidāyat al-tashrīʿīyya*). This form of guidance is necessary because, while man instinctively knows good from evil, he does not know the full consequences of his conduct. He needs a goal to aim for and a model to base his life on. This is the role of a Prophet ﷺ. The Qur'an states:

﴿ يَٰٓأَيُّهَا ٱلنَّبِىُّ إِنَّآ أَرْسَلْنَٰكَ شَٰهِدًا وَمُبَشِّرًا وَنَذِيرًا ﴿٤٥﴾ وَدَاعِيًا إِلَى ٱللَّهِ بِإِذْنِهِۦ وَسِرَاجًا مُّنِيرًا ﴿٤٦﴾ ﴾

O Prophet! Indeed, We have sent you as a witness, and as a bearer of good news and as a warner, and as one inviting to God by His permission, and as a light-giving torch. (Al-Aḥzāb, 33:45,46)

As far as legislative guidance is concerned, from the first day that man walked on earth, God has never left the earth empty of His representative, who would be a witness to the deeds of men, and a bearer of God's knowledge. In this manner, reportedly 124,000 prophets عليهم السلام were sent in all, jointly and successively, many of them bringing Divine books or tracts. The final and most complete message sent by God was through the noblest and last of His prophets, Muhammad ﷺ. He brought a comprehensive religion, and the cornerstone of his teachings was the Qur'an.

3.1 - REVELATION IN QUR'ANIC TERMINOLOGY

The Qur'an itself refers to the nature in which it was revealed, through the Prophet ﷺ, by several terms:

1. SENDING DOWN (*INZĀL, TANZĪL*)

These terms have been used numerously in the Qur'an. Usually, *inzāl* refers to the instantaneous sending down of the Qur'an;

﴿إِنَّآ أَنزَلۡنَٰهُ فِي لَيۡلَةِ ٱلۡقَدۡرِ ١﴾

We have indeed revealed (anzalnāhu) *this [Qur'an] in the Night of Decree.* (Al-Qadr, 97:1)

while the term *tanzīl* refers to the gradual revelation of the Qur'an that occurred over the course of the Prophet's ﷺ mission:

﴿ذَٰلِكَ بِأَنَّ ٱللَّهَ نَزَّلَ ٱلۡكِتَٰبَ بِٱلۡحَقِّ﴾

That is because God has revealed (nazzala) *the Book with Truth.* (Al-Baqara, 2:176)

However, this is not always the case, because the two terms have been used interchangeably:

﴿وَيَقُولُونَ لَوۡلَآ أُنزِلَ عَلَيۡهِ ءَايَةٞ مِّن رَّبِّهِۦۖ﴾

And they say, "Why is a sign not sent (unzila) *to him from his Lord?".* (Yūnus, 10:20)

﴿وَقَالُواْ لَوۡلَا نُزِّلَ عَلَيۡهِ ءَايَةٞ مِّن رَّبِّهِۦ﴾

And they say, "Why has a sign not been sent (nuzzila) *down to him from his Lord?"* (Al-Anʿām, 6:37)

The better distinction between the two terms is that *inzāl* refers to the sending down of the Qur'an, either instantaneously or gradually, in single verses or whole passages, while *tanzīl* refers to the constant revelation of the verses of the Qur'an.[1]

2. INFUSION (*ILQĀ', TALAQQĪ*)

The term *ilqā'* means to infuse and *talaqqī* means to receive, and therefore in the Qur'an, the terms refer to the infusion of guidance into the Prophet's ﷺ heart, and the receiving of this guidance by him. The following are two examples:

﴿ إِنَّا سَنُلْقِي عَلَيْكَ قَوْلًا ثَقِيلًا ۝٥ ﴾

We will infuse (sanulqī) *you with a weighty word.* (Al-Muzzammil, 73:5)

﴿ وَإِنَّكَ لَتُلَقَّى الْقُرْآنَ مِن لَّدُنْ حَكِيمٍ عَلِيمٍ ۝٦ ﴾

And indeed, you are made to receive (latulaqqā) *the Qur'an from the Wise, the all-Knowing.* (Al-Naml, 27:6)

3. READING OR RECITAL (*QIRĀ'A, TILĀWA*)

The term *qirā'a* has been used 4 times in the Qur'an, for example:

﴿ سَنُقْرِئُكَ فَلَا تَنسَىٰ ۝٦ ﴾

We will make you read (sanuqri'uka) *so you shall not forget.* (Al-A'lā, 87:6)

While the term *tilāwa* has been used 6 times in the Qur'an, for example:

﴿ تِلْكَ آيَاتُ اللَّهِ نَتْلُوهَا عَلَيْكَ بِالْحَقِّ ۚ وَإِنَّكَ لَمِنَ الْمُرْسَلِينَ ۝٢٥٢ ﴾

These are the communications of God, We recite them (natlūhā) *to you with truth; for indeed, you are [one] of the messengers.* (Al-Baqara, 2:252)

Both terms mean reading or recital. However, while *qirā'a* can mean reading any text, *tilāwa* is usually confined to reading Divine scriptures.

4. MEASURED RECITAL (*TARTĪL*)

This term refers to the recital of the words of the Qur'an separately, and in a measured style, so that it has an effect on the hearts of the listeners.[2] It has been used in the Qur'an to describe both the style of revelation, as well as the recommended style of recital:

﴿ كَذَٰلِكَ لِنُثَبِّتَ بِهِۦ فُؤَادَكَ ۖ وَرَتَّلْنَٰهُ تَرْتِيلًا ﴿٣٢﴾ ﴾

Thus, We may strengthen your heart by it; and We have recited it on you in a measured recital. (wa rattalnāhu tartīlā). (Al-Furqān, 25:32)

﴿ وَرَتِّلِ ٱلْقُرْءَانَ تَرْتِيلًا ﴿٤﴾ ﴾

And recite (rattil) *the Qur'an in a measured recital* (tartīlā). (Al-Muzzammil, 73:4)

5. BESTOWAL (*ITYĀN, ĪTĀ'*)

These terms, meaning "granting" or "bestowing", have been used 10 times in the Qur'an. The following two examples illustrate the use of both derivatives:

﴿ وَلَقَدْ ءَاتَيْنَٰكَ سَبْعًا مِّنَ ٱلْمَثَانِى وَٱلْقُرْءَانَ ٱلْعَظِيمَ ﴿٨٧﴾ ﴾

And certainly We have granted you (ātaynāka) *seven of the oft-repeated (verses) [*Al-Fātiḥa*], and the exalted Qur'an.* (Al-Ḥijr, 15:87)

﴿ بَلْ أَتَيْنَٰهُم بِذِكْرِهِمْ فَهُمْ عَن ذِكْرِهِم مُّعْرِضُونَ ﴿٧١﴾ ﴾

Nay! We have bestowed (ātaynāhum) *to them their reminder, but from their reminder they turn aside.* (Al-Mu'minūn, 23:71)

6. INSTRUCTION (*TA'LĪM*)

﴿ وَعَلَّمَكَ مَا لَمْ تَكُن تَعْلَمُ ۚ ﴾

And He has instructed you ('allamaka) *about what you did not know.* (Al-Nisā', 4:113)

This term has been used with its derivatives, 4 times in the Qur'an, and indicates that the Prophet ﷺ learnt only from God.

7. NARRATION (*QAṢṢ*)

This term is usually used in the Qur'an when it narrates stories and parables, for example, when the story of Yūsuf ﵇ is narrated:

﴿ نَحۡنُ نَقُصُّ عَلَيۡكَ أَحۡسَنَ ٱلۡقَصَصِ بِمَآ أَوۡحَيۡنَآ إِلَيۡكَ هَٰذَا ٱلۡقُرۡءَانَ ﴾

We narrate (naquṣṣu) *to you the best of narratives, by Our revealing to you this Qur'an .* (Yūsuf, 12:3)

8. OBLIGATION (*FARḌ*)

This term means making compulsory and binding. It is frequently employed for the obligatory acts of worship, such as the daily prayers. In the Qur'an, it refers to the obligation of the Prophet ﷺ to recite the verses and spread God's message.[3]

﴿ إِنَّ ٱلَّذِي فَرَضَ عَلَيۡكَ ٱلۡقُرۡءَانَ لَرَآدُّكَ إِلَىٰ مَعَادٖۚ ﴾

Most surely He Who has made the Qur'an binding (faraḍa) *on you will bring you back to the (promised) destination [Mecca].* (Al-Qaṣaṣ, 28:85)

9. COMING (*MAJĪ'*)

﴿ وَلَقَدۡ جَآءَهُم مِّن رَّبِّهِمُ ٱلۡهُدَىٰٓ ٢٣ ﴾

And certainly the guidance has come to them (jā'ahum) *from their Lord.* (Al-Najm, 53:23)

This term has been used over 35 times in the Qur'an, with different derivatives. Sometimes it refers to guidance coming down to the people, as above, and other times it is used for guidance coming to the Prophet ﷺ:

﴿ وَلَا تَتَّبِعۡ أَهۡوَآءَهُمۡ عَمَّا جَآءَكَ مِنَ ٱلۡحَقِّۚ ﴾

And do not pay heed to their low desires [to turn away from the truth], but judge between them by what has come to you (ja'aka) *[from God].* (Al-Mā'ida, 5:48)

10. REVELATION (*WAḤY*)

﴿ وَلَقَدْ أُوحِيَ إِلَيْكَ وَإِلَى ٱلَّذِينَ مِن قَبْلِكَ ﴾

And certainly, it has been revealed (ūḥiya) *to you and to those before you.*
(Al-Zumar, 39:65)

This basic term for legislative guidance has been used over 70 times in the Qurʾan, with various derivatives, such as *awḥā, yūḥā, awḥaynā,* etc. Because we have a special interest in this term it will be described more fully in the next two sections.

3.2 - DEFINITION OF *WAḤY* AND *ILHĀM*

The term *waḥy* is derived from the root (*w-ḥ-y*). Rāghib Iṣfahānī writes:

> The roots of the word *waḥy* have a meaning of quickness. And *waḥy* therefore, refers to a communication that is swift. It may be secret or allegorical in nature, and the message can be conveyed verbally, in writing or by gestures.[4]

Ibn al-Fāris, the 4th century grammarian, writes:

> Any message transmitted to another in whatever manner, openly or secretly, which is understood clearly by the recipient, can be termed *waḥy*.[5]

Therefore, *waḥy* can be defined as any method of communication, (by words, suggestions, gestures, inspirations, dreams, writings, etc.) that happens swiftly, secretly, and in a concise manner.

Waḥy has been variously translated as Divine guidance, Divine message, revelation and Divine inspiration.[6] We will use the term revelation, especially in the section where we will discuss *waḥy* with respect to God's communications to His prophets ﷺ.

Ilhām has a meaning of a suggestion directed at the heart, which guides the recipient as to the course to follow, without his being aware of the source of guidance. The term *ilhām* is usually translated as inspiration, instinctive desire and Divine revelation.[7] We will translate the term as inspiration, and in the next section, point out some differences between *waḥy* and *ilhām*, because they are occasionally confused with one other.

3.3 - THE DIFFERENCE BETWEEN *WAḤY* AND *ILHĀM*

Legislative guidance, from God to His sentient creatures, takes the form of *ilhām* and *waḥy*. In the Qur'an, when there is a reference to Divine guidance in general, both forms have been referred to as *waḥy*. However, in the context of legislative guidance, *ilhām* can be translated as inspiration, and *waḥy*, as revelation.

In this section we will examine some differences between these two methods of guidance. (While we have discussed *ilhām* as a form of legislative guidance, it must be borne in mind that it is not confined to Divine guidance to the faithful, but can also take the form of evil suggestions from Satan and his accomplices.).[8]

1. *Ilhām* is directed to ordinary human beings only; when it is directed to prophets عليهم السلام, it is no different from *waḥy*. However, *waḥy* is exclusive to prophets عليهم السلام only.

2. The source of inspiration is hidden to the one receiving *ilhām*, whereas the source of revelation is clear to the one receiving *waḥy*. For this very reason, the prophets عليهم السلام never suffer confusion and error in receiving the heavenly message, since they are completely aware of its source, and familiar with the manner in which it is received.[9]

3. For normal individuals, *ilhām* is a personal matter. It has no authority over others, and there is no obligation on the recipient to spread the message he has received, or impose it on others. For the prophets عليهم السلام, however, *ilhām* has the same meaning as *waḥy*; it is an authority over others and is associated with their Divine

commission and mission of proselytization of God's message.

4. Some scholars are of the opinion that *ilhām* is a subliminal command addressed to the unconscious mind.[10] *Waḥy* on the other hand, is always received by the prophets عليهم السلام while they are in a fully aware mental state, even if it is the form of a dream or vision.

3.4 - *WAḤY* AS MENTIONED IN THE QUR'AN

The term *waḥy* appears over 70 times in the Qur'an, and has been used in the discussions of angels, satans, humans, animals and inanimate objects. However, the greatest usage of this term has been in relation to the communication between God and His prophets عليهم السلام. In every instance, an aspect of inspiration, direction or guidance is indicated.

ʿAlī b. Abī Ṭālib divided the usage of the term *waḥy* in the Qur'an into: *waḥy* to the prophets عليهم السلام, inspiration, gestures, destiny, command, falsehood (in the case of Satanic whisperings), and news.[11]

Some instances of the usage of the term *waḥy* in the Qur'an, other than in connection with the prophets عليهم السلام, (which will be discussed in a separate section) are given in the sub-sections which follow.

1. THE DIVINELY-ORDAINED NATURAL ORDER

﴿ وَأَوْحَىٰ فِي كُلِّ سَمَآءٍ أَمْرَهَا ۚ وَزَيَّنَّا ٱلسَّمَآءَ ٱلدُّنْيَا بِمَصَٰبِيحَ وَحِفْظًا ۚ
ذَٰلِكَ تَقْدِيرُ ٱلْعَزِيزِ ٱلْعَلِيمِ ﴿١٢﴾ ﴾

And He inspired in each heaven its affair. And We adorned the lower heaven with brilliant stars and (made it) to guard; that is the decree of the Mighty, the Knowing.
(Fuṣṣilat, 41:12)

Here the mention of the heavens is an allusion to the whole world of creation. The derivative of *waḥy* in this verse refers to the Divinely-ordained natural order that suffuses creation, such as the movement of the sun and the moon, the variation in tides, the orbits of the planets, etc.

2. DIVINELY-GRANTED INSTINCT TO CREATURES

﴿ وَأَوْحَىٰ رَبُّكَ إِلَى ٱلنَّحْلِ أَنِ ٱتَّخِذِى مِنَ ٱلْجِبَالِ بُيُوتًا وَمِنَ ٱلشَّجَرِ وَمِمَّا يَعْرِشُونَ ﴿٦٨﴾
ثُمَّ كُلِى مِن كُلِّ ٱلثَّمَرَٰتِ فَٱسْلُكِى سُبُلَ رَبِّكِ ذُلُلًا ﴾

And your Lord inspired to the bee saying: Make hives in the mountains and in the trees and in what they build: then eat of all the fruits and traverse the ways of your Lord submissively. (Al-Naḥl, 16:68, 69)

Here, the derivative of *waḥy* denotes the natural instinct that He has put into every creature; bees, for example, instinctively live in orderly and disciplined colonies, build hives, gather nectar and make honey. This instinctive guidance is from amongst the secrets of nature. Its amazing manifestations are apparent, but its source remains hidden from the eyes, and so it is called *waḥy*.[12]

3. INSPIRATION (*ILHĀM*)

Occasionally, a human being perceives a message whose source he does not know, especially in the state of desperation or confusion. This sudden inspiration, which provides him with guidance, springs from Divine grace (*luṭf*) and is termed *waḥy* in the Qur'an:[13]

﴿ وَأَوْحَيْنَآ إِلَىٰٓ أُمِّ مُوسَىٰٓ أَنْ أَرْضِعِيهِ ۖ فَإِذَا خِفْتِ عَلَيْهِ فَأَلْقِيهِ فِى ٱلْيَمِّ وَلَا تَخَافِى وَلَا تَحْزَنِىٓ ۖ
إِنَّا رَآدُّوهُ إِلَيْكِ وَجَاعِلُوهُ مِنَ ٱلْمُرْسَلِينَ ﴿٧﴾ ﴾

And we inspired the mother of Mūsā, "Suckle him!" But when you fear for him, then cast him into the river and fear not, nor grieve. Surely, We will bring him back to you and make him one of the messengers. (Al-Qaṣaṣ, 28:7)

Since the mother of Mūsā was not a prophet, *waḥy* in this verse refers to inspiration and insight, and not revelation.[14] This form of communication is very compelling, driving the recipient to fearlessly do what they would not normally consider doing; in this case prompting a mother to cast her infant baby into a river. The inspiration to the disciples of ʿIsā ﷺ was of this type also:

﴿ وَإِذْ أَوْحَيْتُ إِلَى ٱلْحَوَارِيِّـۧنَ أَنْ ءَامِنُوا۟ بِى وَبِرَسُولِى قَالُوٓا۟ ءَامَنَّا وَٱشْهَدْ
بِأَنَّنَا مُسْلِمُونَ ﴿١١١﴾ ﴾

And when I inspired the disciples, saying, "Believe in Me and My messenger", they said, "We believe and bear witness that we submit [ourselves]." (Al-Māʾida, 5:111)

The disciples mentioned in this verse were not prophets, and thus incapable of receiving revelation.[15]

4. SECRETIVE SUGGESTIONS FROM SHAIṬĀN AND HIS ALLIES

Satan and his cohorts are capable of a kind of inspiration:

﴿ وَكَذَٰلِكَ جَعَلْنَا لِكُلِّ نَبِىٍّ عَدُوًّا شَيَـٰطِينَ ٱلْإِنسِ وَٱلْجِنِّ يُوحِى بَعْضُهُمْ إِلَىٰ بَعْضٍ ﴾

And thus We have appointed for every prophet an enemy – satans among mankind and jinn, inspiring one another. (Al-Anʿām, 6:112)

﴿ وَإِنَّ ٱلشَّيَـٰطِينَ لَيُوحُونَ إِلَىٰٓ أَوْلِيَآئِهِمْ لِيُجَـٰدِلُوكُمْ ۖ ﴾

And most surely the satans suggest to their friends that they should contend with you. (Al-Anʿām, 6:121)

In these verses, the word *waḥy* signifies a secretive, insinuative type of influence and inspiration. This is the kind of evil whisper (*waswasa*) that is also referred to elsewhere in the Qurʾan:

﴿ مِن شَرِّ ٱلْوَسْوَاسِ ٱلْخَنَّاسِ ﴿٤﴾ ٱلَّذِى يُوَسْوِسُ فِى صُدُورِ ٱلنَّاسِ ﴿٥﴾
مِنَ ٱلْجِنَّةِ وَٱلنَّاسِ ﴿٦﴾ ﴾

[I seek refuge in God] From the evil of the whisperings of the slinking [Satan]. Who whispers into the hearts of men. [Who is] From among the jinn and the men. (Al-Nās, 114:4-6)

5. COMMUNICATION BY GESTURES AND SIGNS

The following verse is an example of this form of *wahy*:

﴿ فَخَرَجَ عَلَىٰ قَوْمِهِۦ مِنَ ٱلْمِحْرَابِ فَأَوْحَىٰٓ إِلَيْهِمْ أَن سَبِّحُواْ بُكْرَةً وَعَشِيًّا ﴾

He came out unto his people, and communicated to them [by gestures and signs] to glorify God's praises in the morning and afternoon. (Maryam, 19:11)

When God informed Zakariyya ؑ that he would lose his ability to speak (as a sign), he communicated with his people for three days by signing; his gestures to them have been described as *wahy* – here meaning non-verbal communication.

6. GOD'S COMMANDS TO THE ANGELS

﴿ إِذْ يُوحِى رَبُّكَ إِلَى ٱلْمَلَٰٓئِكَةِ أَنِّى مَعَكُمْ فَثَبِّتُواْ ٱلَّذِينَ ءَامَنُواْ ﴾

[And] when your Lord inspired the angels, "I am with you, so keep firm those who have believed." (Al-Anfāl, 8:12)

Here the word *wahy* denotes a command to the angels to strengthen the resolve of the believers.

3.5 - *WAḤY* AND THE PROPHETS OF GOD

We now begin the discussion of *wahy* in the special sense of Divine communication to the prophets ؑ, and henceforth, we will refer to *wahy* as revelation. The following verse outlines the methods by which God communicates with His prophets ؑ:

﴿ وَمَا كَانَ لِبَشَرٍ أَن يُكَلِّمَهُ ٱللَّهُ إِلَّا وَحْيًا أَوْ مِن وَرَآئِ حِجَابٍ أَوْ يُرْسِلَ رَسُولًا فَيُوحِىَ بِإِذْنِهِۦ مَا يَشَآءُ إِنَّهُۥ عَلِىٌّ حَكِيمٌ ﴾

It is not possible for any human being that God should speak to him unless it be by inspiration, or from behind a veil, or [that] He sends a messenger to reveal what He wills by His permission. Verily, He is the Most High, Most Wise. (Al-Shūrā, 42:51)

According to the verse above, God's revelation to the prophets ﷷ occurs in three ways, which are:

1. **Direct revelation.** Here, God reveals directly to the recipient, without an intermediary.

2. **Direct revelation, from behind a veil.** Here, God reveals directly to the recipient, but is heard as a voice from an intermediary object.

3. **Indirect revelation, through a messenger.** Here, God reveals to an intermediary, usually the angel Jibra'īl, who then faithfully relates His words to the recipient.[16]

Each of the three methods of revelation will be discussed in turn.

1. DIRECT REVELATION

This is a method of revelation through which the prophets ﷷ received God's commands directly, without any intermediary. Almost all the prophets ﷷ received this kind of revelation in dreams, but in the wakeful state this was a very difficult experience. The Prophet ﷺ remarked about this method, "The holy spirit (*al-rūḥ al-qudus*)[17] blows into my heart."[18]

The difficulty of this form of revelation is alluded to in the following verse:

﴿ إِنَّا سَنُلْقِي عَلَيْكَ قَوْلًا ثَقِيلًا ۝ ﴾

We will infuse you with a weighty Word. (Al-Muzzammil, 73:5)

Ṭabrisī in the commentary of the above verse, narrates:

> Ḥārith b. Hishām asked the Prophet ﷺ, "In what manner does revelation descend upon you?" The Prophet ﷺ answered, "Sometimes it comes like a ringing sound, and this is the most intense type of revelation for me, so that I become exhausted. In this condition, I memorize all which is said. Other times, an angel appears in the form of a man, and I memorize all that he says."[19]

ʿAbdallāh b. ʿUmar narrates:

> I asked the Prophet ﷺ about the type of sensation during revelation. The Prophet ﷺ answered: "I hear a ringing sound, and at that time I maintain total silence. There is no time that revelation comes to me, except that I feel that it will draw the life out of my body."[20]

Ubāda reports:

> At some moments of revelation the manner of the Prophet ﷺ would be transformed, his face would change colour and he would bow his head. At these times, we too, bowed our heads.[21]

Ṣadūq narrates:

> Zurāra asked Al-Ṣādiq, "Did the Prophet ﷺ experience swooning during revelation? He answered: "This happened on the occasions when there was no intermediary between the Prophet ﷺ and God. It was at these times that the Glory of God would manifest itself to the Prophet ﷺ."[22]

Also, ʿĀyisha narrates that, one day, despite it being very cold, sweat poured from the forehead of the Prophet ﷺ after he had received revelation.[23]

From the traditions above, we can see that direct revelation was the most demanding and difficult for the Prophet ﷺ to bear, and often the strain of it would cause his body to shake and beads of sweat would break out on his blessed forehead. If he was mounted on an animal, it too displayed the strain of the moment. ʿAlī b. Abī Ṭālib reports:

> When chapter Al-Mā'ida, was being revealed, the Prophet ﷺ was mounted on his camel called Al-Shahbā. The heaviness of revelation caused the animal to stop, and its back began to bend in a manner that its stomach almost touched the ground.[24]

Included in this form of revelation, are the true dreams seen by the prophets عليهم السلام. For example, when Ibrāhīm عليه السلام saw in a dream that he was sacrificing his son Ismāʿīl عليه السلام at Munā, both of them understood that it was a direct command from God:

﴿قَالَ يَٰبُنَيَّ إِنِّيٓ أَرَىٰ فِي ٱلۡمَنَامِ أَنِّيٓ أَذۡبَحُكَ فَٱنظُرۡ مَاذَا تَرَىٰۚ قَالَ يَٰٓأَبَتِ ٱفۡعَلۡ مَا تُؤۡمَرُۖ﴾

O my son! Verily, I have seen in a dream that I should sacrifice you; consider then what is your opinion. He said: O my father! Do what you are commanded. (Al-Ṣāffāt, 37:102)

The Prophet ﷺ himself saw a dream in which the Muslims were performing the rites of the ʿumra, and so he set out with the Muslims for Mecca. That year, they could not enter the holy city and instead, the treaty of Hudaybiyya was enacted between the Muslims and the idolaters of Mecca. One of the conditions of the treaty was that, in the following year, the Muslims would return and complete the rites of the ʿumra, and this was what happened. The Qur'an states:

﴿لَّقَدۡ صَدَقَ ٱللَّهُ رَسُولَهُ ٱلرُّءۡيَا بِٱلۡحَقِّۖ لَتَدۡخُلُنَّ ٱلۡمَسۡجِدَ ٱلۡحَرَامَ إِن شَآءَ ٱللَّهُ ءَامِنِينَ﴾

Certainly God had shown to His Messenger the vision with truth: you shall most certainly enter the Sacred Mosque, if God pleases, in security. (Al-Fatḥ, 48:27)

2. DIRECT REVELATION, FROM BEHIND A VEIL

This refers to occurrences where the Prophet ﷺ would hear a low buzzing sound, but there would be no one around him. The sound would then become distinguishable as revelation.[25]

An example of this form of revelation is during the night of his ascension to the heavens, (*miʿrāj*). When the Prophet ﷺ reached the farthest point of his journey, he came to a curtain of light, and there God spoke to him:

﴿ثُمَّ دَنَا فَتَدَلَّىٰ ٨ فَكَانَ قَابَ قَوۡسَيۡنِ أَوۡ أَدۡنَىٰ ٩ فَأَوۡحَىٰٓ إِلَىٰ عَبۡدِهِۦ مَآ أَوۡحَىٰ ١٠﴾

Then he drew near, then he bowed. So he was the measure of two bows or closer still. And He revealed to His servant what He revealed. (Al-Najm, 53:8-10)

This manner of revelation was also experienced by Mūsā ﵇ when God spoke to him through the agency of a burning bush:

﴿فَلَمَّآ أَتَىٰهَا نُودِيَ مِن شَٰطِيِٕ ٱلۡوَادِ ٱلۡأَيۡمَنِ فِي ٱلۡبُقۡعَةِ

﴿ ٱلْمُبَـٰرَكَةِ مِنَ ٱلشَّجَرَةِ أَن يَـٰمُوسَىٰٓ إِنِّىٓ أَنَا ٱللَّهُ رَبُّ ٱلْعَـٰلَمِينَ ﴿٣٠﴾ ﴾

And when he came to it, a voice came from the right side of the valley in the blessed spot of the bush, saying: O Mūsā! Surely I am God, the Lord of the worlds. (Al-Qaṣaṣ, 28:30)

3. REVELATION THROUGH A MESSENGER

This was the customary means of revelation to the Prophet ﷺ, which the archangel Jibraʾīl would bring to him. God says:

﴿ وَإِنَّهُۥ لَتَنزِيلُ رَبِّ ٱلْعَـٰلَمِينَ ﴿١٩٢﴾ نَزَلَ بِهِ ٱلرُّوحُ ٱلْأَمِينُ ﴿١٩٣﴾ عَلَىٰ قَلْبِكَ
لِتَكُونَ مِنَ ٱلْمُنذِرِينَ ﴿١٩٤﴾ ﴾

And most surely this is a revelation from the Lord of the worlds. The Faithful Spirit has descended with it, upon your heart, so that you may be of those who warn. (Al-Shuʿarā, 26:192-194)

and

﴿ قُلْ مَن كَانَ عَدُوًّا لِّجِبْرِيلَ فَإِنَّهُۥ نَزَّلَهُۥ عَلَىٰ قَلْبِكَ بِإِذْنِ ٱللَّهِ
مُصَدِّقًا لِّمَا بَيْنَ يَدَيْهِ وَهُدًى وَبُشْرَىٰ لِلْمُؤْمِنِينَ ﴿٩٧﴾ ﴾

Say: "Whoever is the enemy of Jibrīl", for surely he revealed it to your heart by God's command, verifying that which is before it and guidance and good news for the believers. (Al-Baqara, 2:97)

These verses talk of revelation to the Prophet's ﷺ heart, and this term needs some explanation. Ṭabāṭabāʾī says:

> What is meant by heart (*qalb*) in the language of the Qurʾan, is not the physical heart, but the soul of a person. This "heart" has a perception of its own; and the emotions and the will- power of a person are connected to it. This fact that the revelation is to the heart of the Prophet ﷺ gives an indication that his noble soul received revelation in isolation from his five senses. In other words, the entire soul of the Prophet ﷺ would receive the revelation, and his physical eyes and ears would not have participated in this perception. If it was not like this, then other people too, would have seen and heard what the Prophet ﷺ was seeing and hearing at the time of revelation.[26]

From numerous traditions, we learn that this type of revelation was not very difficult on the Prophet ﷺ, because frequently, Jibra'il would appear before him in the form of a man.

It is narrated from Al-Ṣādiq: "At the time of appearing before the Prophet ﷺ, Jibra'il would wait like a servant, and would not enter without his permission."[27] This tradition is indicative of the great status of the Prophet ﷺ in comparison to Jibra'il.

3.6 - SOME MYTHS ABOUT REVELATION

Unfortunately, several false stories and myths have found their way into the Ḥadīth texts of the Muslims, alleging that the prophets ؑ were susceptible to self-doubt, anxiety, and error. By way of example, we will discuss two famous traditions which concern the last and best of the messengers, Prophet Muḥammad ﷺ.

1. THE STORY OF WARAQA B. NAWFAL

Waraqa b. Nawfal was a paternal cousin of Lady Khadīja. He had some knowledge about the history of the previous prophets. It is narrated that he used to read the [divinely sent] scriptures and attend the sessions of the Christians and Jews.[28]

The story of how he helped the Prophet ﷺ understand what had transpired at the time of the first revelation is narrated in the prominent books of traditions, and the summary of the various narratives is as follows:

> Once when Muḥammad ﷺ was worshipping his Lord in the cave of Ḥirā', he suddenly heard a voice calling out to him. He raised his head in order to see who it was; and encountered a frightening countenance. Everywhere he looked, he saw the same frightening countenance, which seemed to cover the sky. Terrified, he lost consciousness and remained in this state for a long time. Khadīja, who was worried at his delay, sent someone to call him. However, the person did not find the Prophet ﷺ.

Soon after the Prophet ﷺ regained consciousness and went to his house in a state of fear and despair. Khadīja asked, "What is happening to you?" He said, "That which I feared has occurred. I always feared lest I become insane, and now I feel that it has happened." Khadīja said, "Do not give way to evil thoughts about yourself. You are a man of God and God will not leave you. Certainly it must be clear glad tidings of the future..."

Thereafter, in order to remove the Prophet's ﷺ worry completely, she took him to Waraqa b. Nawfal's house and narrated the incident to him. Waraqa asked the Prophet ﷺ some questions, and finally concluded, "Do not worry, this is the very same Divine angel that had come down upon Mūsā ؑ; he has descended on you now, to give you the glad tidings of Apostleship." On hearing this, the Prophet ﷺ relaxed and said: "It is now that I know that I am a Prophet." And then, as his mind became tranquil, and his fear left him, he became confident that he was a Prophet.[29]

As we will presently see, this story does not stand up to critical scrutiny and is contradictory to the verses of the Qur'an and to the high station of Apostleship. This is one of the tens of concocted stories that have entered even respectable collections of traditions. There are several problems with this narration:

1. The tradition itself is *mursal*.[30] Moreover, there are so many different versions as to what may have transpired, that one has no choice but to disregard all of them. It is ironic that Waraqa is supposed to have correctly understood what had transpired at the cave of Ḥirā' and informed the Prophet ﷺ about his Divine calling, yet there is consensus amongst historians that he himself died a Christian.

2. Qāḍī 'Ayyāḍ (d. 544/1149) explaining that this version of events about the first revelation to the Prophet ﷺ is fictitious and unfounded, says, "Certainly the matter (of revelation) was always clear for him, because Divine wisdom necessitates that the matter should become completely clear for him." [31]

3. Ṭabrisī makes the basic point that, in order for the Prophet ﷺ to be

able to guide others through revelation, he himself has to be safe from any kind of anxiety or mistake in receiving the revelation.[32]

4. The verses of Qur'an generally specify the point that the prophets عليهم السلام receive messages from the very beginning of revelation and do not suffer doubt and suspicion. The lofty state of being present near God is a station in which there is no way for imagination, doubt, and fear. When Mūsā عليه السلام was anxious at the start of his mission, God immediately reassured him:

﴿ يَٰمُوسَىٰ لَا تَخَفۡ إِنِّي لَا يَخَافُ لَدَيَّ ٱلۡمُرۡسَلُونَ ١٠ ﴾

O Mūsā! Fear not, for indeed in My presence, [My] messengers have no fear.
(Al-Naml, 27:10)

Hence, at the very moment when he experienced fear, Mūsā عليه السلام was embraced by God's grace and was thereby freed from any kind of anxiety.

2. THE FABLE OF *GHARĀNĪQ* – THE SATANIC VERSES

This legend has also found its way into the Muslim Ḥadīth texts[33], and is particularly disagreeable because it is an obvious concoction designed to cast doubt on the fundamental issue of the authenticity of the revelation of the Qur'an. The gist of this tale is as below:

The Prophet ﷺ was always in the hope of a mutual agreement between himself and the Quraysh, and was distressed due to the division amongst his people. When the chapter Al-Najm was revealed to him, he was seated besides the Ka'ba, while a group of the unbelievers of the Quraysh stood near him. As the chapter was revealed, the Prophet ﷺ began to recite its verses to the people:

﴿ وَٱلنَّجۡمِ إِذَا هَوَىٰ ١ مَا ضَلَّ صَاحِبُكُمۡ وَمَا غَوَىٰ ٢ وَمَا يَنطِقُ عَنِ ٱلۡهَوَىٰٓ ٣
إِنۡ هُوَ إِلَّا وَحۡيٞ يُوحَىٰ ٤ عَلَّمَهُۥ شَدِيدُ ٱلۡقُوَىٰ ٥ ﴾

[I swear] By the star when it goes down, [that] your companion is neither astray nor being misled. He never says (anything) of (his own) desire. This is no less

than revelation sent down to him. He was taught by one Mighty in Power...

Until he reached the verse:

﴿ أَفَرَءَيْتُمُ ٱللَّـٰتَ وَٱلْعُزَّىٰ ۝ وَمَنَوٰةَ ٱلثَّالِثَةَ ٱلْأُخْرَىٰ ۝ ﴾

Have you seen Lāt, and 'Uzzā, and another, Manāt, the third [idol].
(Al-Najm, 53:1-20)

At this point Satan interjected the following line without the Prophet ﷺ being aware of what was transpiring!

تِلْكَ الغَرَانِيْقُ العُلَى وَ اِنَّ شَفَاعَتَهُنَّ لَتُرْتَجَى

These are the high-soaring birds – and their intercession is [also] anticipated. [34]

Then the Prophet ﷺ continued reciting the remaining of the chapter, as it was revealed by Jibra'īl.

As soon as the polytheists heard this sentence, which praised their gods and gave the glad tidings of their intercession, they were overjoyed. They changed their stance towards the Muslims and stretched the hand of brotherhood and unity to them. And all became happy and considered it as a good omen. The news of this incident reached Abyssinia. The Muslims who had migrated there, were also delighted, and all of them returned to live with the polytheists in Mecca as brothers. The Prophet ﷺ was the happiest of all, due to the harmony amongst his community.

At night, when the Prophet ﷺ had returned home, Jibra'īl descended to him and asked him to read the chapter that was revealed earlier. The Prophet ﷺ read the chapter up to the point when he read the Gharānīq verse. On hearing it, Jibra'īl cried in a loud voice, "Silence! What is this speech that you utter?" At this time the Prophet ﷺ became aware of his mistake and realised that he had been deceived by Satan. He exclaimed, "I have said something that God did not say; oh, what a great misfortune!"[35]

Very few Muslim scholars give credence to this incredible story, and most have considered it nothing but a fable.[36]

Here, we will highlight just a few of the contradictions in this story, from the Qur'anic verses. If we study the verses that precede and follow the alleged Gharānīq verse, we see that God emphasises that the Prophet ﷺ is not being misled and that he speaks only what is revealed to him by one Mighty in Power. If it was possible for Satan to lay his influence here, the entire Qur'an would be suspect, and God's word could be denied. The remaining verses up to the end of the chapter also criticize, reproach, and reckon as baseless, the ideology of the polytheists.

The Qur'an specifically denies any kind of dominance on the part of Satan over those believers who are in God's refuge:

﴿ إِنَّ عِبَادِى لَيۡسَ لَكَ عَلَيۡهِمۡ سُلۡطَٰنٌ إِلَّا مَنِ ٱتَّبَعَكَ مِنَ ٱلۡغَاوِينَ ﴿٤٢﴾ ﴾

Verily, as regards My servants, you have no authority over them except those who follow you of the deviators. (Al-Ḥijr, 15:42)

When we compare this verse to the Qur'anic declaration…

﴿ وَٱلنَّجۡمِ إِذَا هَوَىٰ ﴿١﴾ مَا ضَلَّ صَاحِبُكُمۡ وَمَا غَوَىٰ ﴿٢﴾ ﴾

[I swear] By the star when it goes down, [that] your companion is neither astray nor being misled. (Al-Najm, 53:1, 2)

…we see that God has used the same word for deviation in the two verses, thereby excluding the Prophet ﷺ from this kind of error. And Satan himself admits to God:

﴿ وَلَأُغۡوِيَنَّهُمۡ أَجۡمَعِينَ ﴿٣٩﴾ إِلَّا عِبَادَكَ مِنۡهُمُ ٱلۡمُخۡلَصِينَ ﴿٤٠﴾ ﴾

And I will certainly cause them all to deviate. Except Your servants from among them, the purified ones. (Al-Ḥijr, 15:39, 40)

How then is it possible for Satan to triumph over the mind of the Prophet ﷺ of Islam? Moreover, God has guaranteed the protection of the Qur'an as follows:

﴿ إِنَّا نَحۡنُ نَزَّلۡنَا ٱلذِّكۡرَ وَإِنَّا لَهُۥ لَحَٰفِظُونَ ﴿٩﴾ ﴾

We have, without doubt, sent down the Message; and We will assuredly guard it (from corruption). (Al-Ḥijr, 15:9)

﴿ لَّا يَأۡتِيهِ ٱلۡبَٰطِلُ مِنۢ بَيۡنِ يَدَيۡهِ وَلَا مِنۡ خَلۡفِهِۦۖ تَنزِيلٞ مِّنۡ حَكِيمٍ حَمِيدٖ ﴿٤٢﴾ ﴾

No falsehood can approach it from before or behind it: it is sent down by One full of Wisdom, Worthy of all Praise. (Fuṣṣilat, 41:42)

We will end the discussion of the Gharānīq tale at this point and conclude that, the Prophet ﷺ did not make any mistake, nor did he go astray and no evil entity ever prevailed over his intellect and thought. Furthermore, even though Jibra'īl was a trustworthy and capable carrier of the revelation, nevertheless the verses of Qur'an were additionally safeguarded by arrays of angels who accompanied him. This escort ensured the immunity of the Divine revelation from any alteration by Satan or the other *jinn*:

﴿ وَٱلصَّٰٓفَّٰتِ صَفًّا ۝١ فَٱلزَّٰجِرَٰتِ زَجۡرًا ۝٢ فَٱلتَّٰلِيَٰتِ ذِكۡرًا ۝٣ ﴾

By those who range themselves in ranks; and so are strong in repelling, and thus proclaim the Dhikr *(Qur'an)* (Al-Ṣāffāt, 37:1-3)

In fact, the prophets ﷷ were very much aware of the happenings in the spiritual world, as indicated in the following tradition:

> Zurāra asked Al-Ṣādiq: "How was the Prophet ﷺ sure that what he received was Divine revelation and not Satanic insinuations? He replied, "When God chooses His servant as His messenger, He instils tranquillity (*sakīna*) and composure (*waqār*) in his heart, and thus, that which would come in his heart would be as clear as that which he would see by his eye."[37]

In another report, it was asked:

> "How did the prophets ﷷ know that they were indeed, prophets? Al-Ṣādiq replied, "the curtain was unveiled from them…"[38]

In summary, the process of *waḥy* is the method by which God communicates with His creatures. These can take the form of complex detailed messages like the ones sent to His prophets ﷷ, or brief moments of inspiration as to the mother of Mūsā ﷷ. In its main form, legislative guidance, (*waḥy al-tashrīʿī*), requires a special intellect and purity in the recipient to be able to receive it. The purity of heart of the recipient allows him to elevate his spirit to a level where he can begin to accommodate the Divine communication, while his intellect allows him to decipher its meaning. Thus we have a tradition from the Prophet ﷺ:

> God did not appoint a prophet or messenger until he had perfected his intellect and his intellect was superior to that of his people.[39]

NOTES

[1] For a fuller discussion, see Muḥammad Taqī Miṣbāḥ Yazdī, *Qur'an Shināsī*, pp. 65 - 68.

[2] Muḥammad Ḥurr al-Āmilī, *Wasā'il al-Shī'a*, vol. 4, p. 856.

[3] *Qur'an Shināsī*, p. 74.

[4] Rāghib Iṣfahānī, *Al-Mufridāt fī Gharīb al-Qur'an*, p. 515.

[5] Aḥmad ibn al-Fārs, *Mu'jam Maqāyīs al-Lughah.*, root (*w-ḥ-y*).

[6] Akbarī et al, *Farhang-e Iṣṭelāḥāt 'Ulūm wa Tamaddun-e Islāmī*, p. 656.

[7] Ibid., p. 61.

[8] See *Al-'Anām*, 6:113.

[9] Muḥammad Hādī Ma'rifat, *'Ulūm-e Qur'anī*, p. 23.

[10] Ṣubḥī Ṣāliḥ, *Qur'an wa Waḥy*, p. 25 – *op cit* Ardabīlī et al, *Tārīkh wa 'Ulūm-e Qur'anī*, p. 159.

[11] Muḥammad Bāqir al-Majlisī, *Biḥār al-Anwār*, vol. 18, pp. 255 - 256.

[12] *'Ulūm-e Qur'anī*, p. 21.

[13] Ibid.

[14] *Al-Mīzān*, vol. 16, p. 10.

[15] 'Abdullāh and Riḍā, *Tafsīr al-Manār*, vol 7, p. 247.

[16] *Al-Mīzān*, vol. 18, p. 73.

[17] The term "holy spirit" refers to an agency other than the archangel Jibra'īl.

[18] *Al-Itqān*, vol. 1 p. 44.

[19] Ṭabrisī, *Majma' al-Bayān li 'Ulūm al-Qur'an*, vol. 1, p. 570; Abū 'Abdillāh Muḥammad b. Ismā'īl al-Bukhārī, *Ṣaḥīḥ al-Bukhārī*, vol. 1 p. 58.

[20] *Al-Itqān*, vol. 1 p. 141.

[21] Muḥammad b. Sa'd, *Al-Ṭabaqāt al-Kubrā*, vol. 1, p. 131.

[22] *Biḥār al-Anwār*, vol. 18, p. 256; *Al-Mīzān*, vol. 18, p. 79.

[23] *Biḥār al-Anwār*, vol. 18, p. 261; *Al-Mīzān*, vol. 18, p. 79.

[24] Muḥammad b. Mas'ūd al-Samarqandī Al-'Ayyāshī, *Tafsīr*, vol. 1, p. 388.

[25] S. S. Akhtar Rizvi, *Qur'an and Ḥadīth*, p. 4.

[26] *Al-Mīzān*, vol. 15, p. 317.

[27] *Biḥār al-Anwār*, vol. 18, p. 256; *Al-Mīzān*, vol. 18, p. 79.

[28] Abū Muḥammad 'Abd al-Malik Ibn al-Hishām, *Al-Sīrah al-Nabawiyyah*, vol. 1, p. 254.

[29] Bukhārī, *Ṣaḥīḥ*, vol. 1, pp. 3-4; Abū al-Ḥusain b. al-Ḥajjāj al-Muslim, *Ṣaḥīḥ*, vol. 1, pp. 98-99; Abū Ja'far Muḥammad b. Jarīr al-Ṭabarī, *Tārīkh al-Ṭabarī*, vol. 2, pp. 298-300.

[30] A *mursal* tradition is one whose chain of narrators is incomplete.

[31] Qāḍī 'Ayyāḍ was a great scholar of Andalucia. He was the authority at his time on grammar, syntax, traditions and Arab history. See *'Ulūm-e Qur'anī*, p. 28.

[32] *Majma' al-Bayān*, vol. 1, p. 384.

[33] Ṭabarī, *Tafsīr*, vol. 17, p. 131; Ṭabarī, *Tārīkh*, vol. 2, pp 75-78; Al-Suyūṭī, *Durr al-Manthūr*, vol. 4, p. 194; Ibn Ḥajar al-'Asqalānī, *Fatḥ al-Bārī bisharḥ Ṣaḥīḥ al-Bukhārī*, vol. 8, p. 333.

[34] Gharānīq (sing. Ghurnūq) are beautiful white birds, thought to be cranes. Here the term refers to the three bird-shaped idols, Lāt, 'Uzzā and Manāt, which were famous amongst the idol-worshippers of the Quraysh. See *Ulūm-e Qur'anī*, p. 27.

[35] The fabrication begins to disintegrate here. If the Satanic verse was corrected the same night, how did the Muslims in Abyssinia hear about it and come back to Mecca so quickly?

[36] For further details of refutation of this story by the scholars, see Muḥammad b. ʿUmar Fakhr al-Dīn al-Rāḍī, *Tafsīr al-Kabīr,* vol. 23, p. 50; Muḥammad Haikal, *Ḥayat Muḥammad,* pp. 124 - 129, amongst many others.
[37] *Biḥār al-Anwār,* vol. 18, p. 262; Al-ʿAyyāshī, *Tafsīr,* vol. 2, p. 201.
[38] *Biḥār al-Anwār,* vol. 11, p. 56.
[39] Abū Jaʿfar Muḥammad al-Kulaynī, *Uṣūl al-Kāfī,* vol. 1, p. 13.

4

THE REVELATION OF THE QUR'AN

The Qur'an is the speech of God, transmitted through the trustworthy archangel Jibra'il and revealed to the heart of the Prophet ﷺ.

The Qur'an says:

﴿ قُلْ مَن كَانَ عَدُوًّا لِّجِبْرِيلَ فَإِنَّهُۥ نَزَّلَهُۥ عَلَىٰ قَلْبِكَ بِإِذْنِ ٱللَّهِ
مُصَدِّقًا لِّمَا بَيْنَ يَدَيْهِ وَهُدًى وَبُشْرَىٰ لِلْمُؤْمِنِينَ ﴿٩٧﴾ ﴾

Say: Whoever is the enemy of Jibra'il – for surely he revealed it to your heart by God's command, verifying that which is before it and guidance and good news for the believers. (Al-Baqara, 2:97)

As soon as verses were thus revealed to him, the Prophet ﷺ would recite the Divine words to the Muslims. In this manner, the Qur'an was revealed gradually over a period of 23 years. In this respect its revelation was different to other Divine scriptures, such as the Tawrāt, which were sent down instantaneously. The Qur'an states that Mūsā (ʿa) went to the mountain of Sinai for forty nights, at the end of which he brought back inscribed tablets containing the Tawrāt:

﴿ قَالَ يَٰمُوسَىٰٓ إِنِّى ٱصْطَفَيْتُكَ عَلَى ٱلنَّاسِ بِرِسَٰلَٰتِى وَبِكَلَٰمِى فَخُذْ مَآ ءَاتَيْتُكَ وَكُن مِّنَ
ٱلشَّٰكِرِينَ ﴿١٤٤﴾ وَكَتَبْنَا لَهُۥ فِى ٱلْأَلْوَاحِ مِن كُلِّ شَىْءٍ مَّوْعِظَةً وَتَفْصِيلًا لِّكُلِّ شَىْءٍ ﴾

He said: O Mūsā! surely I have chosen you above the people with My messages and with My words, therefore take hold of what I give to you, and be of the grateful ones. And We ordained for him in the Tablets [Tawrāt] admonition of every kind and a clear explanation of all things. (Al-Aʿrāf, 7:144,145)

In fact, one of the objections of the Quraysh was about the fact that the verses of the Qur'an were revealed gradually. The Qur'an states the reason for this in the following verse:

﴿ وَقَالَ ٱلَّذِينَ كَفَرُوا۟ لَوْلَا نُزِّلَ عَلَيْهِ ٱلْقُرْءَانُ جُمْلَةً وَٰحِدَةً ۚ كَذَٰلِكَ لِنُثَبِّتَ بِهِۦ فُؤَادَكَ ۖ ﴾

And those who disbelieve say: Why has not the Qur'an been revealed to him all at once? Thus, that We may strengthen your heart by it... (Al-Furqān, 25:32)

4.1 - THE BEGINNING OF THE REVELATION

The revelation of the Qur'an began in the blessed month of Ramaḍān, in the "night of decree" (*laylat al-qadr*):

﴿ شَهْرُ رَمَضَانَ ٱلَّذِىٓ أُنزِلَ فِيهِ ٱلْقُرْءَانُ هُدًى لِّلنَّاسِ وَبَيِّنَٰتٍ مِّنَ ٱلْهُدَىٰ وَٱلْفُرْقَانِ ﴾

The month of Ramaḍān, in which was sent down the Qur'an; [it was sent] as a guide for mankind, and a clear guidance and criterion [between good and evil]. (Al-Baqara, 2:185)

﴿ إِنَّآ أَنزَلْنَٰهُ فِى لَيْلَةٍ مُّبَٰرَكَةٍ ۚ إِنَّا كُنَّا مُنذِرِينَ ﴿٣﴾ فِيهَا يُفْرَقُ كُلُّ أَمْرٍ حَكِيمٍ ﴿٤﴾ ﴾

We sent it down during a blessed night: for We [always] wish to warn [against evil]. In that [night] is made distinct every affair of wisdom. (Al-Dukhān, 44:3, 4)

﴿ إِنَّآ أَنزَلْنَٰهُ فِى لَيْلَةِ ٱلْقَدْرِ ﴿١﴾ ﴾

We have indeed revealed this [Qur'an] in the night of decree. (Al-Qadr, 97:1)

According to reliable traditions, this night of decree is either the 21st, 23rd, or 27th night of the month of Ramaḍān.

4.2 - THE BEGINNING OF THE DIVINE COMMISSION (*AL-BI'THA*)

According to the most reliable reports, God sent the angel Jibra'īl to the Prophet ﷺ with the first revelation on the 27th of Rajab.[1] At the time, the Prophet ﷺ was 40 years old and this was thirteen years prior to his migration to Medina (609 CE). This day is known as the day of the Divine commission (*al-bi'tha*). Other dates are also mentioned for this event by the historians, such as the 8th of Rabīʿ al-Awwal[2] and the 17th of Ramaḍān.[3]

The events leading to the first revelation are as follows: as was his habit, the Prophet ﷺ had gone for meditation and worship to the cave of Ḥirā, on the mountain of Nūr, at the outskirts of Mecca. The archangel Jibra'īl came to him while he was meditating in the cave, and announced:

﴿ ٱقْرَأْ بِٱسْمِ رَبِّكَ ٱلَّذِى خَلَقَ ۝١ خَلَقَ ٱلْإِنسَـٰنَ مِنْ عَلَقٍ ۝٢ ٱقْرَأْ وَرَبُّكَ ٱلْأَكْرَمُ ۝٣ ٱلَّذِى عَلَّمَ بِٱلْقَلَمِ ۝٤ عَلَّمَ ٱلْإِنسَـٰنَ مَا لَمْ يَعْلَمْ ۝٥ ﴾

Read in the name of your Lord Who created. He created man from a clot. Read and your Lord is Most Honourable. Who taught (to write) with the pen. Taught man what he knew not. (Al-ʿAlaq, 96:1-5)

Thus, the initial revelation comprised of the first five verses of chapter *Al-ʿAlaq*.

4.3 - RECONCILIATION BETWEEN THE DATES OF THE DIVINE COMMISSION (*AL-BIʿTHA*) AND THE NIGHT OF DECREE (*LAYLAT AL-QADR*)

We need to try to understand what is meant by the revelation of the Qur'an on the night of decree, and reconcile it with the date of the first revelation in the cave of Ḥirā. The opinions of the scholars, about the manner in which the Qur'an was revealed, can be summarised into four:

1. The beginning of the revelation of the Qur'an was on the night of decree.

2. Every year, on the night of decree, a portion of the Qur'an was revealed.

3. Most of the verses of the Qur'an were revealed in the month of

Ramaḍān.

4. The Qur'an had two revelations: instantaneous and gradual.

Each of these possibilities will be discussed in turn.

1. THAT THE BEGINNING OF THE REVELATION OF THE QUR'AN WAS ON THE NIGHT OF DECREE (*LAYLAT AL-QADR*)

Some scholars are of the opinion that the beginning of the revelation of Qur'an was in the night of decree, and they cite the following verses as evidence: [4]

﴿ شَهْرُ رَمَضَانَ ٱلَّذِىٓ أُنزِلَ فِيهِ ٱلْقُرْءَانُ ﴾

The month of Ramaḍān, in which was sent down the Qur'an. (Al-Baqara, 2:185)

and

﴿ إِنَّآ أَنزَلْنَٰهُ فِى لَيْلَةِ ٱلْقَدْرِ ۝١ ﴾

We have indeed revealed it [Qur'an] in the night of decree. (Al-Qadr, 97:1)

Their arguments may be summarised as follows:

1. In the verses above, the word "Qur'an" does not refer to the complete Book, and this was what was understood by the Muslims at the time also. The entire Qur'an, with its words, sentences and particularities cannot have been revealed in one place and in one night, except if one resorts to an esoteric interpretation (*ta'wīl*) of the verse.

2. The Qur'an talks of future events (in relation to the first night of decree), in the past tense. Two examples are given below:

﴿ وَلَقَدْ نَصَرَكُمُ ٱللَّهُ بِبَدْرٍ وَأَنتُمْ أَذِلَّةٌ ﴾

God had helped you at Badr, when you were a small force. (Āli 'Imrān, 3:123)

﴿ إِلَّا تَنصُرُوهُ فَقَدْ نَصَرَهُ ٱللَّهُ إِذْ أَخْرَجَهُ ٱلَّذِينَ كَفَرُوا۟ ﴾

If you do not help him (the Prophet), [it is no matter], for God did indeed help him, when the unbelievers drove him out. (Al-Tawba, 9:40)

There are many such verses in the Qur'an that inform us of past occurrences. If they were revealed on the night of decree, they should have couched in the future (or distant future) tense. Otherwise the speech would be far from the truth.

Additionally, there are many abrogating (*nāsikh*) and abrogated (*mansūkh*), general (*ʿām*) and particular (*khāṣṣ*), and absolute (*muṭlaq*) and confined (*muqayyad*), verses in the Qur'an. Now, we know that the abrogating verse requires the abrogated verse to precede it in time. Likewise, in the other cases mentioned above, a temporal interval is necessary. Furthermore, in the verse…

﴿ شَهْرُ رَمَضَانَ ٱلَّذِىٓ أُنزِلَ فِيهِ ٱلْقُرْءَانُ ﴾

The month of Ramaḍān, in which was sent down the Qur'an. (Al-Baqara, 2:185)

…and other similar verses, there is a conundrum. If the entire Qur'an was revealed on the night of decree, then these verses are informing us of themselves too. This would necessitate the wording of the verse to be different, perhaps, "in which, is sent down..." or, "in which, we are sending down...", instead of, "...in which, was sent down". Since this is not the case, we have to conclude that the revelation on the night of decree means the "start of the revelation" and not that the entire Qur'an was revealed at once on this night.

3. There are many traditions that prove that the Qur'an was revealed on different occasions and in different places. Some verses were revealed in Mecca, some in Medina, and occasionally the Prophet ﷺ would await the revelation of verses. Besides, the Qur'an itself clearly states that it was revealed in a gradual form:

﴿ وَقَالَ ٱلَّذِينَ كَفَرُوا۟ لَوْلَا نُزِّلَ عَلَيْهِ ٱلْقُرْءَانُ جُمْلَةً وَٰحِدَةً

كَذَٰلِكَ لِنُثَبِّتَ بِهِۦ فُؤَادَكَ ۖ وَرَتَّلْنَٰهُ تَرْتِيلًا ﴿٣٢﴾

And those who disbelieve say: why has not the Qur'an been revealed to him all at once? Thus, that We may strengthen your heart by it and We have arranged it well in arranging. (Al-Furqān, 25:32)

COMMENT

All the above arguments conclude that the verses of the Qur'an were revealed gradually. While these arguments are all valid for the physical gradual revelation, they do not however, negate the possibility of a separate, instantaneous revelation. It is of course understood that this instantaneous revelation was not in the physical form of words and phrases, but was of a spiritual form, whose exact nature cannot be comprehended fully.

As for the point that, if the Qur'an was revealed on the night of decree, it would not refer to future events in the past tense, this is not strictly true. The Qur'an talks of the day of Judgement in the past tense, but the meaning is that of the distant future. In the Arabic language something which is definitely going to occur in the future is occasionally mentioned in the past tense. For example:

﴿ فَإِذَا بَرِقَ ٱلْبَصَرُ ﴿٧﴾ وَخَسَفَ ٱلْقَمَرُ ﴿٨﴾ وَجُمِعَ ٱلشَّمْسُ وَٱلْقَمَرُ ﴿٩﴾

يَقُولُ ٱلْإِنسَٰنُ يَوْمَئِذٍ أَيْنَ ٱلْمَفَرُّ ﴿١٠﴾ ﴾

So when the sight became (becomes) dazed, and the moon became (becomes) dark, and the sun and the moon were (are) brought together; man shall say on that day, "Where to flee to?" (Al-Qiyāma, 75:7-10)

2. THAT EVERY YEAR, ON THE NIGHT OF DECREE, A PORTION OF THE QUR'AN WAS REVEALED

A group of scholars have mentioned the opinion that annually, that portion of the Qur'an which was necessary for that particular year, was revealed to the Prophet ﷺ on the night of decree.[5] Thereafter, the same verses were gradually revealed during the year, as the occasion would demand. According to this assumption, in the verses 2:185 and 97:1, the month of Ramaḍān and the night of decree does not denote a specific month of Ramaḍān or a specific night of decree; rather every month of Ramaḍān and every night of decree is meant. In other words, the terms have been used in a general sense and not a particular one.

COMMENT

This view is only related to the verse of Al-Baqara which talks about the revelation of the Qur'an in the month of Ramaḍān, but does not tally with the verses of Al-Qadr. In that chapter, the usage of the definite article indicates a particular night of decree and not all of them.

3. THAT MOST OF THE VERSES OF THE QUR'AN WERE REVEALED IN THE MONTH OF RAMAḌĀN.

The opinion that most of the verses of the Qur'an were revealed in the month of Ramaḍān, is mentioned by some scholars.[6]

COMMENT

There is no evidence cited to support this view. Besides, it specifically concerns the verse of Al-Baqara which talks about the revelation of the Qur'an in the month of Ramaḍān, but does not reconcile with the verses of Al-Qadr and Al-Dukhān which both mention a single night in the month of Ramaḍān.

As can be seen from the comments on each, the three opinions above cannot be accepted as the whole solution. That which is more plausible is the fourth and final view discussed below.

4. THAT THE QUR'AN HAD TWO STAGES OF REVELATION; ONE INSTANTANEOUS AND THE OTHER GRADUAL

A group of scholars, who are mentioned below, believe that the Qur'an had two revelations; one instantaneous and the other gradual. The Qur'an was revealed to the Prophet ﷺ all at a once, in a spiritual form, on the night of decree; and then it was revealed gradually, in the form of verses and phrases, throughout the period of his prophethood. This view is the most popular amongst both Sunnī and Shīʿa authorities. Some have adopted this view from the traditions while others have accepted it through esoteric interpretation. Al-Suyūṭī says:

> The most correct and well-known view is this very view, and many traditions support it. Ibn ʿAbbās is reported to have said, "The Qur'an was revealed instantaneously, on the night of decree, to the earthly heaven, where it was kept in the "abode of honour" (*bayt al-ʿizza*); thereafter, Jibra'īl would bring down to the Prophet ﷺ portions of it in response to the questions and actions of the people. This process of gradual revelation lasted for 20 or 23 years.[7]

Kulaynī reports:

> Al-Sadiq was asked, "The Qur'an was revealed within a span of twenty years, then why did God say it was revealed in the month of Ramaḍān?" He replied, "The Qur'an was revealed in one instant to the "abode of immortality" (*bayt al-maʿmūr*), after which its revelation took 20 years.[8]

This is the view accepted by Ṣadūq, Majlisī[9], Shubbar[10], and others.[11]

Concerning the instantaneous and gradual revelation of the Qur'an, a sample of the opinions of some of the prominent scholars is given below:

Ṣadūq says: "What is meant by the instantaneous revelation of the Qur'an on the night of decree, is that the Prophet ﷺ was informed of the general content of the Qur'an. The Qur'an was not revealed to him on the night of decree in the form of letters and statements; rather, he was only bestowed with its knowledge, and he thereby became aware of its contents in general."[12]

Kāshānī believes that the *bayt al-ma'mūr* is the heart of the Prophet ﷺ. He explains that the Prophet ﷺ has attained that high and unique stage, where his heart could contain the Qur'an. Thereafter, over the course of his mission, the Qur'an flowed from the heart of the Prophet ﷺ to his tongue, whenever Jibra'īl would reveal a part thereof.

Zanjānī says: "The spirit of the Qur'an, which is its exalted objectives and which contains universal dimensions, manifested in the pure heart of the Prophet ﷺ on that night:

﴿ نَزَلَ بِهِ ٱلرُّوحُ ٱلْأَمِينُ ﴿١٩٣﴾ عَلَىٰ قَلْبِكَ ﴾

The Trustworthy Spirit [Jibra'īl] brought it [the Qur'an] to your heart.
(Al-Shu'arā', 26:193, 194)

Thereafter, during the course of his mission, it manifested onto his blessed tongue:

﴿ وَقُرْءَانًا فَرَقْنَٰهُ لِتَقْرَأَهُۥ عَلَى ٱلنَّاسِ عَلَىٰ مُكْثٍ وَنَزَّلْنَٰهُ تَنزِيلًا ﴿١٠٦﴾ ﴾

(It is) a Qur'an which We have divided [into segments], in order that you might recite it to the people at intervals. We have revealed it in stages. (Al-Isrā', 17:106)

Ṭabāṭabā'ī also makes the same esoteric interpretation, he says:

> Fundamentally, the Qur'an possesses another existence and reality, hidden behind its apparent form and far from ordinary sight and comprehension. The Qur'an, in its inner reality, is free from any kind of division and detail. It does not possess parts, chapters and verses. Rather, it is a single reality, interconnected and firm, which is firmly placed in its exalted station. God says:

﴿ الٓر ۚ كِتَٰبٌ أُحْكِمَتْ ءَايَٰتُهُۥ ثُمَّ فُصِّلَتْ مِن لَّدُنْ حَكِيمٍ خَبِيرٍ ﴿١﴾ ﴾

Alif Lām Rā. (This is) a Book, whose verses are fundamental [of established meaning], thereafter explained in detail [simplified], from One Who is Wise, Well-acquainted [with all things]. (Hūd, 11:1)

﴿ وَإِنَّهُۥ فِىٓ أُمِّ ٱلْكِتَٰبِ لَدَيْنَا لَعَلِىٌّ حَكِيمٌ ﴿٤﴾ ﴾

And verily, it [the Qur'an] is in the Mother of the Book, in Our Presence, exalted, full of wisdom. (Al-Zukhruf, 43:4)

﴿ إِنَّهُۥ لَقُرْءَانٌ كَرِيمٌ ﴿٧٧﴾ فِى كِتَـٰبٍ مَّكْنُونٍ ﴿٧٨﴾ لَّا يَمَسُّهُۥٓ إِلَّا ٱلْمُطَهَّرُونَ ﴿٧٩﴾ ﴾

That this is indeed a Qur'an most honourable, in a Book well-guarded, which none shall touch but those who are pure. (Al-Wāqiʿa, 56:77-79)

COMMENT

This view conforms to the evidence from both the Qur'an and traditions. Therefore, we can conclude that the Qur'an has two kind of existence; its physical existence, which is in the form of letters, words and phrases, and its non-physical existence, which is stationed in its own place.

Thus, the Qur'an in its original form, which is a single reality, was revealed to the heart of the Prophet ﷺ all at once, on the night of decree. Thereafter, it descended gradually, in its detailed and existing form, at different intervals and occasions during the period of the prophethood.

There are two verses that indicate that the Prophet ﷺ already had the knowledge of the Qur'an even before the gradual revelation. These are:

﴿ وَلَا تَعْجَلْ بِٱلْقُرْءَانِ مِن قَبْلِ أَن يُقْضَىٰٓ إِلَيْكَ وَحْيُهُۥ ۖ ﴾

And do not make haste with the Qur'an before its revelation is made complete to you.

(Ṭā Hā, 20:114)

﴿ لَا تُحَرِّكْ بِهِۦ لِسَانَكَ لِتَعْجَلَ بِهِۦٓ ﴾

Do not move your tongue with it to make haste with it. (Al-Qiyāma, 75:16)

4.4 - THE STAGES OF REVELATION

The Prophet ﷺ was not the first messenger to receive divine revelation, as the Qur'an testifies:

﴿ إِنَّآ أَوۡحَيۡنَآ إِلَيۡكَ كَمَآ أَوۡحَيۡنَآ إِلَىٰ نُوحٖ وَٱلنَّبِيِّـۧنَ مِنۢ بَعۡدِهِۦۚ وَأَوۡحَيۡنَآ إِلَىٰٓ إِبۡرَٰهِيمَ
وَإِسۡمَٰعِيلَ وَإِسۡحَٰقَ وَيَعۡقُوبَ وَٱلۡأَسۡبَاطِ وَعِيسَىٰ وَأَيُّوبَ وَيُونُسَ وَهَٰرُونَ وَسُلَيۡمَٰنَۚ وَءَاتَيۡنَا
دَاوُۥدَ زَبُورٗا ١٦٣
وَرُسُلٗا قَدۡ قَصَصۡنَٰهُمۡ عَلَيۡكَ مِن قَبۡلُ وَرُسُلٗا لَّمۡ نَقۡصُصۡهُمۡ عَلَيۡكَۚ
وَكَلَّمَ ٱللَّهُ مُوسَىٰ تَكۡلِيمٗا ١٦٤ ﴾

Surely We have revealed to you as We revealed to Nūḥ, and the prophets after him, and We revealed to Ibrāhīm and Ismāʿīl and Isḥāq and Yaʿqūb and the tribes, and ʿĪsā and Ayyūb and Yūnus and Harūn and Sulaimān and We gave to Dāwūd Psalms. And (We sent) messengers We have mentioned to you before and messengers we have not mentioned to you; and to Mūsā, God addressed His Word, speaking (to him).
(Al-Nisāʾ, 4:163, 164)

Although this verse only mentions the major prophets amongst the Banū Isrāʾīl, in all, a total of twenty-six prophets ﵈ have been mentioned in the Qur'an. As the verse states, all of them were recipients of revelation, as indeed was every other prophet of God.

The methodology of revelation through the ages does not seem to be different. A study of the traditions suggests that revelation, which is the manifestation of God's speech to man – occurs in several phases. In the case of the Prophet ﷺ of Islam, three stages can be identified:

THE FIRST STAGE

The first stage deals with matters that happen in a realm that is beyond man's understanding. We know that God sent the Qur'an to the "guarded" or "preserved" tablet (*al-lawḥ al-maḥfūẓ*). Little is known about the nature of the tablet; some traditions mention that this is the tablet upon which all the things that will happen until the end of time are written. The Qur'an states:

﴿ بَلۡ هُوَ قُرۡءَانٞ مَّجِيدٞ ٢١ فِي لَوۡحٖ مَّحۡفُوظِۭ ٢٢ ﴾

Nay! It is a glorious Qur'an. In a guarded tablet. (Al-Burūj, 85:21, 22)

THE SECOND STAGE

From the guarded tablet, God transmitted the Qur'an to a more accessible location in the earthly heaven, to a place called "the abode of honour" (*al-bayt al-ʿizza*) or the "abode of immortality" (*al-bayt al-maʿmūr*). As we have discussed, many scholars believe that this "abode" is an allusion to the heart of the Prophet ﷺ. This transference occurred in the night of decree (*laylat al-qadr*) in the month of Ramaḍān.

﴿ شَهْرُ رَمَضَانَ ٱلَّذِىٓ أُنزِلَ فِيهِ ٱلْقُرْءَانُ ﴾

The month of Ramaḍān, in which was sent down the Qur'an. (Al-Baqara, 2:185)

THE THIRD STAGE

In this stage, Jibra'īl communicated the verses of the Qur'an to the Prophet ﷺ, as directed by God. This stage of the revelation lasted for 23 years, throughout the mission of the Prophet ﷺ. The Qur'an states:

﴿ وَرَتَّلْنَٰهُ تَرْتِيلًا ﴿٣٢﴾ ﴾

We have revealed it to you in gradual, well-arranged stages. (Al-Furqān, 25:32)

4.5 - THE BENEFITS OF GRADUAL REVELATION

The Divine books given to the prophets Mūsā ﵇, ʿĪsā ﵇ and Dāwūd ﵇, and the scrolls sent down to Ibrāhīm ﵇ and other messengers are thought to have been revealed in their complete form in one go. It is usually mentioned that the Qur'an is different in this respect, because it was revealed gradually. However, God does not change His practice, as He says:

﴿ فَلَن تَجِدَ لِسُنَّتِ ٱللَّهِ تَبْدِيلًا ۖ وَلَن تَجِدَ لِسُنَّتِ ٱللَّهِ تَحْوِيلًا ﴿٤٣﴾ ﴾

For you shall not find any alteration in the course of God; and you shall not find any change in the course of God. (Al-Fāṭir, 35:43).

It seems likely therefore, that all the divine messages were revealed in the same way; they initially came to the heart of the messenger in their entirety, and then the messenger would formally receive the details, which he would in turn communicate to his people, as and when directed by God.

There are several advantages to this steady and continual revelation. The Qur'an itself refers to the phenomenon as a blessing to the Muslims, in the form of the strengthening of their hearts. When the unbelievers demanded to know why the Qur'an was not revealed all at once like the previous scriptures, the following verse was revealed,

﴿ وَقَالَ ٱلَّذِينَ كَفَرُوا۟ لَوْلَا نُزِّلَ عَلَيْهِ ٱلْقُرْءَانُ جُمْلَةً وَٰحِدَةً ۚ
كَذَٰلِكَ لِنُثَبِّتَ بِهِۦ فُؤَادَكَ ۖ وَرَتَّلْنَٰهُ تَرْتِيلًا ﴿٣٢﴾ ﴾

The unbelievers say: "Why is the Qur'an not revealed to him all at once? (It is revealed) Thus, so that We may strengthen your heart thereby, and [We have revealed it to you in gradual], well-arranged stages. (Al-Furqān, 25:32)

Interestingly, the Qur'an does not reject the objection of the unbelievers. (This is further evidence of the point we have made earlier, specifically, that the Qur'an was revealed in one go, but to the heart of the Prophet ﷺ.) Instead, the verse mentions the benefit of gradual revelation. Some other benefits are given in the following sub-sections.

1. TO GIVE THE MUSLIMS CONSTANT GUIDANCE IN STEP WITH THE SITUATIONS THEY FACED

By the continual revelation of the Qur'an to the Prophet ﷺ, the Muslims felt a sense of constant guidance from God. This answered their doubts and queries, strengthened their resolve and gave them the patience to withstand the hardship that they were facing, especially at the hands of the idolaters in the early years and from the Jews and hypocrites in the later ones.

Verses were revealed in response to many events that took place in the lives of the Muslims, and these form the basis of the branch of the Qur'anic sciences known as *asbāb al-nuzūl,* or occasions of revelation.

2. TO FACILITATE EASE IN RECORDING, MEMORISATION AND UNDERSTANDING OF THE QUR'AN BY THE COMPANIONS

This gradual revelation made it easier for the companions to understand, memorise and put into practice the portions that were revealed. Due to the fact that relatively few people could read and write in those days, interaction with a large amount of text would be difficult. However, because just a few verses were revealed at a time, the Muslims had the opportunity to memorize them, ponder deeply about God's message, and to transform their lives accordingly. Even in later times, when the whole Qur'an was available in a book form, the companions preferred to teach the Qur'an to the successors (*tābiʿūn*) a few verses at a time.

3. TO PROVE THE APOSTLESHIP OF THE PROPHET ﷺ

The unbelievers would ask the Prophet ﷺ questions in an attempt to discredit him, but each time a verse or chapter of the Qur'an would be revealed in answer to their questions. For example, the idolaters of the Quraysh consulted the Jews for information about ancient nations and events, and then challenged the Prophet ﷺ to answer a list of questions, including one about the seven sleepers of the cave. In response, the chapter of Kahf was revealed. Similarly, the Jews instructed the Quraysh to ask how the Banū Isrāʾīl ended up in Egypt, when Yaʿqūb عليه السلام and his sons were residents of Canaan (Kanʿān); in reply a beautiful and comprehensive reply came in the form of chapter

Yūsuf. This remained the practice throughout the Prophet's ﷺ mission, and the Qur'an states:

﴿ وَلَا يَأْتُونَكَ بِمَثَلٍ إِلَّا جِئْنَٰكَ بِٱلْحَقِّ وَأَحْسَنَ تَفْسِيرًا ﴿٣٣﴾ ﴾

And they shall not bring to you any argument, but We have brought to you (one) with truth and best in significance. (Al-Furqān, 25:33)

4. A TESTAMENT TO THE MIRACLE OF THE QUR'AN

One of the most outstanding miracles of the Qur'an is that although it was continually revealed over a period of 23 years – with over 6,000 verses, covering a variety of topics – yet there is no contradiction found in its contents. As a new verse was revealed, it fitted easily with the rest to create, in time, a coherent and perfect whole. Achieving such a seamless harmony over such a long time is a feat that cannot be accomplished by a human being. The Qur'an states:

﴿ أَفَلَا يَتَدَبَّرُونَ ٱلْقُرْءَانَ ۚ وَلَوْ كَانَ مِنْ عِندِ غَيْرِ ٱللَّهِ لَوَجَدُوا۟ فِيهِ ٱخْتِلَٰفًا كَثِيرًا ﴿٨٢﴾ ﴾

Do they not then meditate upon the Qur'an? If it were from any other than God, they would have found in it many discrepancies. (Al-Nisā', 4:82)

5. TO PRESENT THE TEACHINGS OF ISLAM IN A GRADUAL MANNER

The gradual nature of the revelation allowed the Muslims to more easily assimilate the new ideas and directives that Islam brought to their lives. The early Meccan verses continually emphasised the basics of belief; eloquently and persuasively arguing against idolatry and promoting *tawḥīd*. Once the basics were understood and accepted in society, then the articles of worship were introduced one by one to a more ready and receptive audience.

An example that is usually mentioned about the gradual introduction of rulings is the manner in which the use of intoxicants was eventually forbidden. This prohibition was revealed in four stages.

In Mecca, the Qur'an made a mention of the fruit of the date palm and grapes; at that time there was no prohibition in place against drinking intoxicants and some Muslims drank alcohol.[13] Later, the Muslims were instructed not to come to the prayers intoxicated. After some time, intoxicants were labelled a great sin and finally, intoxicants were attributed to the evils of Satan and prohibited outright. The four verses below illustrate this gradual prohibition:

﴿ وَمِن ثَمَرَٰتِ ٱلنَّخِيلِ وَٱلۡأَعۡنَٰبِ تَتَّخِذُونَ مِنۡهُ سَكَرٗا وَرِزۡقًا حَسَنًاۚ
إِنَّ فِي ذَٰلِكَ لَأٓيَةٗ لِّقَوۡمٖ يَعۡقِلُونَ ٦٧ ﴾

And of the fruits of the palms and the grapes – you obtain from (both of) them intoxication and goodly provision; most surely there is a sign in this for a people who ponder (Al-Naḥl, 16:67)

followed by

﴿ يَٰٓأَيُّهَا ٱلَّذِينَ ءَامَنُواْ لَا تَقۡرَبُواْ ٱلصَّلَوٰةَ وَأَنتُمۡ سُكَٰرَىٰ حَتَّىٰ تَعۡلَمُواْ مَا تَقُولُونَ ﴾

O you who believe! Do not approach the prayer while you are intoxicated, [wait] until you know (well) what you say. (Al-Nisā', 4:43)

followed by

﴿ يَسۡـَٔلُونَكَ عَنِ ٱلۡخَمۡرِ وَٱلۡمَيۡسِرِۖ
قُلۡ فِيهِمَآ إِثۡمٞ كَبِيرٞ وَمَنَٰفِعُ لِلنَّاسِ وَإِثۡمُهُمَآ أَكۡبَرُ مِن نَّفۡعِهِمَاۗ ﴾

They ask you about intoxicants and games of chance. Say: In both of them there is a great sin and means of profit for men, and their sin is greater than their profit. (Al-Baqara, 2:219)

and finally,

﴿ يَٰٓأَيُّهَا ٱلَّذِينَ ءَامَنُوٓاْ إِنَّمَا ٱلۡخَمۡرُ وَٱلۡمَيۡسِرُ وَٱلۡأَنصَابُ وَٱلۡأَزۡلَٰمُ رِجۡسٞ مِّنۡ عَمَلِ ٱلشَّيۡطَٰنِ
فَٱجۡتَنِبُوهُ لَعَلَّكُمۡ تُفۡلِحُونَ ٩٠ إِنَّمَا يُرِيدُ ٱلشَّيۡطَٰنُ أَن يُوقِعَ بَيۡنَكُمُ ٱلۡعَدَٰوَةَ وَٱلۡبَغۡضَآءَ فِي

ٱلْخَمْرِ وَٱلْمَيْسِرِ وَيَصُدَّكُمْ عَن ذِكْرِ ٱللَّهِ وَعَنِ ٱلصَّلَوٰةِ ۖ فَهَلْ أَنتُم مُّنتَهُونَ ﴿٩١﴾

O you who believe! Intoxicants and games of chance and [sacrificing to] stones set up and [divining by] arrows are only an uncleanness, the Satan's work; shun it therefore that you may be successful. The Satan only desires to cause enmity and hatred to spring in your midst by means of intoxicants and games of chance, and to keep you off from the remembrance of God and from prayer. Will you then (not) desist? (Al-Mā'ida, 5:90, 91)

6. TO TAKE INTO ACCOUNT THE LEVEL OF LITERACY OF THE MUSLIMS

Al-Suyūṭī mentions that some scholars believe that the Qur'an was revealed gradually, unlike the Tawrāt, because Mūsā ﷺ was literate while the Prophet Muḥammad ﷺ, and most of his nation, were unable to read and write[14]; this seems a far-fetched opinion and the more plausible reasons are those that we have already mentioned above.

CONCLUSION

In conclusion, the strongest reasons for gradual revelation have to be related to the first generation of Muslims and the Prophet ﷺ himself. This is because successive generations of Muslims did not receive the Qur'an gradually; rather, the Divine book was always accessible to them in a complete form. Therefore, the main effect was that of verifying the Prophet's ﷺ claim to prophethood, and inspiring and strengthening the resolve of the early Muslims who had the great responsibility of transferring the religion to future generations.

NOTES

[1] Ṭūsī quotes from al-Ṣādiq: "The Prophet ﷺ was elevated to prophethood on the 27th of Rajab. The reward for one who fasts on this day is like the reward for fasting 60 months." (Ḥurr al-Āmilī, *Wasā'il*, vol. 7, p. 330).

[2] Aḥmad b. abū Ya'qūb al-Ya'qūbī, *Tārīkh al-Ya'qūbī*, vol. 2, p. 17.

[3] Abū al-Fadā', *Tārīkh*, vol. 1, p. 115 - See *'Ulūm-e Qur'anī*, p. 61.

[4] *Al-Kashshāf*, vol. 1, p. 227; 'Abduh, *Al-Manār*, vol. 2, p. 158; *'Ulūm-e Qur'anī*, p. 65.
[5] *Tafsīr al-Kabīr*, vol. 5, p. 85; *Al-Durr al-Manthūr*, vol. 1, p. 189 and *Al-Itqān*, vol. 1, p. 40.
[6] Quṭb, *Fī Ẓilāl al-Qur'an*, vol. 2, p. 79.
[7] *Al-Itqān*, vol. 1, pp. 116 - 117.
[8] *Al-Kāfī*, vol. 2, p. 269; *Al-Mīzān*, vol. 2, p. 29.
[9] *Biḥār al-Anwār*, vol. 18, pp. 250 - 253.
[10] 'Abdallāh Shubbar, *Tafsīr Shubbar*, p. 350.
[11] *Al-Itqān*, vol. 1, p. 40.
[12] Ṣadūq, *Al-I'tiqādāt*, p. 101.
[13] See Ḥujjatī, *Tārīkh-e Qur'an-e Karīm*, p. 51 (citing the exegesis of Abū al-Maḥāsin al-Jurjānī).
[14] *Al-Itqān*, vol. 1, p. 71.

5

OCCASIONS OF REVELATION: *ASBĀB AL-NUZŪL*

The Qur'an, in its original form is free from any kind of division and detail. It does not possess parts, chapters and verses. However, God revealed it in portions which were sent down gradually. The verses were sent according to the events that had a bearing on their revelation. The Qur'an states:

﴿ وَقُرْءَانًا فَرَقْنَـٰهُ لِتَقْرَأَهُۥ عَلَى ٱلنَّاسِ عَلَىٰ مُكْثٍ وَنَزَّلْنَـٰهُ تَنزِيلًا ﴿١٠٦﴾ ﴾

And it is a Qur'an which We have revealed in portions so that you may read it to the people by slow degrees, and We have revealed it, revealing in portions. (Al-Isrā', 17:106)

Of course, there is a basic difference between revealing the Qur'an to the Prophet ﷺ in portions and other methods of guidance, for example, teaching a student a book, piece by piece. In the case of a teacher and student, the teacher prepares and teaches the lessons in sequential order so that the subject is gradually made clear for the student. But the Qur'anic verses do not run in sequential fashion. Therefore, it is useful to know the circumstances under which a verse is revealed, and this is what we are concerned with when we study the occasions of revelation – *asbāb al-nuzūl.* In fact, some scholars are of the opinion that without knowing the *asbāb al-nuzūl* of the verses it is not possible to understand their meaning fully.[1] Indeed, some scholars consider knowing the *asbāb al-nuzūl* of a verse as the best way to understand its meaning.[2]

5.1 - MEANING OF *ASBĀB AL-NUZŪL*

Asbāb (sing. *sabab*) has various meanings which can be found in the verses of the Qur'an, for example: rope[3], access[4], attachment[5], means[6] and path.[7] The common meaning throughout the verses in the Qur'an is "the means of access" to a thing, and indeed, the meaning of *sabab* is anything that provides the means of access to the goal.[8] So, in the study of *asbāb al-nuzūl*, we are concerned with the circumstances of revelation of a specific verse of the Qur'an, in order to "get access" to the meaning of the verse, or at least a preliminary understanding of it. This necessitates the knowledge about the particular events and circumstances and places that are related to the revelation of that verse. In other words, the occasion that prompted the revelation of the verse. That is why we will translate the term *asbāb al-nuzūl* as "occasions of revelation".

5.2 - THE DIFFERENCE BETWEEN THE TERMS, "OCCASION OF REVELATION" (*SABAB AL-NUZŪL*) AND "REASON FOR REVELATION" (*SHA'N AL-NUZŪL*)

Most exegetes do not see any difference between these two terms; and they have used the terms interchangeably for every occasion that has necessitated a verse or verses to be revealed. However, there does exist a subtle difference between the terms; the significance of the reason for revelation (*sha'n al-nuzūl*) is more general than that of the occasion of revelation (*sabab al-nuzūl*).

Whenever a verse or verses are revealed immediately after an incident, that incident is referred to as the occasion of revelation. In other words, the revelation took place as a result of that incident.

Whenever a verse or verses are revealed about an incident concerning a person or an event, whether of the past, present or future, or concerning the obligation of Islamic laws, then that incident is referred to as the reason for revelation.[9]

Therefore, *sabab* is more specific, while *sha'n* is more general. As an example, it cannot be said that the occasion of revelation (*sabab al-nūzūl*) of *Al-Fīl* was the attacking of the Kaʿba by the Christian Yemenite governor, Abrahā, because this event occurred in the year of the birth of the Prophet ﷺ, well before the revelation of the Qur'an. Even though this incident explains the meaning of the verses, it does not qualify as its occasion of revelation, since it did not occur immediately before the revelation of this chapter. In this case, the incident of the attack on the Kaʿba is the reason of revelation, (*sha'n al-nuzūl*), of the chapter.

In this chapter, we will only concern ourselves with the term "occasions of revelation" – the *asbāb al-nūzūl*.

5.3 - TYPES OF OCCASIONS OF REVELATION

Not all the verses of the Qur'an have an occasion of revelation. In fact, many verses, have been revealed purely for guidance and there is no specific question or circumstance that has prompted its revelation. For example:

﴿ الٓر ۚ كِتَٰبٌ أَنزَلۡنَٰهُ إِلَيۡكَ لِتُخۡرِجَ ٱلنَّاسَ مِنَ ٱلظُّلُمَٰتِ
إِلَى ٱلنُّورِ بِإِذۡنِ رَبِّهِمۡ إِلَىٰ صِرَٰطِ ٱلۡعَزِيزِ ٱلۡحَمِيدِ ۝١ ﴾

Alif Lām Rā. (This is) a Book which We have revealed to you that you may bring forth men, by their Lord's permission from utter darkness into the light – to the path of the Mighty, the Praised One. (Ibrāhīm, 14:1)

However, for those verses that do have them, the occasions of revelation are generally one of three types:

1. Actions of individuals;

2. A particular, well-known incident;

3. Questions asked of the Prophet ﷺ.

Each of these will be discussed in turn.

1. GOOD OR EVIL ACTIONS OF INDIVIDUALS, WHICH SERVED TO GUIDE THE MUSLIMS

There were individuals at the time of revelation, whose character and qualities were so sublime, or so corrupt, that verses were revealed about them. For example, the noble conduct of ʿAlī b. Abī Ṭālib when he gave a beggar alms, while in the state of prayer, is famous:

﴿ إِنَّمَا وَلِيُّكُمُ ٱللَّهُ وَرَسُولُهُۥ وَٱلَّذِينَ ءَامَنُواْ ٱلَّذِينَ يُقِيمُونَ ٱلصَّلَوٰةَ وَيُؤْتُونَ ٱلزَّكَوٰةَ وَهُمْ
رَٰكِعُونَ ﴿٥٥﴾ وَمَن يَتَوَلَّ ٱللَّهَ وَرَسُولَهُۥ وَٱلَّذِينَ ءَامَنُواْ فَإِنَّ حِزْبَ ٱللَّهِ هُمُ ٱلْغَٰلِبُونَ ﴿٥٦﴾ ﴾

Indeed God is your Guardian, and His Messenger, and those who believe; those who keep up the prayers and pay the poor-rate while they bow. And whoever takes God, and His messenger, and those who believe, for a guardian, then surely the party of God are they who shall be triumphant. (Al-Māʾida, 5:55, 56)

And as for Abū Lahab and his wife, they were condemned to hell-fire even while they lived. Interestingly, Abū Lahab lived for 10 years after God had revealed a whole chapter in condemnation of their conduct. He could have chosen to reform his character in order to disprove the following verses, but he did not.

﴿ تَبَّتْ يَدَآ أَبِى لَهَبٍ وَتَبَّ ﴿١﴾ مَآ أَغْنَىٰ عَنْهُ مَالُهُۥ وَمَا كَسَبَ ﴿٢﴾ سَيَصْلَىٰ نَارًا ذَاتَ
لَهَبٍ ﴿٣﴾ وَٱمْرَأَتُهُۥ حَمَّالَةَ ٱلْحَطَبِ ﴿٤﴾ فِى جِيدِهَا حَبْلٌ مِّن مَّسَدٍۭ ﴿٥﴾ ﴾

Perdition overtake both hands of Abu Lahab, and he will perish. His wealth and what he earns will not avail him. He shall soon burn in fire that flames. And his wife, the bearer of fuel, upon her neck a halter of strongly twisted rope. (Al-Lahab, 111:1-5)

2. PARTICULAR AND WELL-KNOWN INCIDENTS

To emphasise the lessons to be learnt from a well-publicised incident, God would reveal a verse or chapter about it. For example, after the peace treaty of Hudaybiyya was concluded between the Muslims and the unbelievers of Quraysh in 6 AH, God revealed a notice of victory, even though no battle had been fought:

﴿ إِنَّا فَتَحْنَا لَكَ فَتْحًا مُّبِينًا ۝١ ﴾

Indeed, We have given to you a clear victory. (Al-Fatḥ, 48:1)

Sometimes the well-known events were distasteful, for example when the Jews rekindled the old enmity of the ʿAws and Khazraj Muslim tribes of Medina, and matters reached a point where swords were drawn. At that time, God revealed:

﴿ يَٰٓأَيُّهَا ٱلَّذِينَ ءَامَنُوٓاْ إِن تُطِيعُواْ فَرِيقًا مِّنَ ٱلَّذِينَ أُوتُواْ ٱلْكِتَٰبَ يَرُدُّوكُم بَعْدَ إِيمَٰنِكُمْ كَٰفِرِينَ ۝١٠٠ وَكَيْفَ تَكْفُرُونَ وَأَنتُمْ تُتْلَىٰ عَلَيْكُمْ ءَايَٰتُ ٱللَّهِ وَفِيكُمْ رَسُولُهُۥ ۗ وَمَن يَعْتَصِم بِٱللَّهِ فَقَدْ هُدِىَ إِلَىٰ صِرَٰطٍ مُّسْتَقِيمٍ ۝١٠١ ﴾

O you who believe! If you obey a party from among those who have been given the Book, they will turn you back as unbelievers after you have believed. But how can you disbelieve while it is you to whom the communications of God are recited, and among you is His Messenger? And whoever holds fast to God, he indeed is guided to the right path. (Āli ʿImrān, 3:100, 101)

3. QUESTIONS ASKED OF THE PROPHET ﷺ

Frequently, the Prophet ﷺ was asked questions, both by curious Muslims and also by the unbelievers who were trying to test him. At these times, verses would be revealed in reply to these questions. For example, in reply to the question of the unbelievers about the seven sleepers of the cave, the chapter Al-Kahf was revealed.

There are numerous other examples of verses that were in reply to the queries of the believers. Typically, these verses begin with the phrase, "They ask you..." (*yas'alūnaka*). An important lesson from the usage of this term is that only the Prophet ﷺ had the right to legislate, by God's command, and no one had the authority to subsequently change these laws. An example of a question asked, and replied, is:

﴿ يَسْـَٔلُونَكَ عَنِ ٱلشَّهْرِ ٱلْحَرَامِ قِتَالٍ فِيهِ ۖ قُلْ قِتَالٌ فِيهِ كَبِيرٌ ۖ ﴾

They ask you concerning the sacred month, about fighting in it. Say: "Fighting in it is a grave matter.". (Al-Baqara, 2:217)

5.4 - THE IMPORTANCE OF KNOWING THE OCCASION OF REVELATION OF A VERSE

When available, the knowledge of the occasion of revelation of a verse helps us to understand that verse better. Information about the circumstances behind the revelation sheds some light on the implication and the exegesis of that verse. It helps us to understand:

1. The historical background at the time of the Prophet ﷺ and the development of the early Muslim community.
2. The original intent of the verses.
3. The direct and immediate meaning and implication of the verses.
4. The philosophy and reason underlying some legal rulings.
5. Whether the application of a verse is general or specific, and if it is specific, then under what circumstances it is to be applied.
6. The difference between the fundamental and unchanging needs of human-beings, which have remained constant since the time of the revelation, and the variable needs, which change with time and place.

The first four points are self explanatory. The last two points need some elaboration and are discussed in the next section.

5.5 - THE UNIVERSAL AND ETERNAL APPLICATION OF VERSES THAT HAD A PARTICULAR OCCASION OF REVELATION

Islam is the final religion and the Qur'an is God's last message. Some questions arise here; the Qur'an was revealed to a group of people with a specific culture and language, in a particular location and time segment of history – how then, can it adequately address the needs of Muslims of all backgrounds, of varying cultures and for all time?

Is it enough to understand the verses in the same manner as they were understood at the time of revelation, or is it necessary to interpret the Qur'an in light of modern situations and knowledge? A simple example will highlight the problem. The Qur'an states:

﴿أَفَلَا يَنظُرُونَ إِلَى ٱلْإِبِلِ كَيْفَ خُلِقَتْ ١٧﴾

Will they not then consider the camels, how they are created? (Al-Ghāshiya, 88:17)

The present-day Muslim might wonder why, in the midst of all the amazing natural phenomena, God chooses the example of a camel. However, when we study the culture of the Arabs at the time of revelation, we find that the camel was the single most important animal in their lives – and they knew and understood the marvel of its creation well.[10] Accordingly, they were asked by the verse to study the creation, so as to appreciate its Creator.

The question of the eternal applicability of the Qur'an has come to the forefront in light of the progress of science and technology, and the rethinking of philosophical and social issues. However, there is an important matter to understand here. Man's needs are divided into two – those that are constant and those that are variable.[11] For instance, man's clothing has changed greatly over the course of time, but his need to be clothed has remained constant. This is the same with his need for food and shelter.

Similarly, man's interactions with his fellow human beings may have become more sophisticated with the advent of modern technology, but his basic instincts and emotions have remained the same.

The Qur'an addresses the fundamental and constant needs of man, and is not primarily concerned with the variables. Therefore, it is quite possible that, if the Qur'an was revealed to a community with a different culture and in a different time, different examples would have been used in it.

By knowing the occasions of revelations of different verses, and drawing parallels between those times and our own, we are able to distinguish between the constant needs of man, which are of importance in God's eyes, and the variables, which are ever changing with time and location.

Therefore, we can conclude, that although the verses have particular occasions of revelations, their focus is the fundamental and unchanging psyche of man, and thus the message of the Qur'an is relevant at all times, all places and for all cultures. In the words of Al-Bāqir:

> If a verse was revealed about a community, and if after the passing of that community the verse also passed away, then there would be nothing left of the Qur'an. Whereas, [the truth is that] the whole of the Qur'an is in force and will remain so, as long as the heavens and the earth exist.[12]

5.6 - EXAMPLES OF WHEN THE KNOWLEDGE OF THE OCCASION OF REVELATION HAS HELPED IN THE UNDERSTANDING OF VERSES

There are many examples where the knowledge of the circumstances surrounding the revelation of a verse has helped to clarify its import. A few examples are cited below.

EXAMPLE 1

﴿ وَلِلَّهِ ٱلْمَشْرِقُ وَٱلْمَغْرِبُ ۚ فَأَيْنَمَا تُوَلُّوا۟ فَثَمَّ وَجْهُ ٱللَّهِ ۚ إِنَّ ٱللَّهَ وَٰسِعٌ عَلِيمٌ ١١٥ ﴾

To God belong the East and the West: wherever you turn, there is God's countenance. For God is all-Embracing, all-Knowing. (Al-Baqara, 2:115)

The occasion of revelation of the verse is as follows. The Jews mocked the Muslims, saying that if it had been correct to pray facing the Dome of the Rock (Bayt al-Maqdas), which had been the qibla till then, then the change to face the Kaʿba was incorrect; and if praying while facing the Kaʿba was correct, then it would mean that all the prayers prayed so far were void.

In this verse, God responds by saying that both the acts were, and are correct, for prayer itself is an established reality, whereas the act of facing the Kaʿba, or the Dome of the Rock, is a relative issue, for unifying the ranks of the worshippers. Wherever you turn, you stand facing God. Therefore, facing the east because the Kaʿba is to the east of Medina, or facing the west because the Dome of the Rock is to the west of Medina, is not the real issue. All belongs to God, for He does not occupy a particular area – "For God is all-Embracing, all-Knowing". Based on this verse jurists rule that in the non-obligatory prayers, one can pray in any direction, if the qibla is not known.

EXAMPLE 2

﴿إِنَّ ٱلصَّفَا وَٱلْمَرْوَةَ مِن شَعَآئِرِ ٱللَّهِ ۖ

فَمَنْ حَجَّ ٱلْبَيْتَ أَوِ ٱعْتَمَرَ فَلَا جُنَاحَ عَلَيْهِ أَن يَطَّوَّفَ بِهِمَا﴾

Surely the [mountains of] Ṣafā and the Marwa are among the signs of God; so whoever comes for Ḥaj or 'Umra to the House, there is no blame on him if he goes round them both. (Al-Baqara, 2:158)

The occasion of revelation of the verse is as follows. One of the conditions in the peace treaty of Hudaybiyya that was signed between the Quraysh and the Muslims in 6 AH, was an arrangement allowing the Muslims to return the following year for the minor pilgrimage, the ʿumra. For the duration of the ʿumra it was agreed that the polytheists would remove their idols from the vicinity of the Kaʿba and from the tops of the mountains of Ṣafā and Marwa.

After the three days of the ʿumra were over, the polytheists restored their idols back to their mountain-top positions. Some Muslims had not yet performed the rituals of *sa'ī*, and on seeing the idols standing on the mountains, they thought that they would be committing a sin by walking between Ṣafā and Marwa.

The above-mentioned verse was revealed so that the Muslims would not refrain from performing the *sa'ī*, which is a fundamental and obligatory part of the ʿumra. Therefore, after referring to the occasion of revelation of this verse, the wording "there is no blame on them" which denotes permissibility rather than obligation, becomes completely clear.

As can be seen from the examples above, understanding the occasions of revelation plays a useful role in clarifying the meanings of many verses.

5.7 - RELIABILITY OF *ASBĀB AL-NUZŪL*

Notwithstanding the foregoing, there is some disagreement amongst the scholars about how much importance to place on the *asbāb al-nuzūl* of the verses of the Qur'an. Since the writing of traditions was banned by the Caliphs until the reign of ʿUmar b. ʿAbd al-ʿAzīz (99-101 AH), there are many reports in the Ḥadīth literature that are weak or inauthentic. Ṭabāṭabā'ī writes:

> Many of these [reports] are without a chain of narration and are not accepted as fully trustworthy...Additionally, from the form of many of these traditions it is obvious that the narrator had not learned them through oral transmission but rather based on his own judgement, that the revelation of a certain verse was connected with certain events. Thus the narrator links a certain event to a verse of suitable meaning mentioned in the tradition. This is a subjective view, carried out through *ijtihād* or personal reflection upon the matter, and not the actual reason for revelation learned orally through transmission from the Prophet ﷺ.[13]

It is for this reason that Al-Wāḥidī writes:

> It is not permissible that an event can be considered as the occasion of revelation for a verse, except when it is reported by a sound and reliable tradition which is

narrated by an eye-witness of the actual event.

He then quotes Ibn ʿAbbās reporting from the Prophet ﷺ that he said:

> Refrain from narrating traditions except when you have certainty, because whosoever attributes a lie to me or the Qur'an has prepared a seat for himself in hell.[14]

Al-Suyūtī himself only presents 250 narrations on *asbāb al-nuzūl* and admits that some of these narrations are weak.[15]

Of course, not every tradition about *asbāb al-nuzūl* should be discarded; in fact, there are several useful works that mention such traditions which are somewhat reliable. These include Ṭabarī's *Jāmiʿ al-Bayān,* Al-Suyūṭī's *Durr al-Manthūr,* Ṭabrisī's *Majmaʿ al-Bayān,* and Ṭūsī's *Al-Tibyān,* as well as works dedicated to the subject such as Al-Wāḥidī's *Asbāb al-Nuzūl.*

Maʿrifat has recommended caution in accepting traditions purporting to be *asbāb al-nuzūl* of verses and has formulated some conditions for such a tradition:

1. The tradition must have a sound chain of transmission. Also, it must originate from a source that is reliable; for example an Imam of the household of the Prophet ﷺ or a companion known for his knowledge of the Qur'an, such as ʿAbdallāh ibn al-Masʿūd, Ubayy ibn al-Kaʿb or Ibn ʿAbbās. Or, it must originate from reliable scholars amongst the successors (*tābiʿīn*) such as Mujāhid, Saʿīd b. al-Jubair and Saʿīd b. Musayyab.
2. It must be reported through several successive chains (*tawātur*), even if there is a slight variation in wording amongst the traditions.
3. If the tradition adequately explains and conforms to the verse in question, its chain of transmission need not be very strong, as is the case for the following verse:

﴿ إِنَّمَا ٱلنَّسِيٓءُ زِيَادَةٌ فِى ٱلْكُفْرِ ۖ يُضَلُّ بِهِ ٱلَّذِينَ كَفَرُوا۟ يُحِلُّونَهُۥ عَامًا وَيُحَرِّمُونَهُۥ عَامًا

لِّيُوَاطِـُٔوا۟ عِدَّةَ مَا حَرَّمَ ٱللَّهُ فَيُحِلُّوا۟ مَا حَرَّمَ ٱللَّهُ ۚ زُيِّنَ لَهُمْ سُوٓءُ أَعْمَـٰلِهِمْ ۗ وَٱللَّهُ لَا يَهْدِى ٱلْقَوْمَ ٱلْكَـٰفِرِينَ ﴿٣٧﴾

Postponing (of the sacred month) is only an addition in unbelief, wherewith those who disbelieve are led astray, violating it one year and keeping it sacred another, that they may agree in the number (of months) that God has made sacred, and thus violate what God has made sacred; the evil of their doings is made fair-seeming to them; and God does not guide the unbelieving people. (Al-Tawba, 9:37)

Fighting was forbidden in the sacred months to allow unrestricted passage for pilgrims to come to Mecca for ḥajj and return home in the months of Dhu'l Qaʿda, Dhu'l Ḥijja and Muḥarram, and for ʿumra in the sacred month of Rajab. However, some strong Arab tribes, when they were prevailing in battle against another tribe, and perchance a sacred month would arrive, would alter the sequence of months. For example, they would say, "We are postponing this year's month of Rajab and bringing forward the month of Shaʿbān!". Thereafter, they would continue to fight their enemy, and thus make a mockery of God's law. This unpleasant practice was totally forbidden in 9 AH.[16] This tradition of the *sabab al-nuzūl* is in perfect conformity with the verse and quite plausible as the occasion of revelation for this verse, even though it is a weak tradition.

NOTES

1 Abū al-Ḥasan ʿAlī b. Aḥmad al-Nīshābūrī al-Wāḥidī, *Asbāb al-Nuzūl*, p. 6.
2 Ibn Ratq al-ʿĀyad, *Mabḥath fī ʿUlūm al-Qur'an*, p. 82 – as quoted by Ardabīlī et al, *Tārīkh wa ʿUlūm-e Qur'anī*, p. 281.
3 Al-Ḥaj, 22:15.
4 Al-Kahf, 18:84.
5 Al-Baqara, 2:166.
6 Ṣād, 38:10.
7 Ghāfir, 40:36,37.
8 *Majmaʿ al-Bayān*, vol. 7, p. 102.
9 *Ulūm-e Qur'anī*, p. 100.
10 For further details, see Harūn Yaḥyā, *Camel: A Special Animal in the Service of Man.*
11 Muṭahharī, *Islam wa Muqtaḍiyyāt-e Zamān*, vol. 1, p. 16.

[12] See Ṭabāṭabā'ī, *Qur'an dar Islam*, p. 71.
[13] Ṭabāṭabā'ī, *Qur'an dar Islam*, p. 74.
[14] Wāḥidī, *Asbāb al-Nuzūl*, p. 4.
[15] *Al-Itqān*, vol. 4, p. 214 - 257.
[16] *Majma' al-Bayān*, vol. 5, p. 29.

6

VERSES AND CHAPTERS OF THE QUR'AN

The Qur'an is divided into 114 chapters; each chapter contains several verses, ranging from four, to well over two hundred. There are various opinions about the total number of verses in the Qur'an, depending on the method employed in counting. According to a report from ʿAlī b. Abī Ṭālib, the number is 6,236. This is the number in the main *muṣḥaf* in use today, which is in the calligraphy of ʿUthmān Ṭāhā, and distributed from Saudi Arabia.

There are also varying counts about the number of words, but a recent and comprehensive study concluded that the total number is 77,807.[1] In this chapter, we will look at some of the features of the verses and chapters of the Qur'an.

6.1 - VERSES OF THE QUR'AN (*ĀYA PL. ĀYĀT*)

The term *āya* is usually translated as "verse", although the Qur'an is not a book of poetry. The word also means a miracle or sign, as in the verse:

﴿ وَقَالَ لَهُمْ نَبِيُّهُمْ إِنَّ ءَايَةَ مُلْكِهِۦٓ أَن يَأْتِيَكُمُ ٱلتَّابُوتُ فِيهِ سَكِينَةٌ مِّن رَّبِّكُمْ ﴾

And their prophet said to them: Surely the sign (āyat) *of His kingdom is, that there shall come to you the chest in which there is (means of) tranquillity from your Lord.*
(Al-Baqara, 2:248)

In the context of the Qur'an, *āya* refers to the shortest division of the Qur'anic text – it could be a single phrase or several sentences long.

The longest verse in the Qur'an is the one which discusses debt, verse 282 in the chapter Al-Baqara, (130 words) and the shortest one is verse 64 in the chapter Al-Raḥmān (1 word).

The boundaries of the verses have been delineated by the Prophet ﷺ himself, just as he defined the length of the chapters. For example he would say, "The chapter Al-Fātiḥa has 7 verses, the chapter Al-Mulk has 30 verses, etc."[2]

There are a few verses for which there exists a difference of opinion about their size. These differences stem from conflicting narrations, but do not affect the text in any way. We have traditions that mention that the Prophet ﷺ would pause at particular places in the text when he recited the Qur'an. Those places at which he always stopped in a given passage are unanimously taken to be verse breaks. About those places at which he always continued, it is accepted that they are not verse breaks. The difference of opinion occurs at those places where he sometimes stopped and sometimes continued; some scholars took this to be a pause for breath, and thus did not count it as a verse break, whereas others took this to be the beginning of a new verse.

Another factor is that the early scholars did not consider some of the unconnected letters (*al-ḥurūf al-muqaṭṭa'āt*) as distinct verses. For example, they did not count *alif-lām-mīm-rā* (13:1) and *alif-lām-rā* (10:1, 11:1, 12:1, 14:1, 15:1) as separate verses, while *alif-lām-mīm* (2:1, 3:1, 29:1, 30:1, 31:1, 32:1) and *alif-lām-mīm-ṣād* (7:1) were counted as distinct verses.[3]

However, it is important to note that while these differences result in minor variations in the verse numbers, they do not change the Qur'anic text at all. Due to the above, various counts for the total number of verses of the Qur'an are quoted. As we have mentioned, the most reliable number is 6,236, based on a sound tradition from 'Alī b. Abī Ṭālib, who quoted the Prophet ﷺ as having related this number.[4]

6.2 - THE PRESENT ARRANGEMENT OF THE VERSES

There is some debate amongst the scholars about whether the present arrangement of the verses was directed by the Prophet ﷺ himself (referred to as the *tawqīfī* arrangement), or did it result from the efforts of the companions after his passing (referred to as *ijtihādī*)? Or did both of these arrangements occur to some extent?

Zarkashī writes in *Al-Burhān*, "Whenever verses were revealed, the Prophet ﷺ would call the appointed scribes of revelation and instruct them to place the verse or verses in a particular place in a particular chapter."[5]

Most commentators are of the opinion that the current arrangement was specifically dictated by the Prophet ﷺ himself, and they cite the following proofs:

1. There are many narrations from the Prophet ﷺ that mention the benefits of certain verses at certain places in a particular chapter. For example, we have a narration from the Prophet ﷺ, "He who recites the last verse of the chapter Ḥashr and dies on that day, shall have all his sins forgiven."[6]

2. There are narrations that mention specific directives by the Prophet ﷺ about the placement of verses; for example, he said, "Jibra'īl has informed of the placement of the verse,

﴿ إِنَّ ٱللَّهَ يَأۡمُرُ بِٱلۡعَدۡلِ وَٱلۡإِحۡسَٰنِ وَإِيتَآيِٕ ذِي ٱلۡقُرۡبَىٰ وَيَنۡهَىٰ عَنِ
ٱلۡفَحۡشَآءِ وَٱلۡمُنكَرِ وَٱلۡبَغۡيِۚ يَعِظُكُمۡ لَعَلَّكُمۡ تَذَكَّرُونَ ٩٠ ﴾

Verily, God enjoins the doing of justice and good (to others) and the giving to the kindred, and He forbids indecency and evil and rebellion; He admonishes you that you may be mindful.[7]

6.3 - CHAPTERS OF THE QUR'AN (*SŪRA* PL. *SUWAR*)

There are 114 chapters, or *suwar,* in the Qur'an. There are several opinions about the origins of the word *sūra* as used in the Qur'an. A commonly cited one is that it originates from *sūr,* which was a defensive wall that ringed cities in olden times, and since a *sūra* contains within it its verses, just like a city wall contained the houses, this name was given to the chapters of the Qur'an.[8] Others have said that it derives from *su'r,* meaning a remainder or portion of something, in this case, a portion of the Qur'an.[9] Another opinion is that *sūra* has a meaning of importance and nobleness. Abū al-Futūḥ al-Rāzī cites poetry to prove this meaning.[10]

In its technical usage, a *sūra* or chapter is defined as a self-contained part of the Qur'an that includes a varying number of verses. Another definition is that it is a group of verses that has a distinct and known beginning and end.[11] A number of commentators also define a *sūra* as a group of verses bounded by the *basmala.*[12]

This last definition is not strictly correct because it is not true of the eighth chapter, Al-Anfāl, the ninth chapter, Al-Tawba, and of the last chapter Al-Nās. Perhaps it is more correct to say that all the chapters in the Qur'an begin with the basmala, with the exception of Al-Tawba. (For this reason, some scholars are of the opinion that Al-Anfāl and Al-Tawba are one chapter.)

There are 114 basmalas in the Qur'an – an extra one within Al-Naml, makes up for the one missing in Al-Tawba. These basmalas are not a later addition to the chapters but were present at the time of the Prophet ﷺ and are integral parts of the chapters, as is evident from every copy of the Qur'an.

The 114 chapters themselves are of differing lengths – the shortest consisting of 4 verses (Al-Kawthar) and the longest of 286 verses (Al-Baqara). We will discuss the various opinions about the present arrangement of the chapters themselves, when we look at the compilation of the Quran in Chapter 7.

6.4 - THE NAMES OF CHAPTERS

All the chapters of the Qur'an have distinct names. Some chapters have two or more names. Examples of chapters with two names are:

Chapter 40: Al-Mu'min and Ghāfir
Chapter 42: Al-Shūrā and Ḥā Mīm ʿAin Sīn Qāf
Chapter 45: Al-Jāthiya and Al-Sharīʿa
Chapter 47: Muḥammad and Al-Qitāl
Chapter 76: Al-Insān and Al-Dahr

Some chapters have several names. For example, Al-Suyūṭī lists more than 10 names for Al-Tawba and over 20 names for Al-Fātiḥa.[13] Several names have also been mentioned for clusters of chapters. Some examples are:

Ḥawāmīm – This refers to the seven chapters, Ghāfir, Fuṣṣilat, Al-Shūrā, Al-Zukhruf, Al-Dukhān, Al-Jāthiya and Al-Aḥqāf, which all begin with *Ḥā Mīm.*

Musabbiḥāt – This refers to the seven chapters Al-Isrā', Al-Ḥadīd, Al-Ḥashr, Al-Ṣaff, Al-Jumuʿa, Al-Taghābun and Al-Aʿlā, which all begin with *tasbīḥ* (glorification).

Ḥāmidāt – This refers to the five chapters, Al-Fātiḥa, Al-Anʿām, Al-Kahf, Sabā' and Al-Fāṭir, which all begin with *taḥmīd* (praise).

Ṭawāsīn – This refers to the three chapters, Al-Shuʿarā', Al-Naml and Al-Qaṣaṣ, which all begin with the letters *Ṭā Sīn.*

Muʿawwadhatayn – This refers to the two chapters where refuge is sought with God, Al-Falaq and Al-Nās.

6.5 - CLASSIFICATION OF CHAPTERS

The chapters of the Qur'an are sometimes divided into the following groups.

1. THE SEVEN LONG CHAPTERS (*AL-SAB'Ā AL-ṬIWĀL*)

These are the seven long chapters at the beginning of the Qur'an; Al-Baqara, Āli 'Imrān, Al-Nisā', Al-Mā'ida, Al-An'ām, Al-A'rāf and Al-Anfāl coupled with Al-Tawba. About the seventh, there is a difference of opinion. According to a tradition quoted from Sa'īd b. al-Jubair, it is Yūnus, while others consider it to be Al-Kahf.[14]

2. THE HUNDREDS (*AL-MI'ĪN*)

These are shorter chapters, with approximately 100 verses each. These are the 14 chapters from Yūnus to Al-Mu'minūn.[15]

3. THE OFT-REPEATED (*AL-MATHĀNĪ*)

These are chapters with less than 100 verses, which are approximately 20 in number. They follow the *mi'īn* chapters.

4. THE SEPARATED (*AL-MUFAṢṢAL*)

These are the short chapters that are frequently separated (*mufaṣṣal*) by basmalas. The last of these chapters is Al-Nās, while the first is reckoned by Ma'rifat[16] to be Al-Raḥmān and by Zanjānī[17] and others to be Al-Ḥujurāt.

There is a well-known tradition of the Prophet ﷺ, where he has mentioned these classifications. He said:

> I have been given the seven long chapters (*ṭiwāl*) in place of the *Tawrāt*, the hundred-verse chapters (*mi'īn*) in place of the *Zabūr*, the oft-repeated chapters

(*mathānī*) in place of the *Injīl,* and I have been uniquely honoured with the separated chapters (*mufaṣṣal*).[18]

According to another report, the *mufaṣṣal* chapters mentioned in the tradition above are the *"hawāmīm"* or the 7 chapters beginning with *Ḥā Mīm* (40-46). This report defines the *ṭiwāl* as Al-Baqara to Al-Tawba; the *mi'īn* as Bani Isrā'īl to Al-Mu'minūn, the *mathānī* as the chapters that follow the *mi'īn* and the *mufaṣṣal* as the chapters beginning with *Ḥā Mīm.*[19]

It must be noted that there is much disagreement amongst the various exegetes and Qur'anic scholars about exactly which chapters are included in these four classifications.

6.6 - THE OPENINGS OF CHAPTERS

Al-Suyūṭī mentions that the opening verses of the chapters of the Qur'an are divided into 10 types, which are the following:

1. PRAISE OF GOD (*TAḤMĪD*)

This has taken two forms; firstly, the mention of the praiseworthy attributes of God (*taḥmīd* and *tabārak*), and second, by declaring Him free of any imperfection (*tasbīḥ*). Examples of each type are as below:

﴿ ٱلْحَمْدُ لِلَّهِ ٱلَّذِىٓ أَنزَلَ عَلَىٰ عَبْدِهِ ٱلْكِتَـٰبَ وَلَمْ يَجْعَل لَّهُۥ عِوَجَا ۜ ﴿١﴾ ﴾

(All) praise is due to God, Who revealed the Book to His servant and did not make in it any crookedness. (Al-Kahf, 18:1)

﴿ تَبَـٰرَكَ ٱلَّذِى بِيَدِهِ ٱلْمُلْكُ وَهُوَ عَلَىٰ كُلِّ شَىْءٍ قَدِيرٌ ﴿١﴾ ﴾

Blessed is He in Whose hand is the kingdom, and He has power over all things. (Al-Mulk, 67:1)

﴿ سَبَّحَ لِلَّهِ مَا فِى ٱلسَّمَـٰوَٰتِ وَٱلْأَرْضِ ۖ وَهُوَ ٱلْعَزِيزُ ٱلْحَكِيمُ ﴿١﴾ ﴾

Whatever is in the heavens and whatever is in the earth declares the glory of God, and He is the Mighty, the Wise. (Al-Ḥashr, 59:1)

2. COMMAND (*AMR*)

Five chapters of the Qur'an begin with the command, *"Qul"* or "Say!". These are Al-Jinn (72), Al-Kāfirūn (109), Al-Ikhlāṣ (112), Al-Falaq (113) and Al-Nās (114). An example is:

﴿ قُلْ أُوحِىَ إِلَىَّ أَنَّهُ ٱسْتَمَعَ نَفَرٌ مِّنَ ٱلْجِنِّ فَقَالُوٓا۟ إِنَّا سَمِعْنَا قُرْءَانًا عَجَبًا ۝١ ﴾

Say: It has been revealed to me that a party of the jinn listened, and they said: Surely we have heard a wonderful Qur'an. (Al-Jinn, 72:1)

3. EXHORTION (*NIDĀ'*)

Five chapters begins with a direct address to the Prophet ﷺ; these are, Al-Aḥzāb, Al-Ṭalāq, Al-Taḥrīm, Al-Muzzammil and Al-Muddaththir. An example is:

﴿ يَٰٓأَيُّهَا ٱلنَّبِىُّ لِمَ تُحَرِّمُ مَآ أَحَلَّ ٱللَّهُ لَكَ ﴾

O Prophet! Why do you forbid (yourself) that which God has made lawful for you. (Al-Taḥrīm, 66:1)

Another five chapters begins with an exhortation to mankind; these are, Al-Nisā', Al-Mā'ida, Al-Ḥaj, Al-Ḥujurāt and Al-Mumtaḥana. An example is:

﴿ يَٰٓأَيُّهَا ٱلنَّاسُ ٱتَّقُوا۟ رَبَّكُمْ ۚ إِنَّ زَلْزَلَةَ ٱلسَّاعَةِ شَىْءٌ عَظِيمٌ ۝١ ﴾

O people! Guard against (the punishment from) your Lord; surely the tumult of the hour is a grievous thing. (Al-Ḥaj, 22:1)

4. STATEMENT OR REPORT (*KHABAR*)

About twenty chapters begin with a general statement or announcement. Examples of these openings are:

﴿ يَسْـَٔلُونَكَ عَنِ ٱلْأَنفَالِ ۖ قُلِ ٱلْأَنفَالُ لِلَّهِ وَٱلرَّسُولِ ﴾

They ask you of the spoils of war. Say: The spoils of war belong to God and the messenger. (Al-Anfāl, 8:1)

﴿ قَدۡ أَفۡلَحَ ٱلۡمُؤۡمِنُونَ ۝١ ﴾

Successful indeed are the believers. (Al-Mu'minūn, 23:1)

5. OATH (*QASAM*)

Fifteen chapters of the Qur'an begin with oaths, where God swears by various aspects of creation, such as celestial bodies, special times, etc. For example, there is an oath by stars in Al-Najm, by daybreak in Al-Fajr, by the sun in Al-Shams, by the fig and olive in Al-Tīn, etc. An example is:

﴿ وَٱلتِّينِ وَٱلزَّيۡتُونِ ۝١ وَطُورِ سِينِينَ ۝٢ وَهَٰذَا ٱلۡبَلَدِ ٱلۡأَمِينِ ۝٣ ﴾

I swear by the fig and the olive, And the mount of Sinai; And this secure city (Mecca). (Al-Tīn, 95:1-3)

Oaths have been discussed in greater detail in chapter 12.

6. INTERROGATION

Several chapters begin with a rhetorical question. These include Al-Nabā', Al-Fīl, Al-Ghāshiya, Al-Inshirāḥ and Al-Insān. An example of this kind of opening is:

﴿ أَلَمۡ تَرَ كَيۡفَ فَعَلَ رَبُّكَ بِأَصۡحَٰبِ ٱلۡفِيلِ ۝١ ﴾

Have you not considered how your Lord dealt with the possessors of the elephant? (Al-Fīl, 105:1)

7. CONDITIONAL OR SUBJUNCTIVE STATEMENT (*SHARṬ*)

Seven chapters begin with a statement in this form. They are Al-Wāqʿia, Al-Naṣr, Al-Zalzala, Al-Munāfiqūn, Al-Takwīr, Al-Infiṭār and Al-Inshiqāq. An example is:

﴿ إِذَا وَقَعَتِ ٱلۡوَاقِعَةُ ۝١ لَيۡسَ لِوَقۡعَتِهَا كَاذِبَةٌ ۝٢ خَافِضَةٞ رَّافِعَةٌ ۝٣ ﴾

When the great event comes to pass; there is no belying its coming to pass; Abasing (one party), exalting (the other). (Al-Wāqiʿa, 56:1-3)

8. CAUSATION (*TA'LĪL*)

Only chapter Al-Quraysh is mentioned in this category:

﴿ لِإِيلَٰفِ قُرَيْشٍ ۝١ ﴾

For the protection of the Quraysh. (Al-Quraysh, 106:1)

9. IMPRECATION (*DU'Ā'*)

Some chapters begin with an imprecation or curse from God towards certain groups of people. These are chapters Al-Muṭaffifīn, Al-Humaza and Al-Lahab. For example:

﴿ وَيْلٌ لِّلْمُطَفِّفِينَ ۝١ ٱلَّذِينَ إِذَا ٱكْتَالُوا۟ عَلَى ٱلنَّاسِ يَسْتَوْفُونَ ۝٢ وَإِذَا كَالُوهُمْ أَو وَّزَنُوهُمْ يُخْسِرُونَ ۝٣ ﴾

Woe to the defrauders – who, when they take the measure (of their dues) from men take it fully – but when they measure out to others or weigh out for them, they are deficient. (Al-Muṭaffifīn, 83:1-3)

10. UNCONNECTED LETTERS (*AL-ḤURŪF AL-MUQAṬṬA'ĀT*)

These are dealt with separately in the next section.

Al-Suyūṭī mentions a poem composed by Abū Shāma, in which he brings together all these ten openings:

أثنــى علــى نفسه سُبْحانَهُ بِثُــبو ... تِ الْحَمْدِ والسَّلْبِ لَمَّا استَفْتَحَ السُّوَرا

وَالأَمْرِ وَالشَّرْطِ وَالتَّعْـليلِ وَالْقَسَمِ الدُّ ... عَـا حُرُوفِ التَّهَجِّي استَـفْهَمِ الخَبَرا

God has praised Himself by opening the chapters with His praise and glorification and command, and condition and causation and oath and imprecation and letters and queries and news.[20]

6.7 - THE UNCONNECTED LETTERS: AL-ḤURŪF AL-MUQAṬṬA'ĀT

The presence of the unconnected letters (*al-ḥurūf al-muqaṭṭa'āt*) in the

Qur'an has been the subject of great interest and debate amongst the scholars. Most commentators have devoted a separate section in their books to attempt to explain the meaning and purpose of these cryptic letters. Of the chapters that begin with these letters,

3 chapters begin with a single letter: Ṣād, Qāf, Al-Qalam.

9 chapters begin with two letters: Ṭā Hā, Al-Naml, Yā Sīn, Ghāfir, Fuṣṣilat, Al-Zukhruf, Al-Dukhān, Al-Jāthiya, Al-Aḥqāf.

13 chapters begin with three letters: Al-Baqara, Āli Imrān, Yūnus, Hūd, Yūsuf, Ibrāhīm, Al-Ḥijr, Al-Shuʿarā, Al-Qaṣaṣ, Al-ʿAnkabūt, Al-Rūm, Luqmān, Al-Sajda.

2 chapters begin with four letters: Al-Aʿrāf, Al-Raʿd.

2 chapters begin with five letters: Maryam, Al-Shūrā.

The number of letters used are 14 – half of the Arabic alphabet.

1. THE OCCURRENCE OF THE UNCONNECTED LETTERS

The unconnected letters come at the head of twenty-nine chapters of the Qur'an. The details of their occurrence is as follows:

Alif Lām Mīm	Al-Baqara, Āli ʿImrān, Al-ʿAnkabūt, Al-Rūm, Luqmān, Al-Sajda
Alif Lām Mīm Ṣād	Al-Aʿrāf
Alif Lām Rā	Yūnus, Hūd, Yūsuf, Ibrāhīm, Al-Ḥijr
Alif Lām Mīm Rā	Al-Raʿd
Kāf Hā Yā ʿAin Ṣād	Maryam

Ṭā Hā	Ṭā Hā
Ṭā Sīn Mīm	Al-Shuʿarā, Al-Qaṣaṣ
Ṭā Sīn	Al-Naml
Yā Sīn	Yā Sīn
Ṣād	Ṣād
Ḥā Mīm	Ghāfir, Fuṣṣilat, Al-Zukhruf, Al-Dukhān, Al-Jāthiyā, Al-Aḥqāf
Ḥā Mīm – ʿAin Sīn Qāf	Al-Shūrā
Qāf	Qāf
Nūn	Al-Qalam

Fourteen of the twenty-eight letters of the Arabic alphabet, in various combinations, have appeared at the head of twenty-nine chapters in the Qur'an. Scholars have tried to detect a pattern and have made many observations about the choice of letters. An interesting quality of the letters used is that they are made up from one letter from each morphological subset of the Arabic alphabet, as the figure below indicates. In other words, one letter of each form has been used in the unconnected letters in the Qur'an.

The first row is made up of the unconnected letters found in the Qur'an

ي	ه	ن	م	ل	ك	ق	ع	ط	ص	س	ر	ح	ا
		ب				ف	غ	ظ	ض	ش	د	ج	
		ت				و					ذ	خ	
		ث									ز		

2. POSSIBLE MEANINGS OF THE UNCONNECTED LETTERS

2.1. THAT THEY FORM PART OF GOD'S CHALLENGE TO THE IDOLATERS TO PRODUCE A CHAPTER LIKE THAT FOUND IN THE QUR'AN

This opinion is favoured by many of the scholars like Ṭabāṭabā'ī[21], Ṭabrisī[22], Zamakhsharī[23] and others. They state that, since the text of the Qur'an is formed from the very same alphabet that was familiar to the Arabs, the presence of the unconnected letters was, and is, a challenge to the unbelievers to produce anything similar to the Qur'an, using the very same letters that they employed in their speech and writings.

2.2. THAT THEY WERE A MEANS TO SILENCE THE DISBELIEVERS AND TO CAPTURE THEIR ATTENTION

The unbelievers had decided not to heed the recitation of the Qur'an and as God states:

﴿ وَقَالَ ٱلَّذِينَ كَفَرُوا۟ لَا تَسْمَعُوا۟ لِهَٰذَا ٱلْقُرْءَانِ وَٱلْغَوْا۟ فِيهِ لَعَلَّكُمْ تَغْلِبُونَ ٢٦ ﴾

And those who disbelieve say: Do not listen to this Qur'an, and make noise therein, perhaps you may overcome. (Fuṣṣilat, 41:26)

When the Prophet ﷺ would recite the Qur'an, they would jeer and clap their hands in an effort to drown out his voice. However, the enigmatic nature of the opening of these chapters would grab their attention and arouse their curiosity. They would then give ear to the arresting beauty of the verses, and often turn to Islam.[24]

This view seems plausible, especially when we consider that all the chapters headed by unconnected letters were revealed in Mecca, where the audience was largely non-Muslim. The two exceptions are Al-Baqara and Āli 'Imrān, which were the first chapters revealed in Medina, at a time when a sizeable portion of the audience was made up of Jews.

2.3. THAT THEY REFER TO THE QUR'AN ITSELF

After every occurrence of the unconnected letters, there is an immediate reference to the Qur'an itself, or its verses. For example:

﴿ الٓمٓ ۝١ ذَٰلِكَ ٱلۡكِتَٰبُ لَا رَيۡبَۛ فِيهِۛ ﴾

Alif Lām Mīm. This Book, there is no doubt in it. (Al-Baqara, 2:1, 2)

﴿ الٓمٓصٓ ۝١ كِتَٰبٌ أُنزِلَ إِلَيۡكَ ﴾

Alif Lām Mīm Ṣād. A Book revealed to you. (Al-Aʿrāf, 7:1, 2)

﴿ الٓرۚ تِلۡكَ ءَايَٰتُ ٱلۡكِتَٰبِ ٱلۡحَكِيمِ ۝١ ﴾

Alif Lām Rā. These are the verses of the wise Book. (Yūnus, 10:1)

﴿ الٓرۚ تِلۡكَ ءَايَٰتُ ٱلۡكِتَٰبِ ٱلۡمُبِينِ ۝١ ﴾

Alif Lām Rā. These are the verses of the Book that makes manifest. (Yūsuf, 12:1)

There is a minor exception to this trend in Āli ʿImrān (3) – but, after a brief mention of the creed of Islam, the pattern remains unchanged:

﴿ الٓمٓ ۝١ ٱللَّهُ لَآ إِلَٰهَ إِلَّا هُوَ ٱلۡحَيُّ ٱلۡقَيُّومُ ۝٢ نَزَّلَ عَلَيۡكَ ٱلۡكِتَٰبَ بِٱلۡحَقِّ ﴾

Alif Lām Mīm. Allah, (there is) no god but He, the Ever-living, the Self-subsisting by Whom all things subsist. He has revealed to you the Book with truth. (Āli ʿImrān, 3:1-3)

2.4. THAT THEIR MEANING IS A SECRET ONLY KNOWN TO GOD, AND MAN IS UNABLE TO COMPREHEND THEIR SIGNIFICANCE

This was the opinion of some of the former scholars, who said that these letters were part of the indefinite verses (*mutashābihāt*), whose interpretation (*ta'wīl*) is only known to God. Ṭabrisī has quoted the traditions that form the basis of this view, but has acknowledged them to be from weak sources. [25]

2.5. THAT THEY ARE NAMES OF THE QUR'AN

This opinion has also been mentioned by scholars.[26]

2.6. THAT THEY ARE THE NAMES OF THE CHAPTERS IN WHICH THEY APPEAR

Some scholars, such as Ṭabarī[27] and Ibn al-Kathīr[28] are of this opinion. The weakness in this opinion is that most chapters do not have these letters in their opening and so this cannot be the main purpose of the letters.

2.7. THAT THEY ARE THE LETTERS MOST REPEATED IN THE CHAPTER IN WHICH THEY APPEAR

Based on computer-assisted analyses of the chapters of the Qur'an, researchers like Rashād Khalīfa have presented numerous findings, including the discovery that the letters that appear at the head of a chapter occur the greatest number of times in that chapter. For example, in chapter Al-Baqara, which begins with *alīf-lām-mīm,* the letter *alif* appears more numerously than any other letter, followed by the letter *lām* and then *mīm.* Similarly, in Qāf, the letter *qāf,* which heads the chapter, also appears more number of times within the chapter than any other letter. However, these details are still subject to verification[29] and the phenomenon is not true for all chapters.

2.8. THAT THEY ARE THE ABBREVIATIONS OF NAMES AND ATTRIBUTES OF GOD

It is the opinion of some scholars[30] that the letters abbreviate certain phrases, for example:

Alīf-lām-mīm denotes, *"ana Allāhu a'lamu"* (I am Allah, I am all-Knowing), and

Alīf-lām-mīm-ṣād denotes, "*ana Allāhu a'lamu wa ufaṣṣilu*" (I am Allah; I am all-Knowing and I make manifest).

Ibn 'Abbās is quoted as saying,

> In the phrase (*kāf-hā-yā-'ain-ṣād*), *kāf* represents *kāfin* (sufficient), *hā* represents *hādin* (guide), *yā* represents *hakīm* (wise), *'ain* represents *'aẓīm* (exalted) and *ṣād* represents *ṣādiq* (veracious).[31]

One report states that they form the Names of God, for example, (الـر), (حـم) and (ن) make (الرحمن – the Merciful).[32]

There are various other similar reports[33], with different meanings given for the same letters. On the whole these opinions seem to be based largely on conjecture, and the possibility that the letters stand for the names of God is remote.

CONCLUSION

Interestingly, the Arabs at the time of revelation, both Muslim and non-Muslim, did not seem to question the presence of the letters, possibly because they had encountered this style of address in the poetry of the day.

Of all the possible meanings stated above, the more credible ones seem to be the first three, especially the first one. More recently, Ṭabāṭabā'ī has suggested that the letters may stand for a summary of the main themes of the chapter, and that for example, the chapter A'rāf, which begins with the letters *Alif Lām Mīm Ṣād,* has similar themes to the chapters beginning with *Alif Lām Mīm* as well as chapter Ṣād.[34] This hypothesis remains for researchers to test. In conclusion, we can state that while the true import of the unconnected letters is not known for certain, their presence certainly add to the challenge of the Qur'an where God states:

﴿ وَإِن كُنتُمْ فِي رَيْبٍ مِّمَّا نَزَّلْنَا عَلَىٰ عَبْدِنَا فَأْتُوا بِسُورَةٍ مِّن مِّثْلِهِۦ ﴾

And if you are in doubt as to that which We have revealed to Our servant, then produce a chapter like it." (Al-Baqara, 2:23)

6.8 - THE FIRST VERSES OF THE QUR'AN TO BE REVEALED

There are three reports concerning the first verses that were revealed:

FIRST REPORT

Many scholars report that the first verses to be revealed were the *basmala* followed by the opening three or five verses of Al-ʿAlaq which signalled the start of the Divine commission of the Prophet ﷺ.[35] The archangel Jibraʾīl descended and addressed the Prophet saying: "Read!". The Prophet ﷺ asked, "What should I read?' Then the angel announced:

﴿ ٱقۡرَأۡ بِٱسۡمِ رَبِّكَ ٱلَّذِى خَلَقَ ﴿١﴾ خَلَقَ ٱلۡإِنسَٰنَ مِنۡ عَلَقٍ ﴿٢﴾ ٱقۡرَأۡ وَرَبُّكَ ٱلۡأَكۡرَمُ ﴿٣﴾
ٱلَّذِى عَلَّمَ بِٱلۡقَلَمِ ﴿٤﴾ عَلَّمَ ٱلۡإِنسَٰنَ مَا لَمۡ يَعۡلَمۡ ﴿٥﴾ ﴾

Read! In the name of your Lord, Who created. He created man, out of a [mere] clot of congealed blood. Read! Your Lord is Most Bountiful. He Who taught (the use of) the Pen. He Who taught man that which he did not know. (Al-ʿAlaq, 96:1-5)

It has been narrated from Al-Ṣādiq: "The first verses that were revealed to the Prophet ﷺ were, "*In the name of God, the Most Beneficent, the Most Merciful. Read! In the name of your Lord…*"[36]

SECOND REPORT

It is also reported that the opening verses of Al-Muddaththir were the first verses to be revealed.[37] Jābir b. ʿAbdillāh al-Anṣārī was asked, "Which chapter or verse of the Qur'an was the first to be revealed?" In reply, Jābir recited the opening verse of Al-Muddaththir. He was then asked, "What about the opening verses of Al-ʿAlaq?" Jābir then narrated the speech that he had heard from the Prophet ﷺ, who said:

> I spent some time in the proximity of the cave of Ḥirāʾ, and later, as I descended and reached the ground, I heard a voice. I looked everywhere but saw no one. Thereafter, I raised my face towards the sky and suddenly saw him [Jibraʾīl]. I was trembling all over and went to my house to Khadīja. I asked her to cover me. Then, the following verses were revealed:"

﴿ يَٰٓأَيُّهَا ٱلْمُدَّثِّرُ ۝١ قُمْ فَأَنذِرْ ۝٢ ﴾

O you who are covered up! Arise and warn. (Al-Muddaththir, 74:1, 2)

However, a careful study of this tradition shows that it does not imply that the first chapter revealed to the Prophet ﷺ was Al-Muddaththir; it is Jābir's interpretation of events and it is quite possible that this incident may have taken place some time after the Divine commission, during a subsequent visit to the cave of Ḥirāʾ.

THIRD REPORT

A group of scholars believe that the first chapter to have been revealed was Al-Fātiḥa. Zamakhsharī says, "Many exegetes of the Qur'an believe that Al-Fātiḥa is the first chapter of the Qur'an to have been revealed." 38 Ṭabrisī reports from ʿAlī that he said, "I asked the Prophet ﷺ about the reward (*thawāb*) of reciting the Qur'an. The Prophet ﷺ then enumerated the recompense of every chapter of the Qur'an, in order of their revelation. He began with the first chapter to have been revealed in Mecca, which was Al-Fātiḥa, followed by Al-ʿAlaq, then Al-Qalam." 39

COMMENT

It is possible to combine the three views mentioned above to understand the sequence of events. The revelation of the three or five first verses of Al-ʿAlaq was certainly coincidental with the beginning of the Divine commission. This fact is unanimously accepted by the scholars. Some time after, the opening verses of Al-Muddaththir were revealed, as shown above, in the tradition of Jābir. However, the first complete chapter to have been revealed to the Prophet ﷺ was Al-Fātiḥa.

There is no contradiction here, because the first few verses of Al-'Alaq and Al-Muddaththir revealed in the beginning, given their incomplete form, were not known as chapters. They were only recognised as complete chapters once all their verses had been revealed. Therefore, it follows that the first complete chapter to be revealed was Al-Fātiḥa. This is probably why it is called "the opening of the book"(Al-Fātiḥat al-Kitāb).

In conclusion, if we consider the order of the revelation of the chapters of the Qur'an to be according to the revelation of the opening part of the chapters, then the first chapter to be revealed is Al-'Alaq and the fifth is Al-Fātiḥa. This is how we have indicated the sequence in the table of the order of the revelation of the chapters (see Appendix 1).

However, if we consider the criterion to be the revelation of a complete chapter, then the first complete chapter to be revealed was Al-Fātiḥa.

6.9 - WAS THERE AN INTERMISSION IN THE REVELATION ?

Some scholars are of the view that after the first revelation, there was a pause of three years, when no further revelation came.[40] They have named these three years as, "intermission in revelation" (*fatrat al-waḥy*). During this period, the Prophet ﷺ would invite the people to Islam privately, until the following verse was revealed and he was commanded to openly proclaim his mission:

﴿ فَٱصۡدَعۡ بِمَا تُؤۡمَرُ وَأَعۡرِضۡ عَنِ ٱلۡمُشۡرِكِينَ ٩٤ ﴾

Therefore declare openly what you have been commanded and turn aside from the polytheists. (Al-Ḥijr, 15:94)

However, it is unlikely that there was a gap in revelation for a period of three years, because:

1. There seems to be no purpose for this intermission and there is no firm evidence from history or reliable traditions about any intermission.
2. The Qur'an states that the revelation served to strengthen the heart of the Prophet ﷺ, and this support would be even more important in the beginning of his mission than later on:

﴿كَذَٰلِكَ لِنُثَبِّتَ بِهِۦ فُؤَادَكَ﴾

Thus, so that We may strengthen your heart thereby. (Al-Ḥijr, 15:54)

3. The verse 15:94 that instructed the Prophet ﷺ to openly proclaim his mission, which was the first verse to be revealed after the alleged intermission, is from Al-Ḥijr, which was the 54th chapter in the order of revelation.[41] If there was an intermission, during which there was no revelation, then this chapter would have been 2nd in the order of revelation.

6.10 - THE ORDER OF REVELATION OF THE CHAPTERS OF THE QUR'AN

Most scholars are in agreement that the order of the revelation of the chapters of the Qur'an is to be reckoned according to the beginning of the revelation of each chapter.[42]

Let us suppose a chapter is revealed up to a certain number of verses, and before its completion another chapter is revealed in its complete form, which is followed by other complete chapters, and then the remainder of the first chapter is revealed; in this case, that which will be taken into consideration in the order of revelation is the beginning of the revelation of every chapter. This is the case with Al-ʿAlaq, whose first five verses were revealed in the beginning of the Divine commission, and the rest of the chapter was revealed after some years. The chapters Al-Muddaththir and Al-Muzzammil were also revealed in this manner.

The order of the chapters according to Ibn ʿAbbās, after having been corrected through the use of different reliable works, is shown in Appendix 1.[43]

6.11 - THE LAST CHAPTER OF THE QUR'AN TO BE REVEALED

Most scholars are of the opinion that the last complete chapter to be revealed was Al-Naṣr, which came down in the year of the conquest of Mecca, in 8AH. [44] In this chapter the glad tidings are given of the absolute victory of the religion, whose foundations had become firm, and that the masses were accepting the creed in great numbers:

﴿ إِذَا جَآءَ نَصۡرُ ٱللَّهِ وَٱلۡفَتۡحُ ۝١ وَرَأَيۡتَ ٱلنَّاسَ يَدۡخُلُونَ فِي دِينِ ٱللَّهِ أَفۡوَاجٗا ۝٢
فَسَبِّحۡ بِحَمۡدِ رَبِّكَ وَٱسۡتَغۡفِرۡهُۚ إِنَّهُۥ كَانَ تَوَّابَۢا ۝٣ ﴾

When there comes the help of Allah and the victory, and you see the people enter God's religion in crowds, then celebrate the praises of your Lord, and seek His forgiveness: for He is oft-returning [in Mercy]. (Al-Naṣr, 110)

Ṭabrisī relates:

> At the revelation of this chapter, the companions of the Prophet ﷺ were happy, since it gave them the glad tidings of Islam's absolute victory over the unbelievers, and the stabilization and consolidation of the foundations of the religion. However, ʿAbbās, the uncle of the Prophet ﷺ became extremely sad at the revelation of this chapter. The Prophet ﷺ asked him, "O uncle, why are you weeping?" He replied, "I think that this chapter is informing us about the end of your mission." The Prophet ﷺ agreed, "It is as you have surmised." Thereafter, the Prophet ﷺ did not live for more than two years.[45]

6.12 - THE LAST VERSE OF THE QUR'AN TO BE REVEALED

Since the Prophet ﷺ never expressly stated which was the final verse of revelation, there exist various opinions about the last verse of the Qur'an to be revealed. Some of them are summarised below:

1. Kashānī says that the last verses to be revealed were those of Al-Tawba, the first verses of which were revealed in 9AH, and the Prophet ﷺ sent ʿAlī to recite them to the polytheists in Mecca.[46]

2. Al-Suyūṭī cites three traditions which mention three different verses from *Al-Baqara* as the last verses to be revealed. The three reports are:

   - Bukhārī narrates from Ibn ʿAbbās, that the last verse to be revealed was the verse of interest:

﴿ يَٰٓأَيُّهَا ٱلَّذِينَ ءَامَنُواْ ٱتَّقُواْ ٱللَّهَ وَذَرُواْ مَا بَقِيَ مِنَ ٱلرِّبَوٰٓاْ إِن كُنتُم مُّؤۡمِنِينَ ٢٧٨ ﴾

O you who believe! Be careful of [your duty to] God and relinquish what remains (due) from usury, if you are believers. (Al-Baqara, 2:278)

   - Bukhārī and Al-Ṭabarī narrate from Ibn ʿAbbās, that the last verse revealed was:

﴿ وَٱتَّقُواْ يَوۡمٗا تُرۡجَعُونَ فِيهِ إِلَى ٱللَّهِۖ ثُمَّ تُوَفَّىٰ كُلُّ نَفۡسٖ مَّا كَسَبَتۡ وَهُمۡ لَا يُظۡلَمُونَ ٢٨١ ﴾

And fear the day when you shall be brought back to God. Then shall every soul be paid what it earned, and none shall be dealt with unjustly.
(Al-Baqara, 2:281)

   Jibraʾīl revealed this verse and instructed that it should be placed between the verse of interest and the verse of debt (following verse 280) of *Al-Baqara*. The Prophet ﷺ passed away 9 days later.[47]

   - Ṭabarī narrates from Ibn al-Mussayib that the last verse

revealed was the verse of debt:

﴿ يَـٰٓأَيُّهَا ٱلَّذِينَ ءَامَنُوٓاْ إِذَا تَدَايَنتُم بِدَيْنٍ إِلَىٰٓ أَجَلٍ مُّسَمًّى فَٱكْتُبُوهُ ﴾

O you who believe! when you deal with each other in contracting a debt for a fixed time, then write it down. (Al-Baqara, 2:282)

Al-Suyūṭī states that there is no contradiction between the traditions because these verses were all revealed at the same time, and are about the same topic. Each narrator has mentioned one of the verses as the last one, and each is right in his own way.[48]

4. Ya'qūbī is of the opinion that the last verse to be revealed was:

﴿ ٱلْيَوْمَ أَكْمَلْتُ لَكُمْ دِينَكُمْ وَأَتْمَمْتُ عَلَيْكُمْ نِعْمَتِى وَرَضِيتُ لَكُمُ ٱلْإِسْلَـٰمَ دِينًا ﴾

This day have I perfected your religion for you, and completed my favour upon you, and have chosen for you Islam as your religion. (Al-Mā'ida, 5:3)

Then he continues:

> And this very statement is correct and reliable according to us, and it was revealed on the day when the Prophet ﷺ nominated 'Alī b. Abī Ṭālib as his successor at Ghadīr al-Khum.[49]

CONCLUSION

We can conclude that the last verse concerning Divine legislation to be revealed was,

﴿ وَٱتَّقُواْ يَوْمًا تُرْجَعُونَ فِيهِ إِلَى ٱللَّهِ ۖ ثُمَّ تُوَفَّىٰ كُلُّ نَفْسٍ مَّا كَسَبَتْ وَهُمْ لَا يُظْلَمُونَ ﴾

And fear the day when you shall be brought back to God. Then shall every soul be paid what it earned, and none shall be dealt with unjustly. (Al-Baqara, 2:281)

which was revealed in Munā during the final pilgrimage of the Prophet ﷺ in 10AH.[50]

And, we can conclude that the very last verse revealed to the Prophet ﷺ, which occurred on his way back from the final pilgrimage, was the verse:

﴿ ٱلْيَوْمَ أَكْمَلْتُ لَكُمْ دِينَكُمْ وَأَتْمَمْتُ عَلَيْكُمْ نِعْمَتِي وَرَضِيتُ لَكُمُ ٱلْإِسْلَـٰمَ دِينًا ﴾

This day have I perfected your religion for you, and completed my favour upon you, and have chosen for you Islam as your religion. (Al-Mā'ida, 5:3)

This opinion is probably the most correct one, because the verse talks about the completion of the favour of God and His being satisfied with Islam as the final religion. This emphatic statement clearly suggests that no further revelation was necessary.

6.13 - MECCAN AND MEDINAN CHAPTERS AND VERSES

The Qur'an was revealed over twenty-three years, principally in the holy cities of Mecca and Medina. In each city, the non-Muslim audience was different. In Mecca, the non-Muslim addressees of the Qur'an were the polytheists of the Quraysh. In Medina, the non-Muslim addressees were the people of the Book, mainly the Jews.

In Mecca, the Muslims were very few, they were in the minority and had no government. Conversely, in Medina, the Muslims were the majority and moreover, had established a fledgling Islamic state. Due to these differences, we find that verses revealed in the first period are quite distinct from the verses of the later period in their style of address and content.

According to statistics compiled from the traditions about the order of revelation, eighty-six chapters of the Qur'an are Meccan and twenty-eight are Medinan.[51] In fact, roughly two-thirds of the Qur'an was revealed in the thirteen years of the prophetic mission in Mecca, and the remaining one-third during the ten years that the Prophet ﷺ lived in Medina.

1. DEFINITION OF THE TERMS MECCAN AND MEDINAN

For the definition and classification of the verses of the Qur'an into

Meccan and Medinan, one of three main criteria can be considered. These are:

I. The criterion of location

II. The criterion of addressee

III. The criterion of period

We will discuss each of these criteria in turn.

I. THE CRITERION OF LOCATION

According to this definition, the criterion for a verse being Meccan or Medinan is the place of revelation. If the verse was revealed in Mecca, then it is classified as Meccan, and if it was revealed in Medina, then it is classified as Medinan. It does not matter whether the revelation of the verse was before or after the Prophet's ﷺ migration to Medina. Therefore, the verses revealed at the conquest of Mecca in 8AH, or the farewell pilgrimage in 10 AH, are to be considered Meccan, although they were revealed after the migration.

A problem with this definition is that, if a verse was not revealed either in Mecca or Medina then, according to this definition, it cannot be classified as either Meccan or Medinan. Such verses are few, and in this connection, Al-Suyūṭī narrates that the Prophet ﷺ said, "The Qur'an was sent down in three places: Mecca, Medina, and Shām." And according to Ibn al-Kathīr, Shām refers to Tabūk.[52]

II. THE CRITERION OF THE ADDRESSEE

In this definition, the criterion of a verse being Meccan or Medinan is the addressee of the verse. For instance, if the verse is addressed to the Muslims, Quraysh and the idolaters of Mecca, then the verse is classified as Meccan, and if the verse is addressed to the Muslims, Jews or the hypocrites (*munafiqūn*) of Medina, then the verse is classified as

Medinan. In this connection, a tradition is quoted from ʿAbdullāh ibn al-Masʿūd:

> Every chapter which contains the phrase, "O people!" (*yā ayyuha al-nās*) is Meccan, and every chapter which contains the phrase, "O believers!" (*yā ayyuha al-ladhīna āmanū*) is Medinan."[53]

However, there are Medinan chapters, for example, Al-Baqara, in which the phrase: "O people!" has been employed, which invalidates the universality of this definition.

Another problem with making the addressees a criterion is that there are verses in the Qur'an which do not have a specific addressee, or they are addressed to mankind in general; these verses then cannot be classified as either Meccan or Medinan.

III. THE CRITERION OF PERIOD

Most scholars believe that the criterion of a verse being Meccan or Medinan is the hijra, or the Prophet's ﷺ historic migration from Mecca to Medina. Any verse revealed prior to the migration, is classified as Meccan, and any verse revealed after the migration, is classified as Medinan. This definition is not governed by the place of revelation. In other words, every verse revealed in Mecca is not necessarily classified as a Meccan verse. Therefore, the verses revealed at the conquest of Mecca, in 8AH, or at the farewell pilgrimage, in 10AH, are considered Medinan under this definition. This is because these verses were revealed after the migration, although the actual place of revelation was Mecca.

Additionally, the criterion of the migration is "entering Medina". Therefore, the verses that were revealed during the Prophet's ﷺ migration, are counted as Meccan. As an example, the following verse, which was revealed after the Prophet ﷺ had left Mecca and was on his way to Medina, is classified as Meccan.

﴿ إِنَّ ٱلَّذِى فَرَضَ عَلَيْكَ ٱلْقُرْءَانَ لَرَآدُّكَ إِلَىٰ مَعَادٍ ۚ قُل رَّبِّىٓ أَعْلَمُ مَن جَآءَ بِٱلْهُدَىٰ

وَمَنْ هُوَ فِي ضَلَٰلٍ مُّبِينٍ ﴿٨٥﴾

Most certainly, He Who has made the Qur'an binding on you will bring you back to your home [Mecca]. Say: My Lord knows best the one who has brought the guidance and the one who is in clear error. (Al-Qaṣaṣ, 28:85)

This is the best definition, because it was the time factor that changed the tone of the verses of the Qur'an, as the Muslims grew in strength and faith.

According to this preferred definition, the Meccan phase lasted about 13 years – from the time of the first revelation until the entry of the Prophet ﷺ into Medina after his migration. The Medinan phase lasted about 10 years – from the time of the entry of the Prophet ﷺ into Medina until his death in 11AH.

Using this definition, a Meccan chapter is one in which most of the verses had been revealed before the migration, even though its completion may have occurred after the migration. Similarly, a Medinan chapter is one in which most of the verses were revealed after the migration.

2. THE DIFFERENCES BETWEEN THE MECCAN AND THE MEDINAN VERSES

Each phase of revelation (Meccan or Medinan) catered for a different need, as the circumstances of the Muslims changed greatly after the migration. In the early stages of revelation, Islam had been a relatively new ideology, and its tenets had not yet been firmly established in practice. In addition, the Muslims were oppressed and had very little power, and thus needed continual moral encouragement.

In comparison, after the migration, the Muslims had their own state and were relatively well established. The basic beliefs of Islam had been revealed and now the Muslims were in need of Divine guidance in their daily and social lives. They also needed to know the rules and conduct of jihād and the manner of inter-religious dialogue. As the needs of the Muslim community began to change, so did the style and content of the verses of the Qur'an.

One of the methods for distinguishing between the Meccan and Medinan verses is by referring to authentic traditions. However, in the absence of such traditions, other methods have been employed,[54] which look at different features of the verses themselves. Some of these are mentioned below:

I. **THE THEME OF THE VERSES:** The Meccan verses mostly describe the matters of belief (*uṣūl*). They refute the beliefs of the idolaters. They give evidence of the unity of God (*tawḥīd*) and His attributes. They establish the authority of the Prophet ﷺ. They warn about the accounting on the day of Judgement. The Medinan verses, on the other hand, deal mostly with the matter of legislation and rulings (*furūʿ*). These include the legislation regarding the daily prayers, fasting, pilgrimage, alms, war, family affairs, social conduct and so on.

II. **THE FORM OF ADDRESS:** In the Meccan verses, the audience has usually been addressed as, "O people!" or "O children of Ādam!", while in the Medinan verses the words "O you who believe!" has been used.

III. **THE LENGTH OF THE VERSES AND CHAPTERS:** The Meccan verses tend to be short, whereas the Medinan ones tend to be long (although there are exceptions to this general rule). For example, the whole of the 28th *juz'* (mostly Medinan chapters) contains only 137 verses, while the 29th and 30th *juz'* (mostly Meccan chapters) have 431 and 570 verses respectively. The Meccan chapters are the shorter chapters of the Qur'an, for example, those in the 30th *juz'*, whereas the Medinan chapters are the longer chapters, for example, Al-Baqara and Āli ʿImrān.

IV. **DIRECT REFERENCES ABOUT A CERTAIN PERSON OR**

EVENT IN THE MECCAN OR MEDINAN PERIOD: Some verses make direct references to individuals or events that allow us to classify them as Meccan or Medinan. For example, Al-Lahab is definitely Meccan, because his enmity to Islam was from before the migration, and similarly, the verses mentioning the battle of Badr are Medinan, because the battle occurred after the migration.

3. SOME CHARACTERISTICS OF THE MECCAN VERSES:

I. Verses regarding stories of the previous generations, prophets ﷺ and nations, and the trials and tribulations faced by them and the believers at the hands of the disbelievers, and the warning to the disbelievers of the punishment suffered by the previous disobedient nations, are all considered to be Meccan verses.

II. All the chapters beginning with the unconnected letters (*al-ḥurūf al-muqaṭṭaʿāt*), (with the exception of Al-Baqara and Āli ʿImrān) are Meccan chapters.

III. All the verses where prostration is obligatory or recommended are counted *as Meccan verses.*

IV. All verses containing the word of emphasis, "*kallā*", are Meccan verses.

4. SOME CHARACTERISTICS OF THE MEDINAN VERSES:

I. All verses which make a reference to the hypocrites in the Muslim ranks (*munāfiqūn*) tend to be Medinan.

II. The verses which discuss the shortcomings in the religion practised by the Jews and Christians, by explaining the true teachings of Mūsā ﷺ and ʿIsā ﷺ, are considered to be Medinan verses.

III. The verses about holy war (jihād) were only revealed after the migration, and are therefore, Medinan.

Of course, all the characteristics mentioned above are not universal, and there are exceptions to all of them. However, as a general guide they are useful in differentiating between the Meccan and Medinan verses, and when they do not contradict clear traditions, these characteristics enable us to use the result in jurisprudence and exegesis. Therefore, it is important to recognise which verses are Meccan and which are Medinan, and this factor is discussed in greater detail in the next section.

5. THE IMPORTANCE OF KNOWING IF A VERSE IS MECCAN OR MEDINAN

The advantages of knowing whether a verse is Meccan or Medinan are listed below:

I. To enable us to understand the import of a verse, which plays a fundamental role in jurisprudence and in the inference of Islamic laws. For example, the issue of the unbelievers' obligation to follow Islamic laws is a subject discussed by the jurisprudents, most of whom do not consider it incumbent on unbelievers to follow the *sharī'a*. And they have many proofs and traditions to support their view. However, those who reject this view (and consider it obligatory for the unbelievers to follow Islamic rulings) have resorted to the following verse:

﴿ وَوَيْلٌ لِّلْمُشْرِكِينَ ۝٦ ٱلَّذِينَ لَا يُؤْتُونَ ٱلزَّكَوٰةَ وَهُم بِٱلْءَاخِرَةِ هُمْ كَٰفِرُونَ ۝٧ ﴾

And woe to the polytheists; who do not give alms and do not believe in the hereafter. (Fuṣṣilat, 41:6, 7)

However, the verse above, is from Fuṣṣilat, which is a Meccan chapter; whereas the obligation of alms was made compulsory in Medina. That is, when the said verse was revealed, alms was not compulsory even on the Muslims themselves; and in fact, this verse has a different meaning.

II. To understand the history of the progress of the Muslim community and also the development of Islamic legislation, and how the Prophet ﷺ dealt with different groups of non-Muslims such as polytheists, Christians and Jews.

III. Many Qur'anic issues can only be resolved by knowing whether the chapter or verse is Meccan or Medinan. For example, the issue regarding the abrogation of certain verses of the Qur'an by other verses, where the abrogated verse (*mansūkh*) must have been revealed prior to the abrogating verse (*nāsikh*).

IV. It enables us to understand the verse properly and benefit from its guidance if we know when the verse was revealed, especially when the exegetes encounter different occasions of revelation (*asbāb al-nuzūl*) about the verse.

6. EXCEPTIONS IN THE MECCAN AND MEDINAN CHAPTERS

Most scholars accept that some Meccan chapters contain Medinan verses, and very occasionally, Medinan chapters contain some Meccan verses.[55] For example, in Al-Baqara, a Medinan chapter, the following two verses are counted as Meccan by some scholars:[56]

﴿ وَدَّ كَثِيرٌ مِّنْ أَهْلِ ٱلْكِتَٰبِ لَوْ يَرُدُّونَكُم مِّنۢ بَعْدِ إِيمَٰنِكُمْ كُفَّارًا حَسَدًا مِّنْ عِندِ أَنفُسِهِم مِّنۢ بَعْدِ مَا تَبَيَّنَ لَهُمُ ٱلْحَقُّ ۖ فَٱعْفُوا۟ وَٱصْفَحُوا۟ حَتَّىٰ يَأْتِىَ ٱللَّهُ بِأَمْرِهِۦٓ ۗ إِنَّ ٱللَّهَ عَلَىٰ كُلِّ شَىْءٍ قَدِيرٌ ۝ ﴾

Many of the followers of the Book wish that they could turn you back into unbelievers after your faith, out of envy from themselves, [even] after the truth has become manifest to them; but pardon and forgive, so that God should bring about His command; surely God has power over all things. (Al-Baqara, 2:109)

﴿ لَّيْسَ عَلَيْكَ هُدَىٰهُمْ وَلَـٰكِنَّ ٱللَّهَ يَهْدِى مَن يَشَآءُ ﴾

To make them walk in the right way is not incumbent on you, but God guides aright whom He pleases. (Al-Baqara, 2:272)

The table below summarises the exceptions and is based on the opinions cited in Zamakhsharī in his *Al-Kashshāf* and Zanjānī in his *Tārikh al-Qur'an.*[57]

Type of chapter	Number of chapters	Total number of verses	Number of Meccan verses	Number of Medinan verses
Meccan	51	1683	1683	-
Medinan	26	1419	-	1419
Meccan incl. Medinan verses	35	2930	2776	154
Medinan incl. Meccan verses	2	204	9	195
Total	114	6236	4468	1768

From the table above, we can conclude that the number of exceptions is 163 (= 154 + 9) verses.

NOTES

1 Dr Maḥmūd Rūḥanī, *Al-Mu'jam al-Aḥṣā'ī li al-Qur'an al-Karīm,* vol. 1, p. 25.
2 *Al-Itqān,* vol. 1, p. 115.
3 Zamakhsharī, *Al-Kashshāf,* see Hujjatī in *Tarikh-e Qur'an-e Karīm,* p 64.
4 *Majma' al-Bayān,* vol. 10, p. 406.
5 *Al-Itqān,* vol. 1, p. 104
6 *Biḥār al-Anwār,* vol. 92, p. 309.

[7] *Al-Itqān,* vol. 1, p. 212. Verse is Al-Naḥl, 16/90.
[8] *'Ulūm-e Qur'anī,* p. 110.
[9] Abd al-Futūḥ al-Rāzī, *Rawḍatu al-Jinān,* vol. 1, Introduction, p. 9.
[10] Ibid.
[11] *Al-Itqān,* vol. 1, p. 90.
[12] Ibid.
[13] For details of these and other alternative names for chapters, see *Al-Itqān,* vol. 1, pp. 167-171.
[14] *Al-Itqān,* vol. 1. p. 199.
[15] *Majma' al-Bayān,* vol. 1, p. 14; *Al-Itqān,* vol. 1, p. 109.
[16] *Al-Tamhid,* vol. 1, p. 251.
[17] *Manāhil al-'Irfān,* vol. 1, p. 352.
[18] *Al-Itqān,* vol. 1, p. 197.
[19] *Majma' al-Bayān,* vol. 1, p. 14; *Al-Itqān,* vol. 1, p. 89.
[20] *Al-Itqān,* vol. 1, p. 178.
[21] *Al-Mīzān,* vol. 18, pp. 6-8.
[22] *Majma' al-Bayān,* vol. 1, p. 33.
[23] *Al-Kashshāf,* vol. 1, p. 16.
[24] *Majma' al-Bayān,* vol. 1, p. 33.
[25] *Majma' al-Bayān,* vol. 1, p. 32; *Al-Manār,* vol. 7, p. 351.
[26] *Majma' al- Bayān,* vol. 1, p. 33.
[27] *Jāmi' al-Bayān,* vol. 1, p. 67.
[28] Ibn al-Kathīr, *Tafsīr,* vol. 1, p. 36.
[29] See: www.submission.org. While a mathematical analysis of the verses of the Qur'an based on the number 19 and its multiples initially seems to give startling results, some of the conclusions drawn are absurd, notably that the Qur'an contains two "extra" verses at the end of Al-Tawba.
[30] *Jāmi' al-Bayān,* vol. 4, p. 177.
[31] *Al-Itqān,* vol. 2, p.13.
[32] *Majma' al- Bayān,* vol. 1, p. 33; *Tafsīr Ibn al-Kathīr,* vol. 1, p. 36; *Al-Itqān,* vol. 2, p. 15.
[33] *Jāmi' al-Bayān,* vol. 11, p. 57; *Al-Itqān,* vol. 2, p. 13.
[34] *Mehr-e Tābān,* interviews with Allāma Ṭabāṭabā'ī (post *Al-Mīzān*).
[35] Bukhārī, *Ṣaḥīḥ,* vol. 1, p. 3; Muslim, *Ṣaḥīḥ,* vol. 1, p. 97.
[36] *Al-Kāfī,* vol. 2, p. 628.
[37] Muslim, *Ṣaḥīḥ,* vol. 1, p. 99; Aḥmad b. Ḥanbal, *Musnad,* vol. 3, p. 306.
[38] *Al-Kashshāf,* vol. 4, p. 775.
[39] *Majma' al-Bayān,* vol. 10, p. 405.
[40] *'Ulūm-e Qur'anī,* p. 62; Abū 'Abdillāh Zanjānī, *Tārīkh al-Qur'an,* p. 9.
[41] See Appendix 1: Table of chapters in order of revelation.
[42] *Majma' al-Bayān,* vol. 10, p. 405.
[43] See *'Ulūm-e Qur'anī,* pp. 90, 91.
[44] *Al-Itqān,* vol. 1, p. 27.
[45] *Majma' al-Bayān,* vol. 10, p. 554.
[46] Muḥammad Muḥsin Fayḍ Kāshānī, *Al-Ṣāfī fī Tafsīr al-Qur'an,* vol. 1, p. 680.
[47] Muḥammad al-Zurqānī, *Manāhil al-'Irfān fī 'Ulūm al-Qur'an,* p. 97-100.
[48] *Al-Itqān,* vol. 1, p. 87.
[49] Ya'qūbī, *Tārīkh,* vol. 2, p. 35.
[50] Abū al-Ḥasan 'Alī b. Muḥammad al-Māwardī, *Tafsīr,* vol. 1, p. 63; Zarkashī, *Al-Burhān,* vol. 1, p. 186.

[51] *'Ulūm-e Qur'ānī,* p. 81.
[52] *Al-Itqān,* vol. 1, p. 23.
[53] Abū 'Abdillāh Muḥammad Ḥākim al-Nishābūrī, *Al-Mustadrak 'alā al-Ṣaḥīḥain,* vol. 3, p. 18,19.
[54] *'Ulūm-e Qur'anī,* p. 83.
[55] An exception is Hādī Ma'rifat, see *Al-Tamhīd,* vol. 1, pp. 173 - 203. He argues that such reports are either due to misclassification of Makkī and Medinan verses, or due to weak reports.
[56] *Al-Itqān,* vol. 1, pp. 43 - 52.
[57] Dr Maḥmūd Rūḥānī, *Farhang-e Kalimāt-e Qur'an-e Karīm,* vol. 1, pp. 36, 37.

7

THE COMPILATION OF THE QUR'AN

The Qur'an was the cornerstone of the mission of the Prophet ﷺ and his declared miracle. From the earliest days of revelation, its verses were systematically recorded by specially nominated scribes. As a result, the Qur'an is unique amongst the divinely revealed scriptures in that it has been preserved in its original form, without any loss or distortion. And this is not surprising, because God Himself has guaranteed its protection:

﴿إِنَّا نَحْنُ نَزَّلْنَا ٱلذِّكْرَ وَإِنَّا لَهُۥ لَحَٰفِظُونَ ٩﴾

Indeed, We have revealed the Reminder (Qur'an) and We will most surely be its guardian. (Al-Ḥijr, 15:9)

And it is God, who reassured the Muslims of success in the difficult task of collating a document whose revelation spanned 23 years:

﴿إِنَّ عَلَيْنَا جَمْعَهُۥ وَقُرْءَانَهُۥ ١٧﴾

Surely on Us (devolves) the collecting of it and the reciting of it. (Al-Qiyāma, 75:17)

In addition to the appointment of official scribes, the Prophet ﷺ took several further measures to ensure that the Qur'an did not suffer the fate of the previous scriptures. Some of these were:

1. Upon receiving any revelation, the Prophet ﷺ would formally recite the latest verses to all the men in one assembly, and thereafter convene a second gathering and recite the verses to the women.[1]

2. He stressed the importance and reward of the memorization of the Qur'an. He is reported as saying, "The best of you is the one who learns the Qur'an and teaches it to others."[2] He also said that those who had recited more of the Qur'an and collected and memorized more of it, were more deserving to lead the other Muslims in prayer.[3]

3. The Muslims also had a religious obligation to memorize some parts of the Qur'an; in the five daily prayers, they were required to recite from memory, Al-Fātiḥa, followed by another portion of the Qur'an. The Prophet ﷺ greatly encouraged people to memorize and refresh their memories of the Qur'an. Muslim reports that he said, "Try to refresh your memories of the Qur'an for it is more apt to escape from men's minds than a hobbled camel."[4]

4. He encouraged reciting from written text. As a result, there were many scattered portions and a few complete copies of the Qur'an in the possession of Muslims by the time of the death of the Prophet ﷺ.

5. He made the Qur'an the reference point in the lives of the Muslims and they became familiar with its verses and followed its teachings and guidance in all matters.

6. Whenever someone would migrate to Medina, the Prophet ﷺ would assign a companion to him to teach him the Qur'an. In fact the sound of teaching and recitation of the Qur'an would constantly fill the mosque in Medina; at one point the Prophet ﷺ even asked people to recite quietly so that they would not disturb each other's recitation.[5]

7. He turned non-believers into Muslims by reciting to them the Qur'an, and they never forgot their introduction to the Divine words. When 'Utba b. Rabī'a came to the Prophet ﷺ on behalf of the Quraysh, offering every conceivable temptation in exchange for his abandoning of his mission, the Prophet ﷺ waited patiently and

then said, "Now listen to me," and then recited a few verses of the Qur'an in response.[6]

Similarly, a delegation of 20 Christians from Ethiopia who came to debate with the Prophet ﷺ were reduced to tears by his eloquent replies in the form of Qur'anic verses. The Qur'an says about them:

﴿ وَإِذَا سَمِعُوا مَا أُنزِلَ إِلَى الرَّسُولِ تَرَىٰ أَعْيُنَهُمْ تَفِيضُ مِنَ الدَّمْعِ مِمَّا عَرَفُوا مِنَ الْحَقِّ ۖ يَقُولُونَ رَبَّنَا آمَنَّا فَاكْتُبْنَا مَعَ الشَّاهِدِينَ ﴿٨٣﴾ ﴾

And when they hear what has been revealed to the messenger, you will see their eyes overflowing with tears on account of the truth that they recognize; they say: Our Lord! we believe, so write us down with the witnesses (of truth). (Al-Ma'ida, 5:83)

Even prior to the hijra, while the Prophet ﷺ was in Mecca, the growing Muslim community in Medina avidly awaited news of revelation and would eagerly study and memorize what they received. The hard work of the Prophet's ﷺ envoy, Muṣʿab b. ʿUmair is noteworthy in this regard. His efforts ensured that the Qur'an and Islamic teachings already had roots in the nascent Muslim community in Medina by the time the Prophet ﷺ arrived. After his blessed arrival, attention to the Qur'an become even more structured. Ṭabāṭabāʾī writes:

> This study and devotion to the Qur'an became more ordered and comprehensive after the Prophet ﷺ emigrated to Medina and formed an independent Muslim community. He ordered a considerable number of companions to recite the Qur'an and to learn and teach the laws which were being revealed daily. So important was this activity that, according to special permission granted by God in chapter Al-Tawba, verse 9:122, these scholars were relieved of their obligation to participate in jihād.[7]

As a result of these concerted and deliberate efforts, the Qur'an occupied a central place in the daily lives of the Muslims and a great number of the companions became *ḥuffāẓ,* or those who had committed the entire Qur'an to memory. In just a single battle, which occurred at the time of the Prophet ﷺ at Bi'r Maʿuna, out of all the Muslims who were killed, eighty were *ḥuffāẓ.*

7.1 - THE SCRIBES OF THE PROPHET ﷺ

Throughout the course of the twenty-three years of revelation, the Prophet ﷺ was concerned with every aspect of preserving the Qur'anic text from any sort of corruption. Out of the small pool of people who could read and write, he appointed scribes to note down the verses as they were revealed. He would tell them exactly where the verse was to be fixed in a chapter.

The number of literate Muslims gradually increased; some were taught by prisoners in exchange for their freedom, others learned in order to be able to read the Qur'an. In fact, the Qur'an itself encouraged literacy by introducing the concept of written contracts:

﴿ يَٰٓأَيُّهَا ٱلَّذِينَ ءَامَنُوٓاْ إِذَا تَدَايَنتُم بِدَيۡنٍ إِلَىٰٓ أَجَلٖ مُّسَمّٗى فَٱكۡتُبُوهُۚ ﴾

O you who believe! When you deal with each other in contracting a debt for a fixed time, then write it down. (Al-Baqara, 2:282)

From this growing group of writers, the Prophet ﷺ selected more and more as scribes. He would take an active interest in the accuracy of their rendering, as is evident from his recommendations to a novice scribe who was writing the *basmala*:

> Dip the wool in ink, sharpen the pen, write the *bā'* upright, separate [the teeth] of the *sīn*, do not blind (blot) the *mīm*, write the *Allāh* well, elongate the *raḥmān*, write the *raḥīm* neatly and then replace your pen behind your left ear! (*aliq al-dawāta, wa ḥarrif al-qalam, w'anṣab al-bā', wa farriq al-sīn, wa lā tu'awwir al-mīm, wa ḥassin Allāh, wa mudd al-raḥmān, wa jawwid al-raḥīm, wa ḍa' qalamaka 'alā udhunika al-yusrā*).[8]

The scribes were known as the "recorders of revelation" (*kuttāb al-waḥy*). According to Zanjānī, their number was 43 persons. He writes, "from these, the two scribes who were closest to the Prophet ﷺ were Zaid b. Thābit and 'Alī b. Abī Ṭālib."[9]

Among the names of the scribes that the scholars mention are:

IN MECCA: ʿAlī, Abū Bakr, ʿUmar, ʿUthmān, Sharḥīl b. Ḥasana (d. 18/640), ʿAbdallāh b. Saʿd b. Abī al-Sarḥ (d. 37/657)[10], Khālid b. Saʿīd b. al-Ās, Ṭalḥa b. ʿUbaydallāh (d. 36/656), Zubair b. al-ʿAwwām (d. 36/656), Saʿd b. Abī al-Waqāṣ (d. 55/674), ʿĀmir b. al-Fahīra (d. 4/625), Musʿab b. al-Umair and ʿAbdallāh b. al-Jaḥsh.

IN MEDINA: Ubayy b. al-Kaʿb, Zaid b. al-Thābit, ʿAbdallāh b. al-Rawāha (d. 8/629), Thābit b. al-Qays (d. 12/633), Ḥanẓala b. Abī ʿĀmir (d. 3/624) and Muʿāwiya b. Abī Sufyān (d. 60/679).[11]

Some scribes were called upon for writing letters, contracts, war records and treaties, as well as revelation. Yaʿqūbī writes:

> The Prophet ﷺ had scribes to whom he would dictate revelation, letters and treaties. They were ʿAlī b. Abī Ṭālib, ʿUthmān b. ʿAffān, ʿAmr b. al-ʿĀṣ b. Umayya, Sharḥīl b. Ḥasana, Mughayra b. Shaʿba, Maʿādh b. Jabal, Zaid b. Thābit, Ḥanẓala b. Rabīʿ, Ubayy b. Kaʿb, Juhaym b. Ṣalt and Ḥaṣīn b. Numayr.[12]

7.2 - RECORDING OF THE VERSES

The scribes used several different materials to write the revelation. It is narrated from Zaid b. Thābit that he said, "We would sit in the presence of the Prophet ﷺ and write the verses of the Qur'an on sheets (*riqāʿ*)."[13]A study of some verses of the Qur'an gives us some idea about what writing materials were known at the time. The Qur'an mentions:

- Paper (*qirṭās*) in Al-Anʿām 6:7; Papers (*qarāṭīs*) in Al-Anʿām 6:91
- Pen (*qalam*) in Al-Qalam 68:1 and Al-ʿAlaq 96:4; Pens (*aqlām*) in Luqmān 31:27 and Āli ʿImrān 3:44
- Ink (*midād*) in Al-Kahf 19:109
- Scroll for writing (*sijil*) in Al-Anbiyā 21:104
- Scrolls (*ṣuḥuf*) in Ṭā-Hā 20:133, Al-Najm 53:36, Al-Muddaththir

74:52, ʿAbasa 80:13, Al-Takwīr 81:10, Al-Aʿlā 87:18, 19 and Al-Bayyina 94:2

- Parchment (*raq*) in Al-Ṭūr 52:3

Of course, all these were not necessarily used by the scribes of the Prophet ﷺ. The materials which were commonly used for recording the verses on are mentioned in different narrations. Some of them are:[14]

- *ʿUsub* (sing. *ʿasīb*): These were made from the broad sides of the leaves of the date-palm.
- *Likhāf* (sing. *lakhfa*): These were thin and delicate tablets of white stone.
- *Aktāf* (sing. *katif*): These were the wide and flat thigh bones or shoulder blades of camels or sheep.
- *Aqtāb* (sing. *qatb*): These were wooden boards also used to make litters for camels.
- *Adīm* (sing. *adam* or *udm*): Pieces of tanned animal hide.
- *Riqāʿ* (sing. *raqʿa*): This general term encompasses writing material made of paper, hides or leaves.
- *Aḍlāʿ* (sing. *ḍilʿ*): The rib bones of animals.
- *Ḥarīr*: Silk parchment.
- *Qarāṭīs* (sing. *qirṭās*): Paper.
- *Shiẓāẓ*: A type of wood.

Paper was available to the Muslims, but perhaps it was expensive. Dr Ramyār writes:

> The Arabs knew about paper from ancient times. In those days it was manufactured in India and sent to Yemen. Through the summer and winter trading caravans, it was then transported northwards to Damascus and Rome. At that time, Arabia was the main trade route for trade between the north and the south.[15]

7.3 - THE QUR'AN AT THE TIME OF THE PROPHET ﷺ

There are numerous traditions that indicate that in addition to being memorized by many Muslims, the Qur'an was also available in written form throughout the course of revelation. The Prophet ﷺ himself would also recite from written text. The Qur'an describes him thus:

﴿ رَسُولٌ مِّنَ ٱللَّهِ يَتْلُواْ صُحُفًا مُّطَهَّرَةً ۝٢ ﴾

A messenger from God, reciting pure pages (Al-Bayyina, 98:2)

Some collectors had only few chapters in their possession, while the appointed scribes had complete collections. Zanjānī writes:

> Some companions had collected the entire Qur'an in the lifetime of the Prophet ﷺ, while others had partial collections, which they completed after his demise. Ibn al-Nadīm in his *Al-Fihrist* lists the following collectors of the Qur'an in the lifetime of the Prophet ﷺ: ʿAlī b. Abī Ṭālib, Saʿd b. ʾAmr b. Zaid, Abū al-Dardāʾ, Maʿādh b. Jabal, Abū Zaid b. Nuʿmān, Ubayy b. Kaʿb and Zaid b. Thābit.[16]

The following report narrated by Muslim in his *Ṣaḥīḥ* also indicates that the Qur'an was available in a book form (*kitāb*) amongst the Muslims:

> Ibn ʿAbbas reported: When God's Messenger (may peace be upon him) was about to leave this world, there were persons (around him) in his house, ʿUmar b. al-Khaṭṭāb being one of them. God's Apostle (may peace be upon him) said: Come, I may write for you a document; you would not go astray after that. Thereupon ʿUmar said: "Verily, God's Messenger (may peace be upon him) is deeply afflicted with pain. You have the Qur'an with you. The Book of God is sufficient for us (*ḥasbunā kitāballah*)."[17]

Al-Khūʾī is sceptical of reports that suggest that the task of collecting the Qur'an was begun after the Prophet ﷺ passed away. He has critically evaluated all such reports and concludes that they are inconsistent and contradictory and therefore none of them can be relied upon.[18] He argues:

> Many verses of the Noble Book demonstrate that the chapters of the Qur'an were distinct in form and content from each other, and were widely spread among the people, including the idolaters of Mecca and the people of the Book. Significantly, the Prophet ﷺ had challenged the unbelievers and idolaters to produce the like of the Qur'an, and the like of ten chapters from it, and even one chapter. This means that the chapters of the Qur'an were available to them...Moreover, in the famous tradition of *al-thaqalayn*, the Prophet ﷺ says, "I am leaving among you two things of high estimation; the Book of God (*kitābullāh*) and my Family."[19] In this tradition there is evidence that the Qur'an had been collected and written, because it is not correct to call it *al-kitāb* when it is merely in the [people's] memories...The word *al-kitāb* obviously signifies a single and coherent entity. It is not applied to a text which is scattered and not collected.[20]

He concludes that all that was required for the Qur'an after the demise of the Prophet ﷺ was the putting of two covers on what was already available and known amongst the Muslims.

7.4 - THE COLLECTION AT THE TIME OF ABŪ BAKR

The Prophet ﷺ had willed that the Qur'an be compiled in a book form so that it would not be lost or distorted like other Divine revelations such as the Tawrāt. It is possible that he did this because, although the written Qur'an existed, it was not in the form of a single codex written on a medium that could easily be read.[21] Accordingly, ʿAlī b. Abī Ṭālib declared that he "would not wear his cloak (come out of the house), except for the Friday prayers, until he had compiled the Qur'an"[22], and he finished this task within six months of the passing away of the Prophet ﷺ. His compilation contained explanatory information on the verses, for example, the *asbāb al-nūzūl*.

In the battle of Yamāma, around 80 (or by some accounts, 400) Muslims who had memorized the Qur'an were killed.[23] This caused Abū Bakr to worry that the Qur'an might be forgotten if there were more lives lost, and so he commissioned Zaid b. Thābit to gather the

Qur'an from "the hearts of those who had memorized it" and the pieces of wood and bone on which it was written, and to prepare a single official codex.[24] In this regard, Bukhārī reports:

> Zaid b. Thābit narrated: Abū Bakr sent for me owing to the large number of casualties in the battle of Yamāma, while 'Umar was sitting with him. Abū Bakr said (to me), 'Umar has come to me and said, "A great number of *ḥuffāẓ* (memorizers) of the Qur'an were killed in the battle of Yamāma, and I am afraid that heavier casualties amongst them may occur on other battle-fields, whereby much of the Qur'an may be lost. Therefore, I consider it advisable that you (Abū Bakr) should have the Qur'an collected." I said, "How dare I do something which God's Apostle ﷺ did not do?" 'Umar said, "By God, it is something beneficial." 'Umar kept on pressing me, until God opened my chest for that for which He had opened the chest of 'Umar, and I had the same opinion as he had in that matter." Abū Bakr then said to me (Zaid), "You are a wise young man and we do not have any suspicion about you, and you used to write the Divine revelation for God's Apostle ﷺ. So you should search for the fragmentary scripts of the Qur'an and collect it (in one book)." Zaid added: By God, if Abū Bakr had ordered me to shift a mountain among the mountains from one place to another it would not have been heavier for me than this ordering me to collect the Qur'an. Then I said (to 'Umar and Abū Bakr), "How can you do something which God's Apostle ﷺ did not do?" Abū Bakr said, "By God, it is something beneficial." Zaid added: So he (Abū Bakr) kept on pressing me until God opened my chest for that for which He had opened the chests of Abū Bakr and 'Umar, and I had in that matter, the same opinion as theirs...
>
> So I started compiling the Qur'an by collecting it from the leafless stalks of the date-palm tree and from pieces of leather and hide and from stones, and from the chests of men (who had memorized the Qur'an). I found the last verses of Al-Tawba (*Verily there has come unto you an Apostle (Muḥammad) from amongst yourselves...*[9:128-129]) with Abū Khuzaima al-Anṣārī, and I added to it the rest of the chapter. The scrolls of the Qur'an remained with Abū Bakr till God took him unto Him. Then it remained with 'Umar till God took him unto Him, and then with Ḥafṣa, the daughter of 'Umar."[25]

The Qur'an was thus gathered into a single compilation. It is interesting that there was no immediate rush by Muslims to avail themselves of this official codex, and it passed to the care of 'Umar and then his daughter Ḥafṣa. This clearly demonstrates that the Qur'an was generally known and widely available amongst the Muslims all the time.

One can conclude, assuming this oddly-worded narration is indeed true, that Abū Bakr's actions were designed to ensure that at least one official copy was prepared, in the unlikely event that the Qur'an was not memorized and preserved by future generations of Muslims.

7.5 - THE UNIFICATION OF CODICES BY 'UTHMĀN

The next major event in the history of the compilation of the Qur'an occurred at the time of 'Uthmān. By this time, the Islamic empire stretched across a vast area and several codices were in use in different locations. Ibn al-Athīr writes:

> By 20/640, four codices (*muṣḥaf*s) were in use in four corners of the empire; the *muṣḥaf* of Ubayy [b. Ka'b] in Damascus, of ['Abdullāh] Ibn al-Mas'ūd in Kūfa, of Abū Mūṣā [al-Ash'arī] in Baṣrā and of Miqdād [b. 'Amr] in Ḥamṣ.[26]

In addition to these codices, several others were also available throughout Muslim lands. However, the writing style was still not developed to a point where diacritical marks and vowels were used, and as people from non-Arab lands began to embrace Islam, errors in recitation began to surface. Bukhārī writes:

> Anas b. Mālik narrated: Ḥudhaifa b. al-Yamān came to 'Uthmān at the time when the people of Syria and the people of Iraq were (together) waging war to conquer Armenia and Azerbaijan. Ḥudhaifa was afraid of their (the people of Syria and Iraq) differences in the recitation of the Qur'an, so he said to 'Uthmān, "O chief of the believers! Save this nation before it differs about the Book, as the Jews and the Christians did before."[27]

On hearing this, 'Uthmān consulted the companions who resided in Medina, who all concurred that the various codices in use needed to be checked and confirmed to be authentic. Bukhārī continues:

> So 'Uthmān sent a message to Ḥafṣa saying, "Send us the manuscripts of the Qur'an so that we may compile the Qur'anic materials in perfect copies and return the manuscripts to you." Ḥafṣa sent it to 'Uthmān, who ordered Zaid b.

> Thābit, ʿAbdullāh b. al-Zubair, Saʿīd b. al-Āṣ and ʿAbd al-Rahman b. Ḥārith b. Hishām to make duplicates. He advised the three men of Quraysh, "Should you disagree with Zaid b. Thābit on any point regarding the Qur'an, then write it in the dialect of the Quraysh, because it was revealed in their tongue." They did so, and when they had prepared several copies, ʿUthmān returned the original manuscripts to Ḥafṣa.
>
> ʿUthmān sent to every Muslim province one copy of what they had copied, and ordered that all the other Qur'anic materials, whether written in fragmentary manuscripts or whole copies, be burnt.[28]

Initially, ʿUthmān appointed a committee of four persons, made up of Zaid b. Thābit, ʿAbdullāh b. al-Zubair, Saʿīd b. al-ʿĀṣ, and ʿAbd al-Raḥmān b. al-Ḥārith to transcribe a master copy of the Qur'an. The original codex which was in the possession of Ḥafṣa was also recalled for comparison.[29]

Soon after the committee was set up, it was felt that more people would be required to ensure that this important task was performed accurately and with consensus. Accordingly Ubayy b. Kaʿb and a further seven men were recruited and the final committee comprised 12 persons. The senior scholar Ubayy was kept overall in charge, and he dictated the verses as the others wrote them down.[30]. The team also helped, as time allowed, to correct people's own personal copies of the Qur'an. For example, the slave of ʿUthmān, ʿAbdullāh b. Hānī al-Barbarī, reports:

> I was with ʿUthmān watching while people were comparing their copies with the main copyists. ʿUthmān handed me some bone segments on which verses were written. I took them to Ubayy b. Kaʿb who made three minor corrections as follows: he changed *lam yatasann* to *lam yatasanna* (2:259); *lā tabdīla li'l khalqillāh* to *lā tabdīla likhalqillāh* (30:30); and *fa'amhili'l kāfirīn* to *famahhili'l kafirīn.*[31]

In this manner, in 25/645, five master copies were prepared and all the main hitherto existing fragmentary codices were burnt, erased or melted down. ʿUthmān was criticized by some for destroying the fragments, but his actions were the result of consultation with all the companions. ʿAlī b. Abī Ṭālib says in this regard, "By God! ʿUthmān did not do anything in the matter of the *muṣḥaf* except that it was with our unanimous approval." And in another narration he is reported as saying, "If I had been in charge of the matter of the unification of the codices I would not have acted differently…"[32]

As soon as the official and authentic copies of the codices were ready, one was sent to each of the main Muslim cities, Kūfa, Baṣra, Damascus and Mecca, and the master, or *imām*, copy was kept in Medina.[33]

Ṭabāṭabāʾī adds:

> It is said that beside these five, one copy was also sent to Yemen and one to Bahrain. These copies were called the *Imam* copies and served as original for all future copies. The only difference of order between these copies and the first volume (compiled at the time of Abū Bakr) was that the chapters Al-Anfāl and Al-Tawba were written in one place between Al-Aʿrāf and Yūnus.[34]

ʿUthmān also despatched an expert *qāri* or reciter of the Qurʾan with every *muṣḥaf* so that he could serve as a teacher. Thus, ʿAbdallāh b. Sāʾib accompanied a copy of the *muṣḥaf* to Mecca, ʿĀmir b. ʿAbd al-Qays to Baṣra, Mughayra b. Shahab to Damascus and Abū ʿAbd al-Raḥmān al-Sulamī to Kūfa. Zaid b. Thābit was officially nominated as the *qāriʾ* of Medina.

Due to ʿUthmān's efforts in the unification of the codices, the official codex came to be associated with him and is called the *muṣḥaf* of ʿUthmān.

7.6 - WAS THE ORDER OF THE CHAPTERS IN THE QUR'AN REARRANGED AT THE TIME OF ʿUTHMĀN?

The chapters and verses of the Qurʾan were not revealed in the order in which they are currently set out; in fact, they run roughly opposite to the order of revelation, with the chapters revealed in Medina in the beginning and most Meccan chapters towards the end of the *muṣḥaf.*

While nearly all scholars accept that the arrangement of verses in their respective chapters was as directed by the Prophet ﷺ, they are divided on the issue of whether the present arrangement of the chapters themselves is based on the instructions of the Prophet ﷺ (*tawqīfī*) or was decided on by the deliberations of the companions (*ijtihādī*). Some scholars also present a third possibility; that the order of most chapters is *tawqīfī* and the companions decided on the order of the rest.

The proponents of the *tawqīfī* view state the following as proof:

1. The Qur'an used to be recited and taught at the time of the Prophet ﷺ and this process had to have some order in recitation. Some companions, such as ʿAbdullāh b. Masʿūd and Ubayy b. Kaʿb, would also recite the complete Qur'an in the presence of the Prophet ﷺ, to verify their recitation.

2. There are narrations where the Prophet ﷺ has mentioned some order of the chapters. For example, he has said:

   > "I have been given the seven long chapters (*ṭiwāl*) in place of the *Tawrat,* the hundred-verse chapters (*ma'īn*) in place of the *Zabūr,* the oft-repeated chapters (*mathānī*) in place of the *Injīl,* and I have been uniquely honoured with the separated chapters (*mufaṣṣal*).[35]

   However, it must be said that aside from the seven *ṭiwāl,* this narration does not give much information about the arrangement of the rest of the chapters.

3. There is no discernable pattern in the sequence of the chapters; they do not run in order of revelation, or from the longest to the shortest, etc. If the companions had indeed decided on the arrangement after the passing away of the Prophet ﷺ, surely they would have followed some pattern. In this regard, Al-Suyūṭī writes:

   > Amongst the proofs that the arrangement of chapters was *tawqīfī* is the fact that the *Ḥawāmīm* (40-46) and *Ṭawāsīn* (26-28) chapters are in

> sequence, but the *Musabbiḥāt* (17, 57, 59, 61, 62, 64, 87) are not in sequence....Also, in the *Ṭawāsīn* sequence, *Al-Naml* is the shortest of the three, yet it is found between the other two.[36]

4. The ending of one chapter has a dovetail relationship with the beginning of the next chapter, hence indicating a pre-planned sequential arrangement. For example:
   At the end of Al-Fātiḥa, there is a prayer for guidance to the right path. The next chapter, Al-Baqara, begins with a mention that there can be no doubt that the Qur'an itself is the guidance for the God-fearing.
   Al-Baqara ends with a promise that God will not burden a soul more than its capability, and that it earns reward and punishment according to its own actions. The next chapter, Āli 'Imrān, begins with a description of the punishment that man earns when he ignores the guidance that has been sent down through the divine scriptures, Tawrāt, Injīl and Qur'an.
   Similarly, at the end of Āli 'Imrān, the believers are asked to persevere and adopt piety in order to be successful, and the next chapter, Al-Nisā', continues with the theme of piety leading to social obligations.

   A contemporary scholar, Amīn Aḥsan Iṣlāḥī, has presented an elegant theory of cohesion amongst the chapters on three levels; within an individual chapter, between paired chapters, and within clusters of chapters."[37]

5. There are no conclusive or reliable traditions that prove that there was any discussion by the companions, at the time of the compilation, about the order of the chapters. Dr Ṣubḥī al-Ṣāliḥ, who is a strong proponent of the *tawqīfī* view, writes:

> The order of the chapters is as directed by the Prophet ﷺ and was well known during his lifetime. We do not have conclusive evidence that this was not the case, and so the opinion of some scholars that it was the companions who arranged the chapters, either entirely or partially, is

incorrect.[38]

This argument, of course, can work both ways, and he has not provided evidence that the Prophet ﷺ directed the arrangement of all the chapters.

The arguments of those who hold the *ijtihādī* view appear stronger. They cite the following proofs:

1. The arrangement of chapters is not important, because each is self-contained. This is evidenced by the differing arrangements of the chapters, both within the codices (*muṣḥaf*s) of the main collectors, and the compilations of Abū Bakr and 'Uthmān.[39] For example, 'Alī compiled a *muṣḥaf* with the chapters in chronological order of revelation, starting with Al-Iqrā', then Al-Muddaththir, and so on. But the muṣḥafs of Ubayy b. Ka'b and Ibn al-Mas'ūd started with Al-Baqara, then Al-Nisā', then Āli 'Imrān. These differences clearly show that the sequence of the chapters was not from the Prophet ﷺ, otherwise the companions would have compiled their codices with identical arrangements of chapters.[40]

2. Unlike the order of verses, there is no restriction in reciting the Qur'anic chapters in different sequences, either in prayer or for general recitation. One can start from any chapter and end at any chapter, and this is a strong proof that the order of the chapters is not important.

3. As long as the Prophet ﷺ was alive, there was still a chance that more chapters would be revealed. Therefore, the arrangement of chapters could only be done after he passed away and revelation came to an end. Some scholars mention that the fact that the Qur'anic chapters were arranged in the present form at the time of 'Uthmān, is a reason why it is called the 'Uthmānī *muṣḥaf*.[41]

4. The present arrangement of the chapters does not follow the

sequence of revelation, therefore, the order must have been decided upon at a later time. It follows that the order must have been *ijtihādī*.[42]

7.7 - THE ORIGINAL SCRIPT OF THE QUR'AN AND ITS EVOLUTION

During the course of its history, several helpful and aesthetic changes have been made to the original Qur'anic script, which have greatly facilitated its recital. The modern reader may take for granted the ease with which the Qur'an can be read, but it was not always so.

Palaeography, or the study of ancient forms of writing indicates that Arabic script may originally derive from Nabataean or Syriac scripts. At the time of the Prophet ﷺ the script that was in use was probably a rudimentary form of the one that later came to be known as Kufic.

The earliest copies of the Qur'an, including the first and second official copies, were thus written in Kufic script. This very basic script, without any skeletal dots or diacritical marks, was perfectly adequate for recitation and study by Muslims who were well-versed with the Qur'an, or had memorized it. They had no great difficulty in knowing the precise pronunciation of the words. We must bear in mind that the Arab society was used to memorization. This was partly because, although literacy was not greatly prevalent, they were an eloquent people who appreciated poetry and fine speech and had developed a ready ability to memorize the better poems and turns of phrase.

Untrained readers of the Qur'an, on the other hand, immediately faced some problems. The Kufic script was in its infancy, and the script used by 'Uthmān in the official codex can best be described as a form of shorthand, designed to be an *aide memoire* to a knowledgeable reader. It was not ideally suited for inexperienced readers, because of several reasons:

1. The first was the absence of skeletal dots or *nuqāt al-i'jām*, in the

ʿUthmānic codex or *muṣḥaf,* although these were known to the Arabs prior to Islam, and occasionally used by them, especially when writing letters. However, the early Qurʾanic scribes dispensed with them and that meant that there was no way to tell similar letters apart. For example, the letters ب ت ث and ج ح خ were indistinguishable from one another.

2. Another problem was the absence of diacritical marks, which indicate the vowels, and are vital for the correct vocalization of the words. These were developed firstly as dots and later as the familiar symbols *fatḥa, kasra* and *ḍamma* which are variously called *nuqāt al-iʿrāb, tashkīl* or *ḥarakāt.*

These two essential hurdles had to be overcome because of the rapid spread of Islam across non-Arab lands. In the two decades following the death of the Prophet ﷺ, the Muslim territories had trebled in size, spanning an area of 3.5 million square miles, from Libya in the west, to Afghanistan in the East and stretching northwards to Armenia. Non-Arab Muslims out-numbered Arabs, and there was an urgent need to devise a method for the new converts to be able to study and recite the Qurʾan. (Initial delay in this action could be a reason for the appearance in the Ḥadīth corpus of variant and aberrant readings of certain words and phrases.) In time, modifications and improvements were made to the original script, which allowed for easier reading. Some of these were:

1. THE INTRODUCTION OF DIACRITICAL MARKINGS (*TASHKĪL*)

The first modification that was made was the addition of diacritical marks, which greatly aided vocalization and eliminated many of the errors in recital. The man who is credited with inventing these aids is Abū al-Aswad al-Duʾalī (d. 69/688). He had been taught the basics of Arabic grammar by ʿAlī b. Abī Ṭālib himself, and he was approached by the authorities for a solution to resolve the errors in recitation by the non-Arab Muslims.

It is narrated that Ziyād b. Sumayya, the governor of Baṣra, approached Abū al-Aswad al-Du'alī, complaining "These *ḥamrā* have increased in number and are destroying the Arabic language!"[43] He then requested him to devise a system that would aid in the correct recitation of the Qur'an. Abū al-Aswad initially refused, not seeing the need, but apparently, Ziyād was not a man who gave up easily. He instructed a man to sit at a place which Abū al-Aswad frequently passed by and when the grammarian was within earshot, he should recite the following verse of Al-Tawba:

﴿... أَنَّ ٱللَّهَ بَرِيٓءٌ مِّنَ ٱلْمُشْرِكِينَ وَرَسُولُهُۥ...﴾

...that God is free from liability to the idolaters and so is His Messenger ...

(Al-Tawba, 9:3)

However, Ziyād had instructed the man to recite the last portion with a *kasra* instead of *ḍamma,* i.e. *rasūlihi* instead of *rasūluhū.* Of course, this deliberate mis-recital totally changed the meaning of the verse, which now said, "*...that God is free from liability to the idolaters and (also) to His Messenger...*" instead of, "*...that God is free from liability to the idolaters, and so is His Messenger...*"

The ploy achieved the desired result; Abū al-Aswad was appalled, and rushed back to the governor and told him that he would accept the assignment without delay. A scribe from the tribe of 'Abd al-Qays was hired to assist him and Abū al-Aswad said to the man:

> Take a copy of the Qur'an and add vowel markings to the verses, in a different colour from the text, according to my instructions. When you see that, as I pronounce a letter, my lips are open and raised, then place a dot above that letter (to indicate a *fatḥa*). Whenever you see my lips angle downwards, place a dot beneath that letter (to indicate a *kasra*). And when you see my lips purse, place a dot next to the letter (to indicate a *ḍamma*). And whenever I pronounce these letters with *ghunna* (nasalization), then place two dots in that position, instead of one (to indicate the *tanwīn* or indefinite form).

Thus, Abū al-Aswad recited the Qur'an while his aide added the vocalization dots. As each folio was completed, Abū al-Aswad would check the work for any error. In this manner, the first copy was completed, and others then copied this style.[44]

Not everyone was pleased with this innovation. It is reported that the jurist, Ḥasan al-Baṣrī and the traditionist, Muḥammad b. Sīrīn, who both died in 110/728, disliked this practice and considered it *makrūh* (undesirable). Mālik b. Anas (d. 179/795) also disapproved, saying, "Making marks in the *muṣḥaf* from which people learn and teach others is alright, but it is not desirable to adopt this in every *muṣḥaf*."[45]

Nevertheless, further innovations continued, all with the intention of facilitating the proper recitation of the sacred text. The people of Medina invented a sign for the *tashdīd* (double letter) in the shape of "◡". In time, Abū al-Aswad's students designed symbols for the *sukūn* (a quiescent letter carrying no vowel) as a dash "–" on top of the letter; and when an *alif al-waṣl* was preceded by a consonant with a *fatḥa*, a dash was placed at the top of the *alif*, when it was preceded by a consonant with *kasra*, a dash was placed below the *alif*, and when it was preceded by a letter with *ḍamma*, a dash was put across the *alif*.

In later times, more colours were introduced; in Andalucia (Muslim Spain) for example, four colours were used for writing the verses of the Qur'an; black for the text, red for the diacritical marks, yellow for the *hamza*s and green for the occurrences of *alif al-waṣl*.[46]

2. DOTTING THE LETTERS OF THE QUR'ANIC SCRIPT (*I'JĀM*)

As we have mentioned, in the *muṣḥaf* of 'Uthmān there were no dots to distinguish between similar letters such as *jīm*, *ḥā* and *khā*, etc. There is evidence, however, that the dotting system was prevalent even before Islam, and the Arabs used the dotted version of the script, especially when writing letters or treaties. This, of course, is quite plausible and sensible – one can hardly imagine that the original inventors of the script were so lacking in imagination that they proposed the same shape of letter for various different sounds!

When the first *muṣḥaf*s were written, the dot-less version of the script was used, because the codices were meant for readers who were well versed with the Qurʾan. In time, as we have seen, this led to problems for new, non-Arab, Muslims and it was not long before errors in recitation began to occur.

Although Abū al-Aswad had removed much of the difficulty in recitation by his innovative addition of vocalization aids, the problem of incorrect recitation could only be finally eliminated by dotting, or pointing, the similar letters (*iʿjām*) and then rewriting the *muṣḥaf* in the dotted version of the script.

The scholars write that at the time of Ḥajjāj b. Yūsuf al-Thaqafī (d. 95/714), the scribes of the governor of ʿAbd al-Malik b. Marwan in Iraq were commissioned to prepare a codex in a script that allowed the similar letters to be distinguished from one another. Yaḥyā b. Yaʿmar al-ʿAdawanī (d. 129/746) and Naṣr b. al-ʿĀṣim (d. 79/698), both students of the late Abū al-Aswad, undertook and completed this task.[47]

3. OTHER MODIFICATIONS

The work started by Abū al-Aswad al-Du'alī was further improved by the ideas of the multilingual grammarian Khalil b. Ahmad al-Farahīdī (d. 175/791) who substituted the dotted vowels with the markings that we are more familiar with today (ُ , َ and ِ). He also introduced the *maddā,* (the lengthening of certain letters), and greatly removed the difficulties of reading the Qurʾanic script correctly.

In the earliest *muṣḥaf*s, there was no indication in the text as to where one verse ended and another began. In time, scribes began to indicate the verse endings with small markers. There were many styles used; some showed an ending by four horizontal dots (....), others used dots in a column or triangular shape (∴). Later refinements included the introduction of special markers indicating five and ten-verse intervals.

The end of a chapter would normally be recognised by a gap followed by the *basmala* of the next chapter. Later on some decorative calligraphy and chapter titles began to make an appearance.

CONCLUSION

The revelation was an ongoing process as long as the blessed presence of the Prophet ﷺ was amongst the people. As new verses were revealed, they were added to the record by the scribes. Occasionally, the Prophet ﷺ would direct the scribes to insert the new verse between existing verses, for example, he told them to insert the following verse between the verse about interest (verse 280) and the one about debt (verse 282) in Al-Baqara :

﴿وَٱتَّقُواْ يَوْمًا تُرْجَعُونَ فِيهِ إِلَى ٱللَّهِ ثُمَّ تُوَفَّىٰ كُلُّ نَفْسٍ
مَّا كَسَبَتْ وَهُمْ لَا يُظْلَمُونَ ٢٨١﴾

And guard yourselves against a day in which you shall be returned to God; then every soul shall be paid back in full what it has earned, and they shall not be dealt with unjustly. (Al-Baqara, 2:281)

Since there is no evidence of the Prophet ﷺ ever informing the Muslims that the Qur'an was complete, it was always a work in progress during his lifetime. For their part, the scribes diligently maintained and preserved the sacred text. As verses were revealed, they would commit them to memory and record them on *ṣuḥuf*, or loose folios. It was only with the passing of the Prophet ﷺ that the final process of *jamʿ* (collection) – which was to gather the verses in a single compilation – could begin.

Therefore, we can conclude that the Qur'an was always available amongst the Muslims, both in the hearts of the memorizers and in written form (although not in the form of a book or *muṣḥaf*). It is possible that the arrangement of many chapters was also known to those who had been entrusted by the Prophet ﷺ to collect it. After his passing away, the verses were collected into a single codex. This task, accomplished by the consensus of the Muslims, preserved a record of the Qur'anic text against any subsequent disagreement.

In later times, 'Uthmān unified the existing codices – some of which were incomplete, or contained errors – into a single official compilation that would serve as a master from which subsequent copies could be made for new generations of Muslims. This is the codex available today.

The evolution of the writing style in the *muṣḥaf*s can be clearly seen by studying manuscripts that have survived from the earliest centuries. Many of these rare works are on public display at various museums around the world and are well worth the visit. The authors have spent some time studying the beautiful displays at the Āstān-e Quds-e Raḍavī Qur'an Museum in Mashad, Iran, which has the largest collection of Qur'anic manuscripts (over 11,000) in the world. Other excellent examples can be found at the Great Mosque in San'ā , the Egyptian National Library in Cairo, the British Museum in London and the Bibliothèque Nationale in Paris, amongst many other public and private collections.

7.8 - THE QUR'AN IN THE CALLIGRAPHY OF 'UTHMĀN ṬĀHĀ

The Qur'anic text that is mainly used today, and which we have used throughout this book, is the 'Uthmānic codex in the calligraphy of 'Uthmān Ṭāhā from Damascus and printed and distributed, amongst others, by the King Fahd Holy Qur'an Printing Complex in Riyadh.

At the end of this *muṣḥaf* the following has been written:

> This noble *muṣḥaf* has been recorded by taking into account the reading style of Ḥafṣ b. Sulaymān al-Asadī al-Kūfī, from 'Āṣim b. Abī al-Najūd al-Kūfī, from Abī 'Abd al-Raḥmān 'Abdallāh b. Ḥabīb, from 'Uthmān b. 'Affān and 'Alī b. Abī Ṭālib

and Zaid b. Thābit and Ubayy b. Kaʿb, from the Prophet ﷺ.

Its text has been received through reliable transmitters from the *muṣḥaf*s that the righteous caliph, ʿUthmān b. ʿAffān, despatched to Mecca, Baṣra, Kūfa, Shām and the *muṣḥaf* that was entrusted to the people of Medina, as well as his personal *muṣḥaf*, and copies made from them. And every letter in it conforms to the ʿUthmānic *muṣḥaf* mentioned previously…

7.9 - THE QUR'AN IN BRAILLE

For centuries, the only option for blind Muslims who wanted to recite the Qur'an was to listen to its recital and attempt to follow it. Sometimes, they would memorize parts of what they heard, and indeed, over time many blind people memorized the whole Qur'an. In some parts of the Muslim world, the blind were encouraged to memorize the Qur'an and select public recital as a vocation. One of the most gifted reciters in Egypt between 1930 and 1950 was Shaykh Muhammad Rifʿat, and he was blind from birth.

The options for the blind greatly increased with the introduction of the first Braille Qur'an, printed in Egypt in 1952. Another edition was published in Tunisia in 1978.

In 1991, a special press was commissioned in Saudi Arabia for printing the Qur'an in Braille and distributing it freely in the Muslim lands. 2000 copies of this edition were published in six volumes of 80 pages each. Every volume covers five *juz'* of the Qur'an. The volumes are quite bulky, because printing is only done on one side of the page, each containing 30 lines of text. Unlike the normal printed versions of the Qur'an, the Braille version is set from left to right. The reader is required to scan, using two fingers, two successive lines of Braille in order to receive the proper information about the verse which they are reading. The top line contains the diacritical marks and the second line contains the words. A free copy can be obtained from the Saudi Ministry of Education in Riyadh.

More recently, a 30 volume Braille Qur'an has been printed in Iran.

It was on display at the 2005 International Qur'an Exhibition held in Tehran.

NOTES

[1] See Aʿẓami, *The History of the Qur'anic Text,* p. 62.
[2] Bukhārī, *Ṣaḥīḥ,* vol. 6, bk. 61, no. 545.
[3] See *Shinākhtnāme-ye Qur'an,* p. 36, quoting *Al-Ṭabaqāt al-Kubrā,* vol. 8, p. 89.
[4] Muslim, *Ṣaḥīḥ,* bk. 4 no. 1724.
[5] *Al-Bayān,* p. 274, Zanjānī, *Tārīkh al-Qur'an,* p. 80.
[6] See Aʿẓami, *The History of the Qur'anic Text,* p. 60.
[7] Ṭabāṭabā'ī, *Qur'an in Islam,* p. 107.
[8] Majlisī, *Biḥār al-Anwār,* vol. 9, p. 10.
[9] Zanjānī, *Tarīkh al-Qur'an,* p. 42. (See Ḥujjatī, p. 202).
[10] This man turned apostate in later years.
[11] Dr Ramyār, *Tārīkh-e Qur'an,* pp. 262 - 264. (Some names in this list could well have been added later to appease the Umayyids; for example the names of Ibn Abī al-Sarḥ and Muʿāwiya b. Abī Sufyān.)
[12] Yaʿqūbī, *Tārīkh,* vol. 2, p. 80.
[13] *Al-Itqān,* vol. 1, p. 203.
[14] *Biḥār al-Anwār,* vol. 89, p. 40.
[15] *Tārīkh-e Qur'an,* p. 277.
[16] Zanjānī, *Tārīkh al-Qur'an,* chapter 3, p. 46.
[17] Muslim, *Ṣaḥīḥ,* vol.3, bk. 13. no. 4016.
[18] *Al-Bayān,* English translation, p. 168.
[19] Muslim, *Ṣaḥīḥ,* vol.3, bk. 31, no. 5920.
[20] *Al-Bayān,* tr. *Prolegomena to the Qur'an,* p. 172.
[21] Ḥujjatī, *Tārīkh-e Qur'ān-e Karīm,* p. 232.
[22] *Al-Itqān,* vol. 1, p. 99.
[23] The battle against the false prophet Musaylama in 11/632, in which 960 Muslims lost their lives before victory was achieved. (Ṭabarī, *Tārīkh,* vol. 2, p. 516).
[24] *Fatḥ al-Bārī,* vol. 7, p. 447.
[25] Bukhārī, *Ṣaḥīḥ,* vol. 9, bk. 89, no. 301.
[26] Dr Ramyār, *Tārīkh-e Qur'an,* p. 337.
[27] Bukhārī, *Ṣaḥīḥ,* vol. 6, bk. 61, no. 510.
[28] Ibid.
[29] Ibid.; *Al-Itqān,* vol. 1, p. 187.
[30] *ʿUlūm-e Qur'anī,* p. 137.
[31] *Al-Itqān,* vol. 1, p. 183.
[32] Ibid., p. 138.
[33] *Al-Itqān,* vol. 1, p. 188.
[34] *Qur'an in Islam,* p. 65.
[35] *Al-Itqān,* vol. 1, p. 197.
[36] Ibid., p. 219.
[37] Mustansir Mir, *Coherence in the Qur'ān,* p. 5.
[38] Ṣāliḥ, *Al-Mabāḥith fī ʿUlūm al-Qur'an,* p. 71.
[39] *Al-Mīzān,* vol. 1, p. 194.

40 Dāwūd al-Aṭṭār, *'Ulūm al-Qur'an,* pp.180-181.
41 See *Shinākhtnāme-ye Qur'an,* p. 206, quoting Ibn al-Kathīr.
42 This is the view of Ṭabāṭabā'ī, see *Qur'an in Islam,* p. 89.
43 The Arabs referred to the Persian and Roman converts as "*ḥamrā*" (lit. Ruddy complexioned).
44 Ḥujjatī, *Tārikh al-Qur'an,* p. 467.
45 *Al-Itqān,* vol. 2, p. 291.
46 Ibid., p. 470.
47 Ḥujjatī, *Tārikh al-Qur'an,* p. 469. Yaḥyā was a leading *qari'* of Baṣra, and had studied grammar under Abū al-Aswad. Naṣr was a student of both Yaḥyā and Abū al-Aswad, and collaborated with the former in the project.

8

THE ABSENCE OF DISTORTION (*TAḤRĪF*) IN THE QUR'ANIC TEXT

The allegation of tampering and distortion (*taḥrīf*) of the Qur'anic text is a longstanding one and has been discussed extensively by Muslim and orientalist researchers alike. The vast majority of Muslim scholars, from all sects, have rejected the notion of *taḥrīf* outright; and those who believe that the Qur'an has been subjected to *taḥrīf* have either relied on weak narrations, or have applied literal meanings to traditions that have a figurative interpretation (*ta'wīl*).

It is also important to realise that if one cannot prove the inviolability of the Qur'an from *taḥrīf*, then the whole of the Qur'anic text becomes suspect; one can no longer rely on any verse, because it might well be the one that has been corrupted. In this chapter, we will show that this Divinely-protected text has been preserved in its original form since its revelation and in fact, this phenomenon itself is an integral part of its miraculous nature.

8.1 - LEXICAL AND TECHNICAL DEFINITIONS OF *TAḤRĪF*

Taḥrīf is derived from the root (*ḥ-r-f*), which means an edge or boundary. In the Qur'an, it is used in this sense in the verse:

﴿وَمِنَ ٱلنَّاسِ مَن يَعْبُدُ ٱللَّهَ عَلَىٰ حَرْفٍ﴾

And among men is he who worships God on the verge [that is, he only professes belief orally, but his faith is lacking]. (Al-Ḥaj, 22:11)

In the exegesis of this verse, Zamakhsharī states:

> These people always place themselves at the periphery of religion, not at its heart. This is because of their weak and shaky belief, and therefore they are never truly at ease (neither amongst believers nor amongst unbelievers). They are like those who march at the fringes of the army; if there is victory, they join the rest in gathering the booty, but if there is defeat, they are the first to flee...[1]

Taḥrīf in speech or text therefore, signifies a shift or displacement from its true and intended meaning. In other words, if a speech or text is misinterpreted such that its true or intended meaning is changed, *taḥrīf* has occurred. In the Qur'an, this sort of *taḥrīf* is attributed to the Jews:

﴿ مِّنَ ٱلَّذِينَ هَادُوا۟ يُحَرِّفُونَ ٱلْكَلِمَ عَن مَّوَاضِعِهِۦ ﴾

Of those who are Jews (there are those who) alter words (yuḥarrifūna) *from their places.* (Al-Nisā', 4:46; Al-Mā'ida, 5:13)

In his exegesis of this verse, Ṭabrisī writes that this refers to misinterpretation, and a similar opinion is held by Zamakhsharī, who considers "*mawāḍiʿ*" (places) in the verse above, to be synonymous with "meaning", or "the suitable place for the usage" of a word. *Taḥrīf*, according to this definition, occurs every time anyone explains or interprets the Qur'an incorrectly.[2]

It is important to be clear what is meant by the term *taḥrīf* in common usage, because some types of alteration have occurred in the Qur'an, while other types have not. With reference to the Qur'an, Maʿrifat lists seven technical meanings of *taḥrīf*:

1. ***Taḥrīf* in the meaning of a word or phrase;** that is, its incorrect exegesis or interpretation, without offering any proof or evidence from the narrations. This distortion in meaning has definitely occurred, and ʿAlī b. Abī Ṭālib complains of this happening even at his time, saying. "I complain to Allah about persons who live in ignorance and die misguided. For them nothing is less valuable

than the Qur'an if it is recited as it should be recited, nor anything more valuable than the Qur'an if its verses are removed from their contexts…".[3]

2. **Placing a verse or chapter in a sequence other than that in which it was revealed.** This has definitely occurred because the present arrangement of the Qur'an is different from the order of its revelation. However, it is not strictly *taḥrīf* because it was done at the direction of the Prophet ﷺ (as previously dicussed).

3. **A variant reading from that which is known and accepted.** From the earliest times, there have been slight variations in reading styles amongst the famous readers, or *qurrā'* of the Qur'an. The books of history mention 7, 10, or up to 14 recognised variant readings at one time.

4. **Differences in dialect and pronunciation.** Every tribe had its own dialect, which was distinct from the dialect of the Quraysh. Each would recite the Qur'an in its own dialect, and since the actual words of the text were not being altered at all, the Prophet ﷺ allowed these small differences in pronunciation.

5. **Substitution of words.** This means changing a word for its synonym in order to facilitate reading. According to some reports, ʿAbdullāh b. Masʿūd allowed this sort of substitution as long as the original meaning was unchanged. However, most other scholars forbade this practice, and this sort of *taḥrīf* is not found in the Qur'an.

6. **Additions to the original Qur'anic text.** Some individual codices of the companions contained extra phrases, but on closer examination, it is evident that these were no more than personal explanatory notes, which served as reminders about the occasion of revelation, or meaning, or addressee of the verse.

7. **Omissions from the Qur'anic text.** There are reports that the original text of the Qur'an far exceeded what we have presently, and that these verses have been omitted, either accidentally or purposely, from the present codex.

The main issue when discussing *taḥrīf* is to do with this last type; the essential question is whether any material has been lost from the Qur'an or not? Amongst the Muslims, there was a group of scholars – the Ḥashawiyyah amongst the Sunnis and the Akhbāriyūn amongst the Shīʿa – who have reported that this has happened. In support of their claims, they cited weak and insubstantial traditions. Two books which have become infamous in this genre of Ḥadīth literature are:

1. ***Al-Furqān*** by the Egyptian scholar and heresiographer, Muhammad ʿAbd al-Laṭīf, popularly known as Ibn al-Khaṭīb. He gathered the traditions in the six Sunni canonical works (*ṣiḥāḥ al-sitta*) to attempt to show that *taḥrīf* had occurred in the Qur'an. In addition to alleging that there were distortions in the codex even before the time of ʿUthmān, he also claimed that eleven essential changes were made to the text by Ḥajjāj b. Yūsuf al-Thaqafī (d. 95/714), the Ummayad governor in Iraq. For example, he says that originally, in chapter Shuʿarā', in the story of Nūḥ ﷺ there was the phrase, "*min al-mukhrajīn*", and in the story of Lūṭ ﷺ there was the phrase, "*min al-marjūmīn*". However, Ḥajjāj swapped these phrases with each other and that is how they occur today.

The poor scholarship and controversial nature of this book caused widespread condemnation, and the scholars of Al-Azhar University prevailed on the Egyptian government to get it withdrawn from circulation.

2. ***Faṣl al-Khiṭāb fī Taḥrīf Kitāb Rabb al-Arbāb*** by the Shīʿa scholar, Muhammad Husein Nūrī (d. 1320/1902). Once again, this book is a collection of weak reports, culled from both Sunni and Shīʿa canonical sources, as well as some unreliable works of unknown authorship.[4]

This work was a regrettable slip by an eminent scholar, who should have been more circumspect in considering the actual meaning and worth of the narrations he has cited in making his unsound claims. Its publication caused a furore in the seminaries in Najaf and Qom, and both book and author came under severe criticism. Almost immediately, several books and treatises were written in refutation.

Interest in this hundred year old and almost-forgotten book was revived when it was republished some years ago by mischievous hands. All references from the original about *taḥrīf* narrations in Sunni books were removed by the new publishers in an attempt to make it appear that only Shīʿa sources contained these spurious narrations. Sadly, they achieved their goal to some extent, because the belief in *taḥrīf* is a common allegation against the Shīʿa, found abundantly in articles on the internet and elsewhere. The most regrettable part of it is that many scholars and imams, who should know better, are guilty of propagating these false allegations, that serve only to divide the *ummah*. A final word will not be amiss here. It is the statement of none other than the great theologian Abū al-Ḥasan al-Ashʿarī (d. 323/935), whose teachings the majority of Muslims follow in matters of belief:

> The Twelver-Shīʿa are of two groups: one group is of shallow perception in matters of religion. They ascribe to the belief in *taḥrīf*, relying on traditions that are baseless in the eyes of the scholars of the nation. The other group is of scholars and men of intellect, who deny that any addition or omission has occurred. They state that the Qur'an is the same as that which was revealed to the Prophet ﷺ, and no *taḥrīf* has occurred in it whatsoever.[5]

We will now critically examine some of these reports, and then show that the correct position is the one adopted by the consensus (*ijmāʿ*) of Muslim scholars across all sects, that there has not been any *taḥrīf* in the Qur'an at all, and that the codex found in Muslim hands all over the world is exactly the same as that which was revealed to the Prophet ﷺ.

8.2 - A CRITICAL LOOK AT TRADITIONS ABOUT *TAḤRĪF*

In this section we will briefly look at some reports found in the important books of traditions.

TRADITIONS FROM THE *ṢAḤĪḤ* OF BUKHĀRĪ

1. **The verse of stoning:** The Qur'an does not mention the capital punishment of stoning for adultery; what is mentioned is flogging (for fornication). However, stoning is mentioned in the reliable traditions, and is allowed, in special cases, by the jurisprudents.[6]

It is narrated that 'Umar b. al-Khaṭṭāb believed that there was a verse revealed about stoning, but it was missed out during the collection of the Qur'an. Bukhāri reports:

> Ibn 'Abbās narrated that 'Umar said: "Now then, I am going to tell you something which (God) has written for me to say. I do not know; perhaps it portends my death, so whoever understands and remembers it, must narrate it to the others wherever his mount takes him, but if somebody is afraid that he does not understand it, then it is unlawful for him to tell lies about me. God sent Muhammad with the Truth and revealed the Holy Book to him, and amongst what God revealed, was the verse of the *rajm* (the stoning of married person, male or female, who commits adultery), and we did recite this verse and understood and memorized it. God's Apostle did carry out the punishment of stoning and so did we after him.
>
> I am afraid that after a long time has passed, somebody will say, "By God, we do not find the verse of the *rajm* in God's Book," and thus they will go astray by abandoning an obligation which God has revealed. And the punishment of the *rajm* is to be inflicted to any married person, who commits adultery, if the required evidence is available, or there is conception or confession.[7]

2. **The verse about claiming to be offspring of other than one's father:** 'Umar also claimed that another verse which was missing from the official codex was one that warned people about claiming to be the offspring of any but their own fathers. Bukhāri reports:

> And then we used to recite among the verses in God's Book: "O people! Do not claim to be the offspring of other than your fathers, as it is disbelief (ingratitude) on your part that you claim to be the offspring of other than your real father."[8]

It is obvious from the above that ʿUmar was confusing narrations from the Prophet ﷺ with verses. The words of the two phrases bear no semblance to the Qur'anic style, and moreover, nobody else corroborated his claim, and it was rejected outright by the eminent scribes.

TRADITIONS FROM THE *ṢAḤĪḤ* OF MUSLIM

1. A missing chapter the length of Al-Tawba. Muslim reports that this was the opinion of Abū Mūsā al-Ashʿarī, who also claimed that a chapter the length of one of the Musabbiḥāt (chapters beginning with the glorification of God) had also gone missing. He states:

> Abū Ḥarb b. Abī al-Aswad reported on the authority of his father that Abū Mūsā al-Ashʿarī sent for the reciters of Baṣra. They came to him and they were three hundred in number. They recited the Qur'an and he said: You are the best among the inhabitants of Baṣra, for you are the reciters among them. So continue to recite it. (But bear in mind) that your reciting for a long time may not harden your hearts as were hardened the hearts of those before you. We used to recite a chapter which resembled in length and severity to Al-Barā'a. I have, however, forgotten it with the exception of this which I remember out of it: "If there were two valleys full of riches for the son of Ādam, he would long for a third valley, and nothing would fill the stomach of the son of Ādam but dust (the grave)."
>
> And we used so recite a chapter which resembled one of the chapters of Musabbiḥāt, and I have forgotten it, but remember (this much) out of it: "Oh people who believe, why do you say that which you do not practice, so it is recorded in your necks as a witness (against you) and you would be asked about it on the day of Resurrection".[9]

This last phrase is a Divine statement (*ḥadīth al-qudsī*)[10] which Abū Mūsā has confused with a verse of the Qur'an. The phrase about the children of Ādam not being content until they died (and their bellies filled with dust) has been mentioned as a prophetic tradition by

Muslim himself in the same chapter of his *Ṣaḥīḥ*.

As for the two chapters that were allegedly no longer to be found, one can only imagine the amusement that must have been caused in the minds of the 300 experts that Abū Mūsā had summoned to listen to his rather pretentious speech.

2. The verse about how many times a woman would breast-feed a foster baby before the child would be *maḥram* (forbidden for marriage) to her: ʿĀyisha claimed that there was a verse in the Qurʾan about how many times a foster suckling would have to be nursed before he became *maḥram*. Apparently, it was initially ten times, but this was then abrogated to five clear feedings. Muslim narrates:

> ʿĀyisha reported that it had been revealed in the Holy Qurʾan that ten clear sucklings make the marriage unlawful. Then it was abrogated to five sucklings and when God's Apostle ﷺ died, it (the verse about five sucklings) was still in the Holy Qurʾan (and recited by the Muslims).[11]

However, the leaves on which this verse was recorded were supposedly eaten by a wayward goat at the time of the passing of the Prophet ﷺ and thus, was never entered into the official codex. What can one say about this tradition – which makes a mockery of the Prophet's ﷺ lifelong efforts to preserve the Qurʾan – except to categorically state that it is obviously a false report?

TRADITIONS FROM *AL-KĀFĪ* OF KULAYNĪ

1. That the Qurʾan in the hands of the Muslims is incomplete: In the chapter entitled, "No one has the entire Qurʾan except the Imams, and only they possess its entire knowledge.", Kulaynī reports through his chain of narrators from Al-Ṣādiq that:

> No one claims to possess the entire Qurʾan in the manner that it was revealed, except a liar; no one has collected it and memorized it in the manner that God revealed it except Ali b. Abī Ṭālib, and the Imams who followed him, God's blessings be upon all of them.[12]

This tradition is more about the completeness of knowledge claimed by Al-Ṣādiq than it is about the incompleteness of the Qur'an. A careful study of its text will reveal that what Al-Ṣādiq is saying here is that the correct interpretation, the full knowledge of the occasions of revelation of the verses, etc., of the Qur'an is available only through ʿAlī and the Imams from his progeny. It is well documented[13] that ʿAlī had prepared such a compilation, which in addition to the verses of the Qur'an, also contained information about the exegesis and occasions of revelation of the verses.

2. That the Qur'an originally contained 17,000 [14] verses: The Qur'an contains a little over 6200 verses, but Kulaynī reports from Al-Ṣādiq that:

> The Qur'an that Jibra'īl brought down to the Prophet ﷺ contained 17000 verses.[15]

Similarly exaggerated figures are found in weak reports throughout Muslim Ḥadīth literature. For example, Al-Suyūṭī reports that ʿUmar b. al-Khaṭṭāb said that, "The Qur'an contains one million and twenty seven thousand letters, and whoever recites the Qur'an for the sake of God and with perseverance, will receive for each of these letters a heavenly maiden as a reward."[16] Suffice to say, all such reports can only be considered as false.

In conclusion, we can say that all these eminent *ḥadīth* collectors – Bukhārī, Muslim, Kulaynī and others – were only reporting and recording what they had received through chains of narrators which were of varying reliability. It is to be expected that weak and false traditions have found their way into these valuable Ḥadīth resources, because of the very nature of oral reporting. This is not to say that it was the opinion of these great scholars that the Qur'anic text was incomplete or corrupted, because they never claimed that their own collections were completely authentic. In fact, they encouraged scholars to study and compare their reports against the Qur'an and other reports, and then decide on their reliability.

8.3 - EVIDENCE THAT THE QUR'AN IS FREE FROM *TAḤRĪF*

1. HISTORICAL EVIDENCE

From the very first day of its revelation, the Qur'an was available to believers and non-believers alike. The Prophet ﷺ himself memorized the verses, as did many Muslims. He also arranged for a systematic recording of the verses from the beginning of revelation, and these collections were carefully stored by several scribes.

There were so many records, that even non-Muslims had easy access to the Qur'anic text. Otherwise, how could they be challenged to produce a chapter like it:

﴿ وَإِن كُنتُمْ فِي رَيْبٍ مِّمَّا نَزَّلْنَا عَلَىٰ عَبْدِنَا فَأْتُوا بِسُورَةٍ مِّن مِّثْلِهِۦ وَٱدْعُوا شُهَدَآءَكُم مِّن دُونِ ٱللَّهِ إِن كُنتُمْ صَٰدِقِينَ ﴿٢٣﴾ ﴾

And if you are in doubt as to that which We have revealed to Our servant, then produce a chapter like it and call on your witnesses besides God if you are truthful.
(Al-Baqara, 2:23)

In addition to the foregoing, the Qur'an received an extraordinary amount of attention from scholars from the earliest times. The text was subject to various analyses as the Muslims attempted to understand every facet of its meaning. Every scholar in Muslim lands, whether he was studying botany, history, literature or philosophy, would refer to the Qur'an as a source. This kind of detailed scrutiny, within all Muslim centres of learning, virtually eliminated the possibility of any distortion or incompleteness occurring in the text.

2. THE FACT THAT THE QUR'AN HAS BEEN WIDELY TRANSMITTED IN EVERY GENERATION (*TAWĀTUR*)

An important feature of the Qur'an is that the transmission of its verses is *mutawātir.* This means that it has been transmitted through multiple and diverse sources at every stage following its revelation, and in every generation. Every phrase, word and even vowel of its text has been faithfully passed down from hand to hand by different Muslims in different lands at different times. Therefore, any isolated reports about variations in the text must be disregarded because their reliability does not approach the *mutawātir* nature of the Qur'an's transmission. The eminent theologian, Ḥillī (d. 726/1325) says in this regard:

> The consensus of the scholars is that whatever has reached us of the Qur'an by means of *tawātur* is a *ḥujja* (authority) and anything else is unreliable; (this is) because the Qur'an is a proof of prophethood and the everlasting miracle of Islam, and it can only be such a proof if its transmission is at the level of *tawātur.*[17]

3. THE INIMITABILITY (*I'JĀZ*) OF THE QUR'AN

One of the most important safeguards against any corruption in the Qur'an is its inimitable nature. Any attempt to change, add or remove from its text would immediately cause a disharmony in its perfect eloquence and consistency. If such an attempt is made deliberately, it is bound to fail, for God challenges:

﴿ قُل لَّئِنِ ٱجْتَمَعَتِ ٱلْإِنسُ وَٱلْجِنُّ عَلَىٰٓ أَن يَأْتُوا۟ بِمِثْلِ هَـٰذَا ٱلْقُرْءَانِ
لَا يَأْتُونَ بِمِثْلِهِۦ وَلَوْ كَانَ بَعْضُهُمْ لِبَعْضٍ ظَهِيرًا ﴿٨٨﴾ ﴾

Say: If men and jinn should combine together to bring the like of this Qur'an, they could not bring the like of it, though some of them were helpers of others. (Al-Isra', 17:88)

4. THE DIVINE GUARANTEE OF THE PRESERVATION OF THE QUR'AN

A matter of great peace of mind and contentment for Muslims is God's assurance that He will Himself undertake the responsibility of safeguarding the Qur'an:

﴿ إِنَّا نَحۡنُ نَزَّلۡنَا ٱلذِّكۡرَ وَإِنَّا لَهُۥ لَحَٰفِظُونَ ۝ ﴾

Indeed, We have revealed the Reminder (the Qur'an) and We will most surely be its guardian. (Al-Ḥijr, 15:9)

This argument may be considered somewhat tautological, unless it is established that this one verse is definitely a verse of the Qur'an; and since there has been no doubt recorded in this regard, it suffices to validate the entire book.

5. RELIABLE TRADITIONS ABOUT THE ABSOLUTE AUTHORITY OF THE QUR'AN

Further proofs of the safety of the Qur'anic text from any tampering come from the traditions of the Prophet ﷺ about it. In one report, it is narrated that he said, "For every reality, there is a truth which makes that reality known, and for every goodness there is a light which guides towards it (and the Qur'an is that truth and light). Therefore, accept whatever (in the traditions) conforms to the Qur'an, and reject whatever contradicts it.[18] And the clearest and most compelling proof comes from the celebrated and unanimously reported tradition of the "two weighty things" or *thaqalayn*. Muslim reports:

> One day God's Messenger (may peace be upon him) stood up to deliver sermon at a watering place known as Khumm situated between Mecca and Medina. He praised God, extolled Him and delivered a sermon and exhorted (us) and said: Now to our purpose. O people, I am (just) a human being. I am about to receive a messenger (the angel of death) from my Lord and I will respond to God's call, (would bid farewell to you), but I am leaving among you two weighty things: **the first is the Book of God in which there is true guidance and light, so hold fast to the Book of God and adhere to it.** He exhorted (us) (to hold fast) to the Book of God and then said: The second are the members of my household; I remind you (of your duties) to the members of my family…[19]

There is no doubt that the Prophet ﷺ was clear, as were the Muslims, what Qur'an was being referred to; and for the Muslims there was no ambiguity with regards to its text or its accessibility, because there is no record of anybody raising an objection about this clear directive.

In conclusion, we can categorically and confidently state that the Qur'an which we have amongst us has been faithfully preserved from the time of its revelation to the Prophet ﷺ, and no corruption or *taḥrīf* has occurred in it at all. And this is the view and belief of all the Muslims.

NOTES

[1] Al-*Kashshāf*, v.2, p.142.

[2] Maʿrifat, *ʿUlūm-e Qur'anī*, p.445.

[3] *Nahj al-Balāgha*, sermon 18.

[4] See Maʿrifat, *Ulūm-e Qur'anī*, pp. 468 - 478 for a comprehensive critique of *Faṣl al-Khiṭāb*.

[5] See Maʿrifat, *Ulūm-e Qur'anī*, p. 459, where he quotes from Ashʿarī's *Al-Maqālāt*, vol. 1, p.119.

[6] Most jurists rule that if the adulterer had no avenue to enact a *ḥalāl* and legitimate relationship, then the punishment is flogging; otherwise it is stoning to death.

[7] Bukhārī, *Ṣaḥīḥ*, vol. 8, bk. 82, no. 816.

[8] Ibid.

[9] Muslim, *Ṣaḥīḥ*, bk. 5, no. 2286.

[10] Recorded by Aḥmad in his *Musnad*, vol. 5, p. 219.

[11] Muslim, *Ṣaḥīḥ*, vol. 8, no. 3421.

[12] Kulaynī, *Al-Kāfī*, cf Maʿrifat, *ʿUlūm-e Quranī*, p. 467.

[13] See Yaʿqūbī, *Tārīkh*, vol. 2, p. 113 for a detailed description of this compilation.

[14] Ṣadūq offers an explanation for this report by stating: "We say if all that was revealed to the Prophet was collected, its extent would undoubtedly be 17000 verses ... However, not all that was revealed to him was part of the Qur'an." See *Al-Iʿtiqādāt Al-Imāmiyya*, p. 78.

[15] *Al-Kāfī*, vol 2, p. 634.

[16] *Al-Itqān*, vol. 1, p. 198. The Qur'an actually contains just over 323,600 letters.

[17] *ʿUlūm-e Quranī*, p. 450.

[18] *Al-Kāfī*, vol. 1, p. 69.

[19] Muslim, *Ṣaḥīḥ*, bk. 31, no. 5920.

9

ABROGATION (*NASKH*) AND THE QUR'AN

Muslim scholars and researchers have always been interested in the abrogated and abrogating verses in the Qur'an, not least because they have an impact on jurisprudence. Al-Sulamī narrates that ʿAlī b. Abī Ṭālib once met a jurist of Kūfa and asked him, "Are you conversant with the abrogating and abrogated verses?" When the man replied in the negative, ʿAlī said to him, "You have ruined yourself and ruined others".[1] The same event is narrated by Zarkashī in *Al-Burhān* and Al-Suyūṭī in *Al-Itqān,* except that they mention that the conversation was not with a jurist (*qāḍī*), but a storyteller (*qaṣṣī*).[2]

From the earliest days, scholars have written about *naskh.* In his index, Ibn al-Nadīm (d. 380/990) has listed 17 books on the subject that were available at his time.[3] One of the first to write a book about *naskh* was Qatādah (d. 117/735). Many writers followed, and the early ones amongst them include: Al-Zuhrī (d. 125/742), Ibn Sā'ib al-Kalbī (d. 146/763), Ibn al-Ḥanbal (d. 241/855), Al-Tirmidhī (d. 280/893) and Ibn Ḥazm al-Andalūsī (d. 320/932). This last book is the oldest one still extant.

A comprehensive list of the writers on the subject of *naskh* throughout history, with comments about their books, can be found in Dr Muṣṭafā Zaid's seminal work, *Al-Nāsikh fī al-Qur'an al-Karīm.* Another useful work is an index of 71 works compiled in the compendium, *ʿUlūm-e Qur'ān wa Fehrist-e Manābiʿ* by ʿAbd al-

Wahhāb al-Ṭāliqānī.

9.1 - THE POSSIBILITY OF *NASKH*

Every progressive society undergoes stages of growth; as conditions change, its legislators present new laws, or alter the existing ones, to accommodate fresh needs or to counter the unforeseen effects of previous laws. Such is always the case with man-made constitutions. Does this situation exist for Divinely-ordained law as well? This is one of the key questions that we are concerned with when we discuss the possibility of abrogation or *naskh* in the Qur'an.

The difficulty with abrogation when considering laws ordained by God is a fundamental one; it is inconceivable that God, the Omniscient, may ordain a law that is imperfect, or one that proves to be unworkable and require amendment. Since this sort of abrogation is incompatible with theological principles, it follows that *naskh* can only be explained as an essential requirement for the gradual nurturing of man to perfection. And when the religion is perfected as the mission of a prophet draws to a close, there is no further need for abrogation. Thus, in the case of Divine law, abrogation can be likened to treatments prescribed by a physician – a course of treatment may be necessary at one stage, and when a certain level of physical well-being is achieved, the treatment and medication may be modified by something which is more suitable. This explanation conforms with the Qur'an:

﴿ مَا نَنسَخْ مِنْ ءَايَةٍ أَوْ نُنسِهَا نَأْتِ بِخَيْرٍ مِّنْهَآ أَوْ مِثْلِهَآ ﴾

Whatever communications We abrogate or cause to be forgotten, We bring one better than it or like it. (Al-Baqara, 2:106)

Usually, an abrogated verse will contain a clue that it is a transitory order, which will be abrogated in due course. For example, in verse 4:15, about those women who commit acts of lewdness, God says, "*...confine them to the houses until death takes them away, or Allah opens some way for them*", indicating a temporal nature to the injunction. This verse is considered by some exegetes to have been later abrogated by the verse of flogging:

﴿ ٱلزَّانِيَةُ وَٱلزَّانِى فَٱجْلِدُوا۟ كُلَّ وَٰحِدٍ مِّنْهُمَا مِا۟ئَةَ جَلْدَةٍ ﴾

The fornicatress and the fornicator, flog each of them a hundred stripes....
(Al-Nūr, 24:2)

It is also worth mentioning that in the matter of *naskh*, the opinion of scholars varies between those who mention many instances of *naskh* in the Qur'an[4] and those who, as a matter of principle, deny its existence at all.[5] Al-Suyūṭī lists 21 instances of naskh in his *Al-Itqān*, Shah Walī Allāh (d. 1175/1762) reduces this number to five, while Al-Khụ'ī accepts only one (the *najwā* verse – 58:12), which he states is a special case, revealed to test the character of the Muslims.

A major factor in this difference in opinion is the exact definition and scope of the term *naskh* itself. In early narrations, the mention of *naskh* did not automatically mean abrogation as we understand it today; this fact has led to a vastly exaggerated count for the instances of abrogation in the Qur'an.

Another factor is the exact meaning of "*āya*" in verse 2:106, quoted above. While many exegetes believe that it refers to the verses of the Qur'an, some consider it to also refer to previous prophets and scriptures and not just to the Qur'an itself. In this regard, Ṭabāṭabā'ī says:

> Abrogation is not a thing confined to only the religious laws; it holds its place in the sphere of creation too…Although the abrogative differs from the abrogated in its form, both have one thing in common – the perfection and the benefit. When a prophet dies and another is sent in his place – and both of them are the signs of Allah, one abrogating the other – it takes place in total conformity with the natural system. It all depends on the varying needs of the society's welfare, on the ever-changing level of man's rise to perfection. Likewise, when a religious law is replaced by another, the abrogating one has the same power as the abrogated one had, to lead to the spiritual and temporal well-being of the individual and the society.[6]

Finally, the author of the exegesis, *Jāmiʿ al-Taʾwīl,* Abū Muslim al-Iṣfahānī (d. 934/1527), is of the opinion that *āya* in the verse 2:106 means a "miracle". This is the meaning in verse 17:101, where God states that Mūsā ﵇ was strengthened with nine clear "*āyāt*". In this case, the meaning of the verse 2:106 is that God is able to give each successive prophet a better or equivalent miracle to the last; many of these prophets and their miracles have been long forgotten with the passage of time. Which is why, Iṣfahānī adds, the verse ends with the statement, "*Do you not realize that God is all-Powerful?*"

9.2 - DEFINITION OF *NASKH*

In its lexical meaning, *naskh* denotes removal and cancellation (*izālah*), such as in the phrase, *nasakhat al-rīḥ athar al-masby* (the wind removed the footprint). This is the meaning in the verse:

﴿ وَمَآ أَرْسَلْنَا مِن قَبْلِكَ مِن رَّسُولٍ وَلَا نَبِيٍّ إِلَّآ إِذَا تَمَنَّىٰٓ أَلْقَى ٱلشَّيْطَٰنُ فِىٓ أُمْنِيَّتِهِۦ

فَيَنسَخُ ٱللَّهُ مَا يُلْقِى ٱلشَّيْطَٰنُ ثُمَّ يُحْكِمُ ٱللَّهُ ءَايَٰتِهِۦ ۗ وَٱللَّهُ عَلِيمٌ حَكِيمٌ ﴿٥٢﴾ ﴾

And We did not send before you any apostle or prophet, but when he desired, the Satan made a suggestion respecting his desire; but Allah cancels (fayansakhu) that which the Satan casts, then does Allah establish His signs; and Allah is Knowing, Wise.
(Al-Ḥaj, 22:52)

It also signifies progression and substitution (*tanāsukh*), relocation (*naql*) and transformation (*taḥwīl*) of something from one state to another, while its essence remains unchanged, as in the term *tanāsukh al-arwāḥ* (reincarnation).[7] Finally, it signifies transcribing (*istinsākh*) or copying (*intisākh*). In the following verse, the term has been used in this latter sense:

﴿ هَٰذَا كِتَٰبُنَا يَنطِقُ عَلَيْكُم بِٱلْحَقِّ ۚ إِنَّا كُنَّا نَسْتَنسِخُ مَا كُنتُمْ تَعْمَلُونَ ﴿٢٩﴾ ﴾

This is Our book that speaks against you with justice; surely We wrote (nastansikhu) what you did. (Al-Jāthiya, 45:29)

In the early days of exegesis, the term *naskh* was applied to all general ordinances which were restricted or qualified by a later verse. In actuality, this was not abrogation, but specification (*takhṣīṣ*). It was also used when a verse was revealed that changed an existing custom or norm in society.

Over time, the usage of the term *naskh* has came to be restricted to "the complete abolition, or suspension, of a previous religious ruling – which had apparently been of a permanent nature – by a new religious command, in a manner that it replaces the former ruling and the two cannot exist together."[8] Ṭabāṭabā'ī is of the opinion that *naskh* may also signify that the time period of an order has come to its end; that it is no longer valid or in force. Of course, this definition does not include those rulings which are not in force because their external conditions no longer apply, such as the end of the obligation to fast once the month of Ramaḍān has passed, or the end of the obligation to pray the *ṣalāt* when the appointed time has elapsed.

With reference to the Qur'an, *naskh* does not result in the obliteration of a verse, turning it into a non-being. Its only effect is the cancellation of the directive contained in the abrogated verse. To understand better what *naskh* signifies with regards to the Qur'an, we need to consider the verses:

﴿ مَا نَنسَخْ مِنْ ءَايَةٍ أَوْ نُنسِهَا نَأْتِ بِخَيْرٍ مِّنْهَآ أَوْ مِثْلِهَآ ۗ
أَلَمْ تَعْلَمْ أَنَّ ٱللَّهَ عَلَىٰ كُلِّ شَىْءٍ قَدِيرٌ ﴿١٠٦﴾ ﴾

Whatever communications We abrogate or cause to be forgotten, We bring one better than it or like it. Do you not know that Allah has power over all things?
(Al-Baqara, 2:106)

Ṭabāṭabā'ī states about this verse that:

> It should be noted that the Qur'anic verse has been described as a "sign", that is, a mark that points to another thing; a verse is a sign pointing to a Divine command. When abrogated, the verse remains in existence as before, but loses its quality as a sign – no longer does it point to an order, as the order is now cancelled.[9]

Of course, the abrogated verse still plays a part in as a feature of the inimitability and challenge of the Qur'an, amongst other things.

The difference between the terms *naskh* (abrogation) and *insā'* (forgotten) in the verse, is that in the case of *naskh*, a previously existing and known ruling has been substituted by a new one, while *insā'* refers to a ruling that has been forgotten or distorted over time.

9.3 - THE CONDITIONS FOR *NASKH*

With regards to the Qur'an, there are several conditions which are required for *naskh* to take place.

1. The abrogated (*mansūkh*) verse must be a ruling of the *sharī'a*. Therefore, rational principles, moral truths or historical events cannot be abrogated. However, if a ruling is qualified or confined) in any way by the new verse, then this is not strictly *naskh*, but specification (*takhṣīṣ*).

2. The conditions for which the two verses apply must be the same, as there can exist different rulings in different conditions, without *naskh*.

3. The abrogated verse must not have been a ruling that was meant for a limited time only. If it was temporary to begin with, its replacement by a new verse is not *naskh*.

4. The two verses must be mutually exclusive so that both rulings cannot exist simultaneously, otherwise *naskh* has not occurred.

5. The abrogating verse (*nāsikh*) must have been revealed later than the verse it abrogates (*mansūkh*). Although obvious, knowing which verse was revealed earlier allows exegetes and jurists to decide whether *naskh* has occurred.

6. In jurisprudence, abrogation applies only to the Qur'an and *sunna*. Its application to rulings derived by *'aql* (reason) or *ijmā'*

(consensus) is not valid. Furthermore, *qiyās* (analogy), for the jurists who allow it, cannot abrogate the Qur'an and *sunna*, because its principal function is to extend the existing rulings of these two primary sources to similar cases for which no ruling exists.

7. Finally, the possibility of *naskh* is confined to the lifetime of the Prophet ﷺ only. Only he had the authority to repeal an existing ruling.[10]

9.4 - THE MODES OF *NASKH* IN THE QUR'AN

There are four kinds of *naskh* mentioned in relation to the Qur'an:

1. Abrogation of the verse and the ruling
2. Abrogation of the verse only
3. Abrogation of the ruling only
4. Conditional abrogation

We will consider each of these in turn.

1. ABROGATION OF THE TEXT OF THE VERSE AND ITS RULING

In this type of abrogation – which has not occurred in the Qur'an, in our opinion – the verse no longer exists in the Qur'an, and the ruling it contained has also been repealed. In other words, both its *tilāwa* (recital) and *ḥukm* (ruling) have been rescinded. The usual example quoted for this kind of abrogation is the report by Muslim from ʿĀyisha:

> ʿĀyisha reported that it had been revealed in the Holy Qur'an that ten clear sucklings make the marriage (between a male and female nursed by the same mother) unlawful. Then the verse was abrogated to "five clear sucklings" and (when) God's apostle ﷺ died, the "five sucklings" was still in the Holy Qur'an

(and recited by the Muslims).[11]

The verses were written on some leaves that were stored under the bed. These were allegedly eaten by a goat and thus both the abrogating and abrogated verses were lost forever.[12]

It is clear that this narration is baseless, for it portrays the Qur'an as a document that was stored so precariously that it became vulnerable to the foraging of a domestic animal! Moreover, it brings the authenticity and completeness of the whole of the Qur'an into doubt. The scholars who hold this narration to be correct have forgotten that the Qur'an was memorised and recorded by many Muslims. The narration itself states that Muslims used to recite this verse; if so, how could it have been excluded from the compiled copy without objections from many quarters?

In fact, no such abrogation has taken place in the Qur'an and the best evidence for this is the reassurance of God, Himself:

﴿إِنَّا نَحْنُ نَزَّلْنَا ٱلذِّكْرَ وَإِنَّا لَهُۥ لَحَـٰفِظُونَ ٩﴾

Indeed, We have revealed the Reminder and We will most surely be its guardian.
(Al-Ḥijr, 15:9)

2. ABROGATION OF THE TEXT OF THE VERSE ONLY

In this type of abrogation, the verse no longer exists in the Qur'an, but the ruling it contained exists and is in force. In other words, the verse is abrogated but the ruling is not. The common example cited for this type of abrogation is the "stoning" verse – *al-shaykhu wa'l shaykhatu idhā zaniyā farjumūhumā* (if the married man and married woman commit adultery, then stone them) – in a narration attributed to Ibn ʿAbbās, quoting ʿUmar b. al-Khaṭṭāb:

> God sent Muhammad with the Truth and revealed the Holy Book to him, and amongst what God revealed was the verse of the *rajm* (the stoning of a married person, male or female, who commits adultery), and we did recite this verse and understood and memorized it. God's Apostle carried out the punishment of

stoning and so did we after him.

I am afraid that after a long time has passed, somebody will say, "By God, we do not find the verse of the *rajm* in God's Book," and thus they will go astray by abandoning an obligation which God has revealed. And the punishment of the *rajm* is to be inflicted to any married person, who commits adultery, if the required evidence is available or there is conception or confession.[13]

Other verses are also mentioned in this category, for instance, Bukhārī adds that ʿUmar said:

And then we used to recite among the verses in God's Book: *"an lā targhabū ʿan ābāʾikum fa innahu kufrun bikum"* – (Do not claim) to be the offspring of other than your fathers, as it is disbelief (ingratitude) on your part ..."[14]

The Qurʾan only talks about flogging the adulterer; there is no verse about stoning. It is quite possible that these were narrations from the Prophet ﷺ that ʿUmar was recalling, and confusing with actual verses. This is clear because not a single companion, not even Zaid b. Thābit (who had embarked on an official compilation at the behest of Abū Bakr and ʿUmar) agreed with him that these were verses of the Qurʾan. For this reason, subsequent scholars were compelled to conjecture that this was a verse which was abrogated, while its ruling remained in force. However, this is unlikely, and furthermore, the report about the allegedly missing verse about stoning is a solitary report (*khabar al-wāḥid*) and neither *naskh* nor any Qurʾanic text can be proved by such a report.

Another narration states that the phrase, *"al-waladu liʾl firāsh wa liʾl ʿāhir al-ḥajr"* (the child belongs to the marriage, and for the adulterer there is stoning), was a verse that has been lost.[15] In fact, this is a well known *ḥadīth* from the Prophet ﷺ and is not a verse of the Qurʾan.

3. ABROGATION OF THE RULING ONLY

This is the kind of abrogation that has been generally accepted by all the jurists and exegetes, at least as a possibility. In this kind of abrogation, the original verse remains part of the Qur'an, but its ruling has been replaced, or abrogated, by a different ruling. There are three ways this can happen:

I. THE ORIGINAL RULING IS ABROGATED BY A RELIABLE TRADITION FROM THE PROPHET ﷺ (*SUNNA*)

The example quoted here is the following verse:

﴿ وَٱلَّذِينَ يُتَوَفَّوْنَ مِنكُمْ وَيَذَرُونَ أَزْوَٰجًا وَصِيَّةً لِّأَزْوَٰجِهِم مَّتَٰعًا إِلَى ٱلْحَوْلِ غَيْرَ إِخْرَاجٍ ۚ فَإِنْ خَرَجْنَ فَلَا جُنَاحَ عَلَيْكُمْ فِى مَا فَعَلْنَ فِىٓ أَنفُسِهِنَّ مِن مَّعْرُوفٍ ۗ وَٱللَّهُ عَزِيزٌ حَكِيمٌ ﴾

And those of you who die and leave wives behind, (make) a bequest in favour of their wives of maintenance for a year without turning (them) out, and if they themselves go away, there is no blame on you for what they do of lawful deeds by themselves, and Allah is Mighty, Wise. (Al-Baqara, 2:240)

It is reported that according to the prevailing practice at that time, the inheritance of the widow was confined to a year's maintenance from her husband's estate, and no more. Her waiting period (*'idda*) was also one year. When verse 4:12 was revealed, which fixed the widow's inheritance at one-quarter in the absence of any issue, and the period of *'idda* for a widow was stipulated as four months and ten days in verse 2:234, the whole contents of the verse was considered as abrogated, based on several traditions in this regard.

II. THE ORIGINAL RULING IS ABROGATED BY ANOTHER VERSE, WHICH IS ADDRESSING THE SAME ISSUE.

An example of this, where all scholars are agreed that *naskh* has taken place is the "private audience (*najwā*)" verse: [16]

﴿ يَٰٓأَيُّهَا ٱلَّذِينَ ءَامَنُوٓا۟ إِذَا نَٰجَيْتُمُ ٱلرَّسُولَ فَقَدِّمُوا۟ بَيْنَ يَدَىْ نَجْوَىٰكُمْ صَدَقَةً ۚ ذَٰلِكَ خَيْرٌ لَّكُمْ وَأَطْهَرُ ۚ فَإِن لَّمْ تَجِدُوا۟ فَإِنَّ ٱللَّهَ غَفُورٌ رَّحِيمٌ ﴾

O you who believe! when you consult the Messenger privately, then offer something in charity before your consultation; that is better for you and purer; but if you do not find, then surely God is Forgiving, Merciful. (Al-Mujādila, 58:12)

which was abrogated a few days later by the next verse:

﴿ءَأَشْفَقْتُمْ أَن تُقَدِّمُوا۟ بَيْنَ يَدَىْ نَجْوَىٰكُمْ صَدَقَـٰتٍ ۚ فَإِذْ لَمْ تَفْعَلُوا۟ وَتَابَ ٱللَّهُ عَلَيْكُمْ
فَأَقِيمُوا۟ ٱلصَّلَوٰةَ وَءَاتُوا۟ ٱلزَّكَوٰةَ وَأَطِيعُوا۟ ٱللَّهَ وَرَسُولَهُۥ ۚ وَٱللَّهُ خَبِيرٌۢ بِمَا تَعْمَلُونَ ١٣﴾

Do you fear that you will not (be able to) give in charity before your consultation? So when you do not do it and God has turned to you (mercifully), then keep up prayer and pay the poor-rate and obey God and His Messenger; and God is Aware of what you do. (Al-Mujādila, 58:13)

Ṭabarī reports about these verses:

> ʿAlī, may God be pleased with him, said, "There is a verse in the Book of God, on which no one has acted before me nor shall anyone after me. I had a dinar which I exchanged for ten dirhams. Whenever I came to the Prophet ﷺ, I gave one dirham in charity. Then it was abrogated, and no one had acted upon it before me: (The verse was) " *When you consult the Messenger privately...*"[17]

It is clear that *naskh* has taken place, because the two rulings cannot exist side by side, and the second verse does not make sense if isolated from the first.

Another example of this type of abrogation is the verse about the number of the enemy that perseverant Muslims may overcome:

﴿يَـٰٓأَيُّهَا ٱلنَّبِىُّ حَرِّضِ ٱلْمُؤْمِنِينَ عَلَى ٱلْقِتَالِ ۚ إِن يَكُن مِّنكُمْ عِشْرُونَ صَـٰبِرُونَ يَغْلِبُوا۟ مِا۟ئَتَيْنِ ۚ
وَإِن يَكُن مِّنكُم مِّا۟ئَةٌ يَغْلِبُوٓا۟ أَلْفًا مِّنَ ٱلَّذِينَ كَفَرُوا۟ بِأَنَّهُمْ قَوْمٌ لَّا يَفْقَهُونَ ٦٥﴾

O Prophet! Urge the believers to war; if there are twenty patient ones of you they shall overcome two hundred, and if there are a hundred of you they shall overcome a thousand of those who disbelieve, because they are a people who do not understand. (Al-Anfāl, 8:65)

Despite the encouragement offered in this verse, the Muslims displayed reluctance and did not feel that they could overcome that many. As a result of their weak resolve and faith, God reduced the expectation from a Muslim warrior from facing ten enemies to two:

﴿ ٱلْـَٔـٰنَ خَفَّفَ ٱللَّهُ عَنكُمْ وَعَلِمَ أَنَّ فِيكُمْ ضَعْفًا ۚ فَإِن يَكُن مِّنكُم مِّا۟ئَةٌ صَابِرَةٌ يَغْلِبُوا۟
مِا۟ئَتَيْنِ ۚ وَإِن يَكُن مِّنكُمْ أَلْفٌ يَغْلِبُوٓا۟ أَلْفَيْنِ بِإِذْنِ ٱللَّهِ ۗ وَٱللَّهُ مَعَ ٱلصَّـٰبِرِينَ ﴿٦٦﴾ ﴾

For the present God has made light your burden, and He knows that there is weakness in you; so if there are a hundred patient ones of you they shall overcome two hundred, and if there are a thousand they shall overcome two thousand by God's permission, and God is with the patient. (Al-Anfāl, 8:66)

This set of verses is very similar to the two verses about the private audience (najwā); in both cases, the shortcoming in the resolve of the believers was evident and the ruling was abrogated to lighten their burden, permitting Muslim soldiers to stop resisting if the number of enemy was double theirs.

Al-Khū'ī, however, disagrees that *naskh* has occurred, stating that it is not certain that the two verses were not revealed together; moreover, for abrogation to occur, the ruling in the first verse has to have been acted upon, and there is no evidence that that ever happened. He believes that the two verses were revealed together; the first ruling is the recommended and commendable act, while the second sets out the duty and obligation of the Muslim.[18]

However, Al-Khū'ī's opinion is problematic; first, he has not presented evidence that the verses were revealed together, in fact, the tone of the verses seems to suggest the contrary. Only after the Muslims displayed the weakness of their resolve was the burden lightened. Secondly, it is not necessary for the first ruling to be acted upon for *naskh* to be valid; abrogation may occur even if the first ruling was not acted upon, for example, if it proved too difficult for the Muslims.[19]

III. THE ORIGINAL RULING IS ABROGATED BY ANOTHER VERSE, WHICH IS NOT ADDRESSING THE SAME ISSUE, BUT APPEARS TO CONTRADICT THE FIRST VERSE.

In these cases, the verse which was revealed later is considered as abrogating (*nāsikh*) and the earlier verse as abrogated (*mansūkh*).

Several examples have been mentioned in this regard. We will only quote two such verses:

﴿ إِنَّ ٱلَّذِينَ ءَامَنُوا۟ وَهَاجَرُوا۟ وَجَـٰهَدُوا۟ بِأَمْوَٰلِهِمْ وَأَنفُسِهِمْ فِى سَبِيلِ ٱللَّهِ
وَٱلَّذِينَ ءَاوَوا۟ وَّنَصَرُوٓا۟ أُو۟لَـٰٓئِكَ بَعْضُهُمْ أَوْلِيَآءُ بَعْضٍ ﴾

Surely those who believed and fled (their homes) and struggled hard in Allah's way with their property and their souls, and those who gave shelter and helped - these are guardians (awliyā) *of each other;* (Al-Anfāl, 8:72)

This verse contained a ruling about inheritance between brothers-in-faith. The word *awliyā*, plural of *wali*, denotes close relatives, who may inherit. At the time of migration, the Prophet ﷺ established bonds of brotherhood between one each from the migrants (*muhājirūn*) and their helpers from the host Muslim community in Medina (*anṣār*). Such was the strength of these bonds, that when this verse was revealed, every migrant would appoint his adopted brother from amongst the helpers as his heir, in preference to his relatives back in Mecca who were unbelievers and idolaters.[20] This directive was in force until the following verse was revealed, restricting inheritance to blood relatives (*ulu'l arḥām*) only:

﴿ وَأُو۟لُوا۟ ٱلْأَرْحَامِ بَعْضُهُمْ أَوْلَىٰ بِبَعْضٍ فِى كِتَـٰبِ ٱللَّهِ مِنَ ٱلْمُؤْمِنِينَ وَٱلْمُهَـٰجِرِينَ ﴾

... and the possessors of relationship have the better claim in the ordinance of God to inheritance, one with respect to another, than (other) believers, and (than) those who have fled (their homes)... (Al-Aḥzāb, 33:6)

Al-Khū'ī has discussed all these three methods of abrogation at some length, and only recognises the second type – the abrogation of a verse by another verse about the same issue.[21]

With regards to the first type, Al-Shāfi'ī and Aḥmad b. Ḥanbal consider that even a *mutawātir* (successively-narrated) tradition cannot abrogate the Qur'an, citing the following verse:

﴿ وَإِذَا بَدَّلْنَآ ءَايَةً مَّكَانَ ءَايَةٍ ۙ وَٱللَّهُ أَعْلَمُ بِمَا يُنَزِّلُ قَالُوٓا۟ إِنَّمَآ أَنتَ مُفْتَرٍۭ

بَلْ أَكْثَرُهُمْ لَا يَعْلَمُونَ ﴿١٠١﴾

And when We change (one) communication for (another) communication, and Allah knows best what He reveals, they say: You are only a forger. Nay, most of them do not know. (Al-Naḥl, 16:101)

Al-Khū'ī, however, allows that there is no rational or textual problem with a *mutawātir* tradition abrogating a Qur'anic ruling, but he cannot find a single instance of this having occurred. In the example we quoted about the inheritance of a widow, Al-Khū'ī maintains that this was a recommended ruling and not a binding one, because of the words, "*and if they themselves depart*". He finds no contradiction between this verse and the two verses that supposedly abrogated it, and concludes that no abrogation has taken place.

He also rejects strongly the idea that there can be any contradictions between verses (the third type, where abrogation is assumed because of a supposed contradiction between two verses), because the Qur'an itself states:

﴿أَفَلَا يَتَدَبَّرُونَ ٱلْقُرْءَانَ ۚ وَلَوْ كَانَ مِنْ عِندِ غَيْرِ ٱللَّهِ لَوَجَدُوا۟ فِيهِ ٱخْتِلَٰفًا كَثِيرًا ﴿٨٢﴾﴾

Do they not then meditate on the Qur'an? And if it were from any other than God, they would have found therein much incongruity. (Al-Nisā', 4:82)

4. CONDITIONAL ABROGATION

This idea has been mentioned by Maʿrifat, who describes certain verses having undergone a conditional abrogation (*naskh al-mashrūṭ*), and if the original conditions resume or prevail at a later time and location, then the earlier verse is no longer abrogated and comes back in force.[22] For example, he cites the initial weakness of the Muslims as the reason why they were urged to be cautious and ignore the behaviour of the disbelievers, but as Muslims gained strength, they were instructed to confront them. In the case of war, initially permission was given to fight the enemy:

﴿ أُذِنَ لِلَّذِينَ يُقَـٰتَلُونَ بِأَنَّهُمْ ظُلِمُوا۟ ۚ وَإِنَّ ٱللَّهَ عَلَىٰ نَصْرِهِمْ لَقَدِيرٌ ﴿٣٩﴾ ﴾

Permission (to fight) is given to those upon whom war is made because they are oppressed, and most surely God is well able to assist them (Al-Ḥaj, 22:39)

Later on, pre-emptive measures were ordained against those who would harm the Muslims:

﴿وَأَعِدُّوا۟ لَهُم مَّا ٱسْتَطَعْتُم مِّن قُوَّةٍ وَمِن رِّبَاطِ ٱلْخَيْلِ تُرْهِبُونَ بِهِۦ عَدُوَّ ٱللَّهِ وَعَدُوَّكُمْ وَءَاخَرِينَ مِن دُونِهِمْ لَا تَعْلَمُونَهُمُ ٱللَّهُ يَعْلَمُهُمْ ۚ وَمَا تُنفِقُوا۟ مِن شَىْءٍ فِى سَبِيلِ ٱللَّهِ يُوَفَّ إِلَيْكُمْ وَأَنتُمْ لَا تُظْلَمُونَ ﴿٦٠﴾ وَإِن جَنَحُوا۟ لِلسَّلْمِ فَٱجْنَحْ لَهَا وَتَوَكَّلْ عَلَى ٱللَّهِ ۚ إِنَّهُۥ هُوَ ٱلسَّمِيعُ ٱلْعَلِيمُ ﴿٦١﴾﴾

And prepare against them what force you can and horses tied at the frontier, to frighten thereby the enemy of God and your enemy and others besides them, whom you do not know (but) God knows them; and whatever thing you will spend in God's way, it will be paid back to you fully and you shall not be dealt with unjustly. And if they incline to peace, then incline to it and trust in God; surely He is the Hearing, the Knowing. (Al-Anfāl, 8:60, 61)

Finally, as soon as the time was right, idols and idolaters were removed from Mecca for all time:

﴿ فَإِذَا ٱنسَلَخَ ٱلْأَشْهُرُ ٱلْحُرُمُ فَٱقْتُلُوا۟ ٱلْمُشْرِكِينَ حَيْثُ وَجَدتُّمُوهُمْ وَخُذُوهُمْ وَٱحْصُرُوهُمْ وَٱقْعُدُوا۟ لَهُمْ كُلَّ مَرْصَدٍ ۚ فَإِن تَابُوا۟ وَأَقَامُوا۟ ٱلصَّلَوٰةَ وَءَاتَوُا۟ ٱلزَّكَوٰةَ فَخَلُّوا۟ سَبِيلَهُمْ ۚ إِنَّ ٱللَّهَ غَفُورٌ رَّحِيمٌ ﴿٥﴾ ﴾

So when the sacred months have passed away, then slay the idolaters wherever you find them, and take them captives and besiege them and lie in wait for them in every ambush, then if they repent and keep up prayer and pay the poor-rate, leave their way free to them; surely God is Forgiving, Merciful. (Al-Tawba, 9:5)

Thus, according to Maʿrifat, if this former weakness comes back, then the previous rulings apply once more.

9.5 - ABROGATION IN CREATION (*BADĀ'*)

Finally, abrogation is not a phenomenon confined to only religious laws (*shari'ah*); it can apply in the sphere of creation (*takwīn*) too. The doctrine of *badā',* which can be considered as a type of *naskh* or modification in the sphere of creation, is a contentious one amongst the scholars. Often, it is poorly understood, and rejected because, once more, it seems incompatible with God's omniscience.

Of course, there is no doubt that the entire universe is under God's constant sovereignty and also that His knowledge has eternally encompassed everything. The continued existence of any existent being is constantly dependent on the will of God. God's omnipotence means that at every moment, He is in full control of his creation; it is not as the Jews say, that since everything is already destined to happen, all existents, including God Himself, are mere spectators:

﴿وَقَالَتِ ٱلْيَهُودُ يَدُ ٱللَّهِ مَغْلُولَةٌ ۚ غُلَّتْ أَيْدِيهِمْ وَلُعِنُوا۟ بِمَا قَالُوا۟ ۘ بَلْ يَدَاهُ مَبْسُوطَتَانِ

يُنفِقُ كَيْفَ يَشَآءُ﴾

And the Jews say:The hand of God is tied up! Their hands shall be shackled and they shall be cursed for what they say. Nay, both His hands are spread out, He expends as He pleases... (Al-Mā'ida, 5:64)

In fact, *badā'* is not at all incompatible with God's omniscience. To understand it further, we must examine the nature of Divine knowledge and decree. The first kind of Divine decree is the one whose knowledge is exclusively for God and He does not disclose it to any of His creatures. There is no question of *badā'* in this kind of decree, and in fact, *badā'* springs from this absolute knowledge. About this, God says:

﴿قُل لَّا يَعْلَمُ مَن فِى ٱلسَّمَٰوَٰتِ وَٱلْأَرْضِ ٱلْغَيْبَ إِلَّا ٱللَّهُ ۚ

وَمَا يَشْعُرُونَ أَيَّانَ يُبْعَثُونَ ﴿٦٥﴾﴾

Say: No one in the heavens and the earth knows the unseen but God; and they do not know when they shall be raised. (Al-Naml, 27:65)

The second type of divine decree is the one about which God informs His prophets and His angels. He gives them information about matters that will definitely occur. Once more, there is no occurrence of *badā'* in this either. The only difference is that *badā'* does not originate from this knowledge. About this, God says:

﴿ عَٰلِمُ ٱلْغَيْبِ فَلَا يُظْهِرُ عَلَىٰ غَيْبِهِۦٓ أَحَدًا ﴿٢٦﴾ إِلَّا مَنِ ٱرْتَضَىٰ مِن رَّسُولٍ فَإِنَّهُۥ يَسْلُكُ مِنۢ بَيْنِ يَدَيْهِ وَمِنْ خَلْفِهِۦ رَصَدًا ﴿٢٧﴾ ﴾

The Knower of the unseen! So He does not reveal His secrets to any, except to him whom He chooses as a messenger; for surely He makes a guard to march before him and after him. (Al-Jinn, 72:26, 27)

The final type of divine decree, which God has also informed His prophets and His angels about, is one which may materialize if God wills. This is the type which is influenced by man's actions; his supplications, his offering of charity (*ṣadaqa*) and his deeds. It is in this conditional decree (*al-qaḍā' al-mawqūf*) that *badā'* occurs. And in this regard, God says:

﴿ يَمْحُوا۟ ٱللَّهُ مَا يَشَآءُ وَيُثْبِتُ ۖ وَعِندَهُۥٓ أُمُّ ٱلْكِتَٰبِ ﴿٣٩﴾ ﴾

God effaces whatever He pleases and establishes whatever He pleases; and with Him is the Essence of the Book (Umm al-Kitāb). (Al-Ra'd, 13:39)

The belief in *badā'* is a clear acknowledgement that the survival and well-being of creation is dependent on the continual attention of God, and that His will ultimately affects everything. This belief rejects fatalism and encourages man to foster and maintain his relationship with God, knowing that his supplications will make a difference to his destiny. The fact that his destiny is not predetermined is clear from the following verse, which mentions two terms, one decreed and one variable:

﴿ هُوَ ٱلَّذِى خَلَقَكُم مِّن طِينٍ ثُمَّ قَضَىٰٓ أَجَلًا ۖ وَأَجَلٌ مُّسَمًّى عِندَهُۥ ۖ ثُمَّ أَنتُمْ تَمْتَرُونَ ﴿٢﴾ ﴾

He it is Who created you from clay, then He decreed a term;

and there is a term named with Him; still you doubt. (Al-Anʿām, 6:2)

Al-Ṣadūq relates a narration from Al-Bāqir that, "God has not been worshipped more fervently for any other reason than *badāʾ*."[23] In simplified terms, we may think of *badāʾ* in our own lives in the following manner: we make many modifications to our circumstances and destiny through our free will and by supplication, offering *ṣadaqa* and by acting virtuously and avoiding vice. These acts will bring about *badāʾ* in our existence. For example, being grateful for God's bounties, brings about an increase, as God announces:

﴿ وَإِذْ تَأَذَّنَ رَبُّكُمْ لَئِن شَكَرْتُمْ لَأَزِيدَنَّكُمْ ۖ وَلَئِن كَفَرْتُمْ إِنَّ عَذَابِي لَشَدِيدٌ ۝٧ ﴾

And when your Lord made it known: If you are grateful, I would certainly give to you more, and if you are ungrateful, My chastisement is truly severe. (Ibrāhīm, 14:7)

Despite all these modifications, when the book that contains the sum total of our life's activities is compared to the one that God possesses, the two will be exactly identical:

﴿ وَمَا يُعَمَّرُ مِن مُّعَمَّرٍ وَلَا يُنقَصُ مِنْ عُمُرِهِۦٓ إِلَّا فِى كِتَٰبٍ ۚ إِنَّ ذَٰلِكَ عَلَى ٱللَّهِ يَسِيرٌ ۝١١ ﴾

And no one whose life is lengthened has his life lengthened, nor is aught diminished of one's life, but it is all in a book; surely this is easy for God. (Fāṭir, 35:11)

9.6 - WHY IS THERE NO *NASKH* IN THE POST-PROPHET ERA?

Two issues about *naskh* require further deliberation. First, what is the benefit of the presence of the abrogated verses in the Qurʾan? Secondly, if we accept that the basis for abrogation was the natural weakness of mankind who need to be nurtured by gradual instruction, how is this explanation compatible with the post-Prophet era, where new generations of Muslims, up to our times, have not been granted this favour. As we have seen previously, there can be no abrogation after the death of the Prophet ﷺ. In answer to the first question, Maʿrifat states the following:

> The presence of both the abrogating and the abrogated verses in the Qur'an highlights the gradual nature of Islamic legislation and is a valuable historical record of the stages through which the *sharī'ah* was perfected. Secondly, it must be mentioned that an important aspect of the Qur'an is the inimitability of its rhetoric, and for this, it must be studied in its entirety. Thirdly, most of the mansūkh verses were abrogated due to the change in conditions. If the original situation was to prevail again, the verses would once more be in force.[24]

As for the second issue, the special treatment of the early Muslims should cause no surprise. This small group of believers were the forerunners of the great movement and religion that we have inherited today. Just like a young sapling needs to be carefully supported and nurtured so that it may grow into a mighty tree, so it was with the companions of the Prophet ﷺ.

In this regard, Iṣlāḥī makes the following points, although in some cases, his examples are more appropriate to specification (*takhṣīṣ*) rather than *naskh*:

> In some cases, laws evolved and developed into their ultimate form considering the general human nature. For instance, Arabs were addicted to drinking. Therefore, initially, it was forbidden only during the prayer. As it was hard to fast in the hot and dry Arabian desert so atonement was allowed for the sick and the wayfarer. Later, when the people became familiar with these obligations, the permission of atonement for fasting was taken back and complete prohibition of drinking, and fasting for the whole month of Ramaḍān was made compulsory.

> In some cases, the Prophet ﷺ was allowed to put any of the decrees of previous Divine laws in practice for sometime. Later on it was repealed and replaced with a permanent injunction of the Islamic *sharī'ah*, as in the matter of the direction of prayer. It was only to test Muslims and make a clear distinction between those who follow the Prophet ﷺ and those who turn on their heels in adherence to the previous traditions. Obviously this is an essential part of training.

> Similarly, some laws were enforced to make up for the lack of people, which increased the devotion and enabled a small number of Muslims to bear more responsibilities. For example, initially all Muslims were required to offer the *tahajjud* prayer at night. One Muslim fighter was initially required to face ten disbelievers in the battlefield. Alms giving was advised before having a confidential talk with the Prophet ﷺ in order to strengthen and purify the

> Muslims. Later, when the number of Muslims increased and they grew disciplined and purified, these transitory directives were replaced with permanent ones.[25]

In conclusion, *naskh* is a device found in the Qur'an where, for various reasons, a verse is superseded by another. There are very few instances of true *naskh*, and the majority of verses that are usually cited as abrogated are either about a different situation, or are temporal in nature, or *takhṣīṣ* has occurred. The phenomenon of *naskh* does not detract from God's omniscience in any manner, and the abrogating verse contains all the benefits and guidance towards perfection that was found in the abrogated verse.

In fact, both *naskh* and *bada'* have a reality only in the apparent sense; that is, in the eyes of the people, it appears that there has been a change. In reality, and in God's knowledge, it is not *naskh* at all – it was a ruling or matter that was always meant to be temporary in nature.

NOTES

1 *Tafsīr al-ʿAyyāshī*, vol. 1, p. 12.

2 *Al-Burhān*, vol. 2, p. 158; *Al-Itqān*, vol. 2, p. 700.

3 Ibn al-Nadīm, *Al-Fihrist*, "Introduction".

4 In his book, *Al-Nāsikh wa al-Mansūkh*, Abū Bakr al-Naḥḥās mentions that there are 137 verses that have been abrogated.

5 Al-Khū'ī, *Al-Bayān*, p.194.

6 *Al-Mīzān*, vol. 2, p. 260.

7 See *Al-Qāmūs al-Muḥīṭ*, Fīrūz Ābādī.

8 *ʿUlūm-e Qur'anī*, p. 103.

9 *Al-Mīzān*, vol. 2, p. 260.

10 We have not discussed the issue of the the Sunna abrogating the Qur'an – a possibility that is usually rejected by Muslim scholars, with some Hanafi scholars allowing it only when there is a *mutawātir* report to that effect. In practice, these scholars have applied the rule to specification, rather than abrogation.

11 Muslim, *Ṣaḥīḥ*, vol. 8, no. 3421.

12 Ibid.; Tirmidhī, *Ṣaḥīḥ*, vol. 3, p. 456 and others.

13 Bukharī, *Ṣaḥīḥ*, vol. 8, tradition 816.

14 Ibid.

15 Al-Suyūṭī, *Al-Durr al-Manthūr*, vol. 1, p. 106.

16 Al-Khū'ī is of the opinion that this is the only true instance of *naskh* in the Qur'an. He has exhaustively discussed the main verses that are said to be abrogated and argued that either the actual purport of these verses has been misunderstood, or that many of them

were temporary injunctions, meant to test the resolve of the Muslims. See *Al-Bayān*, pp. 193-248, for a discussion of thirty-six such verses.

[17] See *Al-Bayān*, Ṭabarī, *Tafsīr*, vol. 28, p. 15; also narrated by Al-Ḥākim in his *Mustadrak*.

[18] *Al-Bayān*, p. 196.

[19] *'Ulūm-e Qur'anī*, p. 265.

[20] *Majma' al-Bayān*, quoting a narration from Al-Bāqir, vol. 4, p. 561.

[21] *Al-Bayān*, p. 193.

[22] *'Ulūm-e Qur'anī*, p. 265.

[23] Ṣadūq, *Al-Tawḥīd*, p. 272 *vide Al-Bayān*, p. 259.

[24] Ma'rifat, *Āmuzesh-e 'Ulūm-e Qur'anī*, p. 103.

[25] Ṭāriq Hashmī, *Renaissance*, www.renaissance.com, July 2002, adapted from Amīn Aḥsan Iṣlāhī's *Tadabbur-e Qur'an*.

10

DEFINITE AND INDEFINITE VERSES IN THE QUR'AN: *MUḤKAMĀT* AND *MUTASHĀBIHĀT*

One of the interesting features of the Qur'an is that its verses are divided into two types – *muḥkam* and *mutashābih*. The Qur'an states:

﴿ هُوَ ٱلَّذِىٓ أَنزَلَ عَلَيْكَ ٱلْكِتَٰبَ مِنْهُ ءَايَٰتٌ مُّحْكَمَٰتٌ هُنَّ أُمُّ ٱلْكِتَٰبِ وَأُخَرُ مُتَشَٰبِهَٰتٌ ﴾

He it is Who has revealed the Book to you; some of its verses are muḥkam, *they are the basis of the Book, and others are* mutashābih. (Āli ʿImrān, 3:7)

At the same time, the Qur'an also states that all its verses are made *muḥkam*, and thereafter, plain:

﴿ كِتَٰبٌ أُحْكِمَتْ ءَايَٰتُهُۥ ثُمَّ فُصِّلَتْ مِن لَّدُنْ حَكِيمٍ خَبِيرٍ ۝١ ﴾

(This is) a Book, whose verses are made muḥkam, *then are they made plain, from the Wise, All-aware.* (Hūd, 11:1)

In another place, the Qur'an states that all its verses are *mutashābih*:

﴿ ٱللَّهُ نَزَّلَ أَحْسَنَ ٱلْحَدِيثِ كِتَٰبًا مُّتَشَٰبِهًا مَّثَانِىَ تَقْشَعِرُّ مِنْهُ
جُلُودُ ٱلَّذِينَ يَخْشَوْنَ رَبَّهُمْ ۝٢٣ ﴾

God has revealed the best announcement, a book mutashābih *in its various parts, repeating, whereat do shudder the skins of those who fear their Lord.* (Al-Zumar, 39:23)

Although these verses may initially seem contradictory, this is not the case at all. With the aid of these and other verses, we will discuss in this chapter, the meanings of these two terms and their important role in the Qur'an.

10.1 - LEXICAL MEANINGS OF *MUḤKAM* AND *MUTASHĀBIH*

Muḥkam is derived from the root (*ḥ-k-m*), whose original meaning is to forbid or prevent. Words deriving from this root carry a meaning of steadfastness and resistance against any external influence. For example, *ḥikma* (wisdom) refers to that kind of knowledge that prevents ignorance, *ḥukm* (rule) means that kind of authority that forestalls disobedience, etc. Therefore, *muḥkam* denotes a kind of firmness that does not allow an external force to undermine it.[1]

Mutashābih is derived from the root (*sh-b-h*), which means "resembling" or "indistinguishable". For example, the Qur'an mentions that the fruits of heaven will be similar to the fruit of this world (although the taste and nutritional content will be very different):

﴿ كُلَّمَا رُزِقُوا۟ مِنْهَا مِن ثَمَرَةٍ رِّزْقًا قَالُوا۟ هَـٰذَا ٱلَّذِى رُزِقْنَا مِن قَبْلُ وَأُتُوا۟ بِهِۦ مُتَشَـٰبِهًا ﴾

Whenever they shall be given a portion of the fruit thereof, they shall say: This is what was given to us before; and they shall be given the like (mutashābih) *of it.*
(Al-Baqara, 2:25)

Therefore, *mutashābih* refers to two things which resemble each other. It is also used to refer to something that cannot be immediately distinguished as different from something else.[2]

Maʿrifat adds:

> In indefinite verses, the *tashābuh* (resemblance) is between truth and falsehood itself. This resemblance both obscures the true meaning, as well as makes the verse equivocal. In the case of definite verses, *tafsīr* (exegesis) reveals the meaning, but in the case of the indefinite verses, their true meaning can only be understood by resorting to both *tafsīr* and *ta'wīl* (figurative interpretation).[3]

Based on these definitions, in the context of the Qur'anic sciences, the term *muḥkam* denotes a verse whose meaning is clear and definite, while *mutashābih* indicates a verse whose import is not immediately clear; it is indefinite.

10.2 - THE TERM *MUḤKAM* IN THE QUR'AN.

The term *muḥkam* appears in two meanings in the Qur'an:

1. Verses whose meanings are definite and not open to dispute. In this context, the term *muḥkam* is contrasted against *mutashābih*, when it refers to a verse whose meaning is indefinite and equivocal:

﴿ هُوَ ٱلَّذِىٓ أَنزَلَ عَلَيْكَ ٱلْكِتَٰبَ مِنْهُ ءَايَٰتٌ مُّحْكَمَٰتٌ هُنَّ أُمُّ ٱلْكِتَٰبِ وَأُخَرُ مُتَشَٰبِهَٰتٌ ﴾

He it is Who has revealed the Book to you; some of its verses are definite, they are the basis of the Book, and others are indefinite. (Āli ʻImrān, 3:7)

2. Verses which are decisive and must be followed in deed and word. The term *muḥkam* has been used in this meaning in the verse:

﴿ كِتَٰبٌ أُحْكِمَتْ ءَايَٰتُهُۥ ثُمَّ فُصِّلَتْ مِن لَّدُنْ حَكِيمٍ خَبِيرٍ ﴿١﴾ ﴾

(This is) a Book, whose verses are made decisive, then are they made plain, from the Wise, All-aware. (Hūd, 11:1)

This second meaning of *muḥkam* embraces all the verses of the Qur'an.

10.3 - THE TERM *MUTASHĀBIH* IN THE QUR'AN

The term *mutashābih* has been used in the Qur'an with two meanings:[4]

1. Verses that resemble and conform to each other in their manner and effect:

﴿ ٱللَّهُ نَزَّلَ أَحْسَنَ ٱلْحَدِيثِ كِتَٰبًا مُّتَشَٰبِهًا مَّثَانِىَ تَقْشَعِرُّ مِنْهُ جُلُودُ ٱلَّذِينَ يَخْشَوْنَ رَبَّهُمْ ﴾

God has revealed the best announcement, a book conformable in its various parts, repeating, whereat do shudder the skins of those who fear their Lord.
(Al-Zumar, 39:23)

In this verse, *mutashābih* refers to the coherence and lack of contradiction within the verses of the Qur'an.

2. The second meaning of *mutashābih* in the Qur'an is when one thing is indistinguishable from another thing, and its true nature is not easily discerned, as in the verse:

﴿ إِنَّ ٱلْبَقَرَ تَشَٰبَهَ عَلَيْنَا ﴾

For surely to us the cows are all alike. (Al-Baqara, 2:70)

In this verse, the Banī Isrā'īl were saying that they could not distinguish one cow from another.

It is with the same meaning that *mutashābih* has been used in the following verse:

﴿ هُوَ ٱلَّذِىٓ أَنزَلَ عَلَيْكَ ٱلْكِتَٰبَ مِنْهُ ءَايَٰتٌ مُّحْكَمَٰتٌ هُنَّ أُمُّ ٱلْكِتَٰبِ وَأُخَرُ مُتَشَٰبِهَٰتٌ ﴾

He it is Who has revealed the Book to you; some of its verses are definite, they are the basis of the Book, and others are indefinite. (Āli ʿImrān, 3:7)

The lack of clarity of the indefinite verses stems from the fact that within them, the truth is hidden. However, those who do not know where and from whom to acquire this truth, and whose hearts are perverse, choose to interpret these verses to suit themselves, in an attempt to mislead:

﴿ فَأَمَّا ٱلَّذِينَ فِى قُلُوبِهِمْ زَيْغٌ فَيَتَّبِعُونَ مَا تَشَٰبَهَ مِنْهُ ٱبْتِغَآءَ ٱلْفِتْنَةِ وَٱبْتِغَآءَ تَأْوِيلِهِۦ ﴾

Then as for those in whose hearts there is perversity, they follow the part of it which is indefinite, seeking to mislead and seeking to give it (their own) interpretation.
(Āli ʿImrān, 3:7)

The true import and interpretation of these words is known only to God, Who may give this knowledge to "those firmly rooted in knowledge":

﴿ وَمَا يَعْلَمُ تَأْوِيلَهُۥٓ إِلَّا ٱللَّهُ ۗ وَٱلرَّٰسِخُونَ فِى ٱلْعِلْمِ يَقُولُونَ ءَامَنَّا
بِهِۦ كُلٌّ مِّنْ عِندِ رَبِّنَا ۗ وَمَا يَذَّكَّرُ إِلَّآ أُو۟لُوا۟ ٱلْأَلْبَٰبِ ٧ ﴾

But none knows its interpretation except God, and those who are firmly rooted in knowledge, they say: We believe in it, it is all from our Lord; and none do mind except those having understanding. (Āli ʿImrān, 3:7)

10.4 - QUALITIES OF THE DEFINITE AND INDEFINITE VERSES

The exegetes have various opinions about the definitions of the definite and indefinite verses. In this section we will mention some of the commonly cited features of the two.

DEFINITE VERSES:

1. The definite verses can be understood without any external support. For example, it has been narrated from Ibn ʿAbbās that an example of a definite verse is the following: [5]

   ﴿ قُلْ تَعَالَوْا۟ أَتْلُ مَا حَرَّمَ رَبُّكُمْ عَلَيْكُمْ ۖ أَلَّا تُشْرِكُوا۟ بِهِۦ شَيْـًٔا ۖ
   وَبِٱلْوَٰلِدَيْنِ إِحْسَٰنًا ۖ وَلَا تَقْتُلُوٓا۟ أَوْلَٰدَكُم مِّنْ إِمْلَٰقٍ ۖ ﴾

   Say: Come I will recite what your Lord has forbidden to you; that you do not associate anything with Him, and show kindness to your parents, and do not slay your children for (fear of) poverty. (Al-Anʿām, 6:151)

2. The definite verses have a single obvious meaning and the scholars have no difference of opinion about it.

3. The definite verses are those that have not been abrogated by other verses (*ghayr al-mansūkh*). In fact, some scholars are of the opinion that the definite verses are the abrogating (*nāsikh*) ones.

4. The definite verses are those that discuss commands and

prohibitions, for example:

﴿ وَأَقِيمُوا۟ ٱلصَّلَوٰةَ وَءَاتُوا۟ ٱلزَّكَوٰةَ ﴾

And establish the prayer and pay the poor-rate. (Al-Baqara, 2:43, 83, 110, 177)

5. The definite verses are those relating the stories of the prophets عليهم السلام and the communities of the past.

6. The definite verses are those whose apparent meaning and exegesis (*tafsīr*) and inner reality (*ta'wīl*) are the same, and the listener understands a single meaning from it, for example:

﴿ لَيْسَ كَمِثْلِهِۦ شَىْءٌ ۖ ﴾

There is no likeness to Him. (Al-Shūrā, 42:11)

INDEFINITE VERSES:

1. The indefinite verses are those that describe the qualities, attributes and actions of God.

2. The indefinite verses are those that deal with stories, parables and hidden matters, such as the details of the day of judgement and the hereafter.

3. The indefinite verses are those that cannot be acted upon because they have been abrogated (*mansūkh*).

4. The indefinite verses are the unconnected letters that appear at the head of some of the chapters.

5. The indefinite verses only need to be believed in, not understood.

6. The indefinite verses are those whose literal meanings are not implied.

7. The indefinite verses are those that have multiple meanings, some

of which are not immediately apparent and so require further explanation and commentary. Hence, there is a difference of opinion amongst the scholars about their true meaning.

8. The indefinite verses are those whose true meanings cannot be understood, except by God, as its real significance cannot be encompassed by the human intellect.

COMMENTS ABOUT THE QUALITIES STATED ABOVE

Ṭabāṭabā'ī has collected these opinions and discussed them at some length.[6] A summary of his critique of these definitions is presented below:

1. The definition that abrogated verses are indefinite and abrogating verses are definite, is problematic, because many verses of the Qur'an are neither abrogating nor abrogated, and we know from the following verse that there can be no third category:

﴿ هُوَ ٱلَّذِىٓ أَنزَلَ عَلَيۡكَ ٱلۡكِتَٰبَ مِنۡهُ ءَايَٰتٌ مُّحۡكَمَٰتٌ هُنَّ أُمُّ ٱلۡكِتَٰبِ وَأُخَرُ مُتَشَٰبِهَٰتٌ ﴾

He it is Who has revealed the Book to you; some of its verses are definite, they are the basis of the Book, and others are indefinite. (Āli ʿImrān, 3:7)

2. Some of the definitions have no basis or proof, for example, that the definite verses deal with stories of the prophets ﷺ and the past communities.

3. Many of the definitions are only partial, for example, that the indefinite verses deal with qualities of God, or that they deal with the day of judgement.

4. Some of the definitions are repetitive, for example, that the indefinite verses are vague, or that they have hidden meanings, or have multiple meanings, or their literal meanings are not implied and so on.

5. Also, if the indefinite verses can only be understood by God, why place them in the Qur'an, which is a clear guide for mankind and a criterion to judge between good and evil:

﴿ هُدًى لِّلنَّاسِ وَبَيِّنَٰتٍ مِّنَ ٱلْهُدَىٰ وَٱلْفُرْقَانِ ﴾

(The Qur'an is) a guidance for man and a clear guide and criterion. (Al-Baqara, 2:185)

Therefore, it is necessary to come up with a better and more comprehensive definition of what is meant by definite and indefinite verses. Possibly the best and most comprehensive definition is the same as that given by Ṭabāṭabā'ī, a summary of which is given below:

> The definite (*muḥkam*) verses are those whose purport is firm and decisive; and their meaning cannot be mistaken. In contrast, indefinite (*mutashābih*) verses can have several possible meanings, which may be similar to each other. In other words, the true meaning of a definite verse is understood immediately by the listener, while the true meaning of an indefinite verse is not grasped immediately by the listener.
>
> Since their true meaning is not immediately apparent, these verses must be referred back to the definite verses in order to understand their correct meaning. Then, when its meaning is understood, these verses also become definite (*muḥkam*).[7]

10.5 - INDEFINITE VERSES AND HOW THEY SHOULD BE UNDERSTOOD

As we have mentioned, the indefinite verses have to be referred back to the definite verses in order to remove the vagueness from them, and in the process, turn them also into definite verses. This is the course described in the verse:

﴿ كِتَٰبٌ أُحْكِمَتْ ءَايَٰتُهُۥ ثُمَّ فُصِّلَتْ ﴾

(This is) a Book, whose verses are made decisive, then are they made plain. (Hūd, 11:1)

Some examples of indefinite verses are given below:

1. VERSES THAT SUGGEST ANTHROPOMORPHISM

There are several verses where God ascribes limbs to Himself, such as:

EYE AND EYES

To Mūsā ﵇, God says:

﴿ وَلِتُصْنَعَ عَلَىٰ عَيْنِىٓ ﴾

And that you might be brought up before My eye. (Ṭā-Hā, 20:39)

And to Nūh ﵇, He says:

﴿ وَٱصْنَعِ ٱلْفُلْكَ بِأَعْيُنِنَا ﴾

And make the ark before Our Eyes. (Hūd, 11:37)

HAND AND HANDS

At the time of the Pledge of Riḍwān, God revealed to the Muslims:

﴿ إِنَّ ٱلَّذِينَ يُبَايِعُونَكَ إِنَّمَا يُبَايِعُونَ ٱللَّهَ يَدُ ٱللَّهِ فَوْقَ أَيْدِيهِمْ ۚ ﴾

Surely those who swear allegiance to you do but swear allegiance to God; the Hand of God is above their hands. (Al-Fatḥ, 48:10)

And about the slander of the Jews, God says:

﴿ وَقَالَتِ ٱلْيَهُودُ يَدُ ٱللَّهِ مَغْلُولَةٌ ۚ غُلَّتْ أَيْدِيهِمْ وَلُعِنُوا۟ بِمَا قَالُوا۟ ۘ
بَلْ يَدَاهُ مَبْسُوطَتَانِ يُنفِقُ كَيْفَ يَشَآءُ ۚ ﴾

And the Jews say: The Hand of God is tied up! Their hands shall be shackled and they shall be cursed for what they say. Nay, both His Hands are spread out, He expends as He pleases. (Al-Mā'ida, 5:65)

COUNTENANCE

﴿ وَلِلَّهِ ٱلْمَشْرِقُ وَٱلْمَغْرِبُ ۚ فَأَيْنَمَا تُوَلُّوا۟ فَثَمَّ وَجْهُ ٱللَّهِ ۚ ﴾

And God's is the East and the West, so, wherever you turn, there is God's Countenance. (Al-Baqara, 2:115)

All these verses remain indefinite until they are referred to the definite verse,

﴿ لَيۡسَ كَمِثۡلِهِۦ شَيۡءٞۖ ﴾

Nothing is like a likeness of Him. (Al-Shūrā, 42:11)

and then, we understand that the eyes, hands and countenance of God cannot be limbs like ours – since there is no likeness of Him. These words are metaphors for the presence, power and pleasure of God.

Some commentators have literally translated these terms, for example, some early Ashʿarī scholars who subscribe to the notion of anthropomorphism; but even they would have surely had difficulty explaining the disappearance of His hands in the following verse!

﴿ لَآ إِلَٰهَ إِلَّا هُوَۚ كُلُّ شَيۡءٍ هَالِكٌ إِلَّا وَجۡهَهُۥۚ ﴾

There is no god but He, everything will perish but His Countenance. (Al-Qaṣaṣ, 28:88)

2. VERSES THAT MENTION THE PHYSICAL PRESENCE OF GOD

﴿ وَجَآءَ رَبُّكَ وَٱلۡمَلَكُ صَفّٗا صَفّٗا ﴾

And your Lord will come and (also) the angels in ranks. (Al-Fajr, 89:22)

﴿ هَلۡ يَنظُرُونَ إِلَّآ أَن يَأۡتِيَهُمُ ٱللَّهُ فِي ظُلَلٖ مِّنَ ٱلۡغَمَامِ وَٱلۡمَلَٰٓئِكَةُ ﴾

They do not wait aught but that God should come to them in the shadows of the clouds along with the angels. (Al-Baqara, 2:210)

These verses are also misunderstood to mean that God will somehow appear on the Day of Judgement to greet the believers. However, when compared with the verse that describes how God destroyed the plot of the Jews to kill the Prophet ﷺ, it becomes immediately clear that the "coming" of God refers to the manifestation of His Glory and Power:

﴿ وَظَنُّوٓا۟ أَنَّهُم مَّانِعَتُهُمْ حُصُونُهُم مِّنَ ٱللَّهِ فَأَتَىٰهُمُ ٱللَّهُ مِنْ حَيْثُ لَمْ يَحْتَسِبُوا۟ ۖ وَقَذَفَ فِى قُلُوبِهِمُ ٱلرُّعْبَ ۚ ﴾

They were certain that their fortresses would defend them against God; but God came to them whence they did not expect, and cast terror into their hearts. (Al-Ḥashr, 59:2)

ANOTHER EXAMPLE

﴿ وُجُوهٌ يَوْمَئِذٍ نَّاضِرَةٌ ﴿٢٢﴾ إِلَىٰ رَبِّهَا نَاظِرَةٌ ﴿٢٣﴾ ﴾

(Some) faces on that day shall be bright; looking to their Lord. (Al-Qiyāma, 75:22,23)

This verse is understood better when we study the verse where God says to Mūsā ﵇:

﴿ قَالَ رَبِّ أَرِنِىٓ أَنظُرْ إِلَيْكَ ۚ قَالَ لَن تَرَىٰنِى ﴾

He [Mūsā] said: My Lord! show me [Yourself], so that I may look upon You. He said: You cannot see Me. (Al-Aʿrāf, 7:143)

Here the Prophet ﵇ may be asking for the manifestation that could only be perceived in the next world. Indeed, in attempting to explain this verse the Ashʿarīs claim that the verse refers to this world only.[8] However, the "looking" at God, by the successful believers on the day of judgement is clearly different from the vision of the eyes, because a definite verses tell us:

﴿ لَّا تُدْرِكُهُ ٱلْأَبْصَٰرُ ﴾

The eyes cannot perceive Him. (Al-Anʿām, 6:103)

Therefore, the correct meaning of "looking" at God, is the perception of His presence by the hearts, and not the physical eyes.

10.6 - THE DANGER OF FOLLOWING THE INDEFINITE VERSES

The Qur'an warns:

﴿ فَأَمَّا ٱلَّذِينَ فِي قُلُوبِهِمْ زَيْغٌ فَيَتَّبِعُونَ مَا تَشَٰبَهَ مِنْهُ ٱبْتِغَآءَ ٱلْفِتْنَةِ وَٱبْتِغَآءَ تَأْوِيلِهِۦ ﴾

Then as for those in whose hearts there is perversity, they follow the part of it which is indefinite, seeking to mislead and seeking to give it (their own) interpretation.
(Āli ʿImrān, 3:7)

When we reflect over the sectarian beliefs and schisms that have splintered the Muslim community ever since the moment the Prophet ﷺ left this world, and try to discover the cause of the differences in matters of belief and law, we will find that most of them have resulted from following the indefinite verses and from seeking to interpret them without returning the verses to the definite verses.

As Ṭabāṭabāʾī succinctly summarises:

> Every sect proves its beliefs from the Qurʾanic verses. A party finds in it evidence that God has a body; a group proves from it that man has no free-will concerning his actions, while another faction tries to show that man is totally independent of God in this respect; some people argue that the prophets ﷺ committed mistakes and sins, and they quote verses in their support; a group says, and proves it from the Qurʾan, that God is so sublime that even "Divine Attributes" should not be attributed to Him, while another faction says, and also proves it from the Qurʾan, that God is just like His creatures and His attributes are separate from His Person. And so on and so forth. All this is a result of following the indefinite verses without "returning" them to the definite, decisive ones.[9]

10.7 - THE WISDOM OF HAVING INDEFINITE VERSES IN THE QUR'AN

The Qurʾan is a book of guidance and illumination for all mankind, and it states:

﴿ هُدًى لِّلنَّاسِ وَبَيِّنَٰتٍ مِّنَ ٱلْهُدَىٰ وَٱلْفُرْقَانِ ﴾

(The Qurʾan is) a guidance to men and clear proofs of the guidance and the distinction.
(Al-Baqara, 2:185)

Therefore, the question arises; why does the Qurʾan contain verses that are not immediately clear in their meaning? There are several possible answers:

1. While the Qur'an has been sent for all mankind, and for all time, the capacity and understanding of every individual is not the same. Accordingly, the Qur'an needs to employ a style that caters for the entire spectrum of its audience, and this can only be done through the use of metaphors and similes.[10]

2. Man has been given intellect by God so that he may attain perfection by understanding his own nature and through the guidance of God. The Qur'an invites man to exercise this intellect by presenting the challenge of the indefinite verses and urging him to ponder on them.[11]

3. The presence of the indefinite verses obliges the ordinary Muslim to refer to the righteous scholars and sources to learn what the Qur'an means by these verses.[12]

4. Man cannot understand realities outside his own experience. Therefore, to explain these realities, terminologies need to be employed which he can relate to and understand. Therefore, we find that the verses of the Qur'an which discuss non-materialistic and abstract matters – such as the attributes of God, heaven and hell, etc. – are usually indefinite. This last explanation is probably the most accurate one.

CONCLUSION

To best understand the meanings of the verses of the Qur'an, we need to distinguish those verses that are definite from those that are indefinite. By understanding the definite verses, we can then refer the indefinite verses to them, so that they too, can become definite verses. This is best possible through "the exegesis of the Qur'an by the Qur'an".

We will conclude this chapter with the thoughts of the contemporary scholar Jawādī Āmulī on this matter. He says:

If all of mankind had the insight of the Prophet ﷺ, they would find no indefinite verses in the Qur'an. However, due to the varying capacity, intellect and understanding of the people, the possibility of indefinite verses has arisen. The whole concept under discussion can be understood by considering the parable set out in the verse:

﴿ أَنزَلَ مِنَ ٱلسَّمَآءِ مَآءً فَسَالَتْ أَوْدِيَةٌۢ بِقَدَرِهَا فَٱحْتَمَلَ ٱلسَّيْلُ زَبَدًا رَّابِيًا ۚ وَمِمَّا يُوقِدُونَ عَلَيْهِ فِى ٱلنَّارِ ٱبْتِغَآءَ حِلْيَةٍ أَوْ مَتَٰعٍ زَبَدٌ مِّثْلُهُۥ ۚ كَذَٰلِكَ يَضْرِبُ ٱللَّهُ ٱلْحَقَّ وَٱلْبَٰطِلَ ۚ فَأَمَّا ٱلزَّبَدُ فَيَذْهَبُ جُفَآءً ۖ وَأَمَّا مَا يَنفَعُ ٱلنَّاسَ فَيَمْكُثُ فِى ٱلْأَرْضِ ۚ كَذَٰلِكَ يَضْرِبُ ٱللَّهُ ٱلْأَمْثَالَ ﴾

He sends down water from the cloud, then watercourses flow (with water) according to their measure, and the torrent bears along the swelling foam, and from what they melt in the fire for the sake of making ornaments or apparatus arises a scum like it; thus does God compare truth and falsehood; then as for the scum, it passes away as a worthless thing; and as for that which profits the people, it tarries in the earth; thus does God set forth parables. (Al-Ra'd, 13:17)

In this thought-provoking verse, several interesting points emerge. The drops of rain in themselves contain no impurity, and if they were captured in a pure vessel, they would remain in a pure state. Similarly, the verses of the Qur'an were revealed containing distinctive truths and there was no vagueness or possibility of falsehood about them, when they were contained in the heart of the Prophet ﷺ.

It is only when the rain becomes part of the watercourses that flow on the unclean land that the scum appears. Similarly, when the Qur'an is exposed to hearts and minds that are not pure and pristine, the possibility of unclearness in its verses arises.

Each valley and plain takes water according to its capacity – and the scum passes away, leaving the original goodness behind. In the same way, the people absorb of the teachings of the Qur'an according to their capacity. The indefinite verses are part of the same Qur'an and their vagueness can be easily dispelled by looking to the definite verses.

In this process, recourse to those who are "firmly established in knowledge" is vital, if the correct interpretation of the indefinite verses is to be found."[13]

10.8 - INTERPRETATION (*TA'WĪL*)

When mentioning the indefinite verses, God states that their "*ta'wīl*" is only known to Him. In this section we will take a closer look at this term and its usage in the Qur'an.

In the past, the term *ta'wīl* was used interchangeably with *tafsīr* or exegesis. For example, Ṭabarī named his commentary of the Qur'an, "*Jāmiʿ al-Bayān ʿan Ta'wīl Āy al-Qur'an*" – ("*A Comprehensive Discourse on the Ta'wīl of the Verses of the Qur'an*") – and often, while mentioning the *tafsīr* of a verse, he has used the phrase, "the report about the *ta'wīl* of this verse is...".

The early scholars and exegetes argued that the Qur'an itself has used both *tafsīr* and *ta'wīl* in the sense of exposition and elucidation, quoting the following two verses:

﴿وَلَا يَأْتُونَكَ بِمَثَلٍ إِلَّا جِئْنَاكَ بِالْحَقِّ وَأَحْسَنَ تَفْسِيرًا ﴿٣٣﴾﴾

And they shall not bring to you any argument, but We have brought to you (one) with truth and best in significance (tafsīr). (Al-Furqān, 25:33)

﴿وَمَا يَعْلَمُ تَأْوِيلَهُ إِلَّا اللَّهُ وَالرَّاسِخُونَ فِي الْعِلْمِ﴾

But none knows its interpretation (ta'wīl) *except God, and those who are firmly rooted in knowledge.* (Āli ʿImrān, 3:7)

However, in time, *ta'wīl* acquired a specialised meaning, distinct from *tafsīr*. The term *tafsīr* was used when referring to the explanation of the words and concepts in a verse, while *ta'wīl* was used when referring to the esoteric or profound interpretation of a verse whose apparent meaning was doubtful and unclear.

In other words, for *tafsīr*, the verse itself contains the material necessary to understand the text, while in *ta'wīl*, the verse is only fully understood by acquiring information from an external source.

1. DEFINITIONS OF *TA'WĪL*

Ta'wīl is derived from the root (*a-w-l*) which means "to return to the origin". The *ta'wīl* of a matter is to return it to its original place or meaning. Therefore, the *ta'wīl* of an unclear word is to consider its apparent meaning as one that alludes and leads to its real and original meaning.[14]

Some have held *ta'wīl* to mean the interpretation of the indefinite verses of the Qur'an (*mutashābihāt*), and the finding of a second meaning for the text which is its inward or esoteric sense (*bāṭin*), as opposed to its apparent and literal meaning (*ẓāhir*).[15] In this latter sense, both types of verse have *ta'wīl*.

Some scholars have said that *ta'wīl* means to "take a matter to its final interpretation".[16]

2. THE OCCURRENCE OF THE TERM *TA'WĪL* IN THE QUR'AN

The word *ta'wīl* has occurred 17 times in the Qur'an and can be broadly grouped into three meanings:[17]

1. Four times in the sense of interpreting unusual speech or behaviour:

These occur in 3:7 (twice), 18:78 and 18:82. An example of this usage is when the sage Khizr says to Mūsā عليه السلام:

﴿ قَالَ هَٰذَا فِرَاقُ بَيْنِي وَبَيْنِكَ ۚ سَأُنَبِّئُكَ بِتَأْوِيلِ مَا لَمْ تَسْتَطِع عَّلَيْهِ صَبْرًا ﴿٧٨﴾ ﴾

He said: This shall be separation between me and you; now I will inform you of the interpretation of that with which you could not have patience. (Al-Kahf, 18:78)

2. Eight times in the sense of interpreting dreams:

All of these occurrences are in Yusūf, 12:6, 12:21, 12:36, 12:37, 12:44, 12:45, 12:100 and 12:101. An example of this meaning is the verse:

﴿ قَالَ أَحَدُهُمَآ إِنِّيٓ أَرَىٰنِيٓ أَعْصِرُ خَمْرًا ۖ وَقَالَ ٱلْـَٔاخَرُ إِنِّيٓ أَرَىٰنِيٓ أَحْمِلُ فَوْقَ
رَأْسِى خُبْزًا تَأْكُلُ ٱلطَّيْرُ مِنْهُ ۖ نَبِّئْنَا بِتَأْوِيلِهِۦٓ ۖ إِنَّا نَرَىٰكَ مِنَ ٱلْمُحْسِنِينَ ﴿٣٦﴾ ﴾

One of them said: I saw myself pressing wine. And the other said: I saw myself carrying bread on my head, of which birds ate. Inform us of its interpretation; surely we see you to be of the doers of good. (Yūsuf, 12:36)

3. Five times in the sense of the ultimate outcome and interpretation of events:

These occur in 4:59, 17:35, 7:35 (twice) and 10:39, for example:

﴿ بَلْ كَذَّبُوا۟ بِمَا لَمْ يُحِيطُوا۟ بِعِلْمِهِۦ وَلَمَّا يَأْتِهِمْ تَأْوِيلُهُۥ ﴾

Nay, they reject that of which they have no comprehensive knowledge, and the final interpretation of it has not yet come to them. (Yūnus, 10:39)

3. IS THE *TA'WĪL* OF THE QUR'AN KNOWN TO ANYONE BUT GOD?

The verse that is usually the subject of the discussion about *ta'wīl* is:

﴿ هُوَ ٱلَّذِىٓ أَنزَلَ عَلَيْكَ ٱلْكِتَـٰبَ مِنْهُ ءَايَـٰتٌ مُّحْكَمَـٰتٌ هُنَّ أُمُّ ٱلْكِتَـٰبِ وَأُخَرُ مُتَشَـٰبِهَـٰتٌ ۖ فَأَمَّا ٱلَّذِينَ فِى قُلُوبِهِمْ زَيْغٌ فَيَتَّبِعُونَ مَا تَشَـٰبَهَ مِنْهُ ٱبْتِغَآءَ ٱلْفِتْنَةِ وَٱبْتِغَآءَ تَأْوِيلِهِۦ ۗ وَمَا يَعْلَمُ تَأْوِيلَهُۥٓ إِلَّا ٱللَّهُ ۗ وَٱلرَّٰسِخُونَ فِى ٱلْعِلْمِ يَقُولُونَ ءَامَنَّا بِهِۦ كُلٌّ مِّنْ عِندِ رَبِّنَا ۗ وَمَا يَذَّكَّرُ إِلَّآ أُو۟لُوا۟ ٱلْأَلْبَـٰبِ ﴾

He it is Who has revealed the Book to you; some of its verses are definite, they are the basis of the Book, and others are indefinite; then as for those in whose hearts there is perversity they follow the part of it which is indefinite, seeking to mislead and seeking to give it (their own) interpretation; but none knows its interpretation (ta'wīl) *except God, and those who are firmly rooted in knowledge. They say: We believe in it, it is all from our Lord; and none do mind except those having understanding.*

About the issue of the reading of the verse, there are three views.

I. THE READING WITH THE HALT AT THE *WAW* (*WAW AL-WAQF* OR *WAW AL-FAṢL*)

One group says that after the phrase, "except God", there is a stop. They read the verse as follows: "none knows its *ta'wīl* except God."

This groups includes Ṭabarī, Al-Suyūṭī, Fakhr al-Din al-Rāzī and Qurtūbī. Accordingly, Pickthall translates this verse as:

> But those in whose hearts is doubt pursue, forsooth, that which is allegorical seeking (to cause) dissension by seeking to explain it. None knoweth its explanation save Allah. And those who are of sound instruction say: We believe there in; the whole is from our Lord."

Therefore the meaning will be that the real interpretation of the verses is only known to God.

II. THE READING WITH CONTINUATION AT THE *WAW* (*WAW AL-ʿATF* OR *WAW AL-WAṢL*)

Another group believes that the phrase continues to include those individuals who are "firmly rooted in knowledge" – *al-rāsikhūna fī al-ʿilm* – and they read it as follows: "none knows its *taʾwīl* except God and those who are firmly rooted in knowledge." This is the view of Zamakhsharī, Ṭabrisī, Ibn Abī al-Ḥadīd, Zarkashī (in *Al-Burhān*), Ālūsī, Muhammad ʿAbduh, and the Shīʿa scholars Ayyāshī, Kāshānī and Shubbar. Accordingly, Mīr Aḥmad ʿAlī translates the verse as:

> But those in whose hearts there is perversity, they are after that which is ambiguous therein seeking to interpret (to suit their selfish motives) while none knoweth its (hidden) interpretation except God and those firmly rooted in knowledge; say they: "We believe in it, all is from our Lord.".

It is narrated that Ibn ʿAbbās would engage in *taʾwīl*. One of the companions said to him, "None knows the interpretation of the Qurʾan except God." Ibn ʿAbbās replied, "And those who are firmly rooted in knowledge; and I am one of those who are firmly rooted in knowledge."[18]

The proponents of this second view cite the following arguments, amongst others:

1. There are verses in the Qurʾan which mention those who have a special knowledge and who know the inner meanings of the

Qur'an. Some examples are:

﴿ بَلْ هُوَ ءَايَـٰتٌۢ بَيِّنَـٰتٌ فِى صُدُورِ ٱلَّذِينَ أُوتُوا۟ ٱلْعِلْمَ ﴾

Nay, rather they are clear signs in the breasts of those who have been given knowledge.
(Al-ʿAnkabūt, 29:49)

﴿ فَسْـَٔلُوٓا۟ أَهْلَ ٱلذِّكْرِ إِن كُنتُمْ لَا تَعْلَمُونَ ﴾

Question the people of the Remembrance if you do not know.
(Al-Naḥl, 16:43, also Al-Anbiyā, 21:7)

﴿ وَلَوْ رَدُّوهُ إِلَى ٱلرَّسُولِ وَإِلَىٰٓ أُو۟لِى ٱلْأَمْرِ مِنْهُمْ لَعَلِمَهُ ٱلَّذِينَ يَسْتَنۢبِطُونَهُۥ مِنْهُمْ ﴾

If they had referred it to the Messenger and those in authority among them, those of them whose task it is to investigate would have known the matter.
(Al-Nisāʾ, 4:83)

2. The Qur'an is a book revealed by God for the guidance for the people. If its *taʾwīl* cannot be known even to the best of them, for example, the Prophet ﷺ himself, then it would contradict the repeated claim of the scripture that it is a clear Book, distinguishing between truth and falsehood. Moreover, the Divine command to contemplate on the verses and reflect upon their meanings is only a reasonable invitation if it be possible to understand them, even if the entire meaning is only accessible to a select few.

3. The context of the verse leads one to expect the *rāsikhūna fī al-ʿilm* to know the *taʾwīl* of the Qur'an rather than to be ignorant of it, because otherwise, their qualification of being well-grounded in knowledge would be pointless. This is because, many believers who lack learning but possess a sound faith also declare, "We believe, and all of it is from our Lord". Hence, Mujāhid has said, "If the only distinction of the *rāsikhūna fī al-ʿilm* is that they declare, 'we believe', then there is nothing wrong if others also make this declaration; and then there would be no difference between the *rāsikhūn* and others.

III. THE NEUTRAL VIEW

Some scholars are of the view that both recitations are acceptable. This is the view of Ṭūsī and more recently, Ṭabāṭabā'ī, the eminent Qur'anic scholar and author of *Tafsīr al-Mīzān,* whose views are summarised below:

The verse 3:7 restricts the knowledge of *ta'wīl* to God; however, it does not mean that He does not teach it to others. In fact, it is similar to the issue of the knowledge of the unseen (*'ilm al-ghayb*), which God attributes to Himself, but does divulge to His special servants, as we see on comparing the following two verses:

﴿ قُل لَّا يَعْلَمُ مَن فِي ٱلسَّمَٰوَٰتِ وَٱلْأَرْضِ ٱلْغَيْبَ إِلَّا ٱللَّهُ ﴾

Say: No one in the heavens and the earth knows the unseen except God. (Al-Naml, 27:65)

﴿ عَٰلِمُ ٱلْغَيْبِ فَلَا يُظْهِرُ عَلَىٰ غَيْبِهِۦٓ أَحَدًا ۝٢٦ إِلَّا مَنِ ٱرْتَضَىٰ مِن رَّسُولٍ ﴾

The Knower of the unseen! So He does not reveal His secrets to any, except to him whom He chooses as a messenger. (Al-Jinn, 72:26, 27)

Therefore, despite the apparent restriction in the first verse, the second verse mentions that the prophets ﷺ are taught this information.[19]

The verse 3:7 wants to say that the Book is divided into two categories – the definite (*muḥkam*) and the indefinite (*mutashābih*) – and also the people are of two types: there is a group which, because of perversity of hearts, seeks to follow the indefinite verses; and there is another group that is firmly rooted in knowledge and therefore follows the definite verses and believes in the indefinite ones. It is clear, in this light, that the phrase, "those who are firmly rooted in knowledge", is used here primarily to describe their good faith and behaviour with respect to the Qur'an, and to extol their virtue in contrast to those in whose hearts there is perversity. The phrase aims at nothing else. Ṭabāṭabā'ī's concluding statement is:

> Interpretation is that reality to which a verse refers; it is found in all verses, the decisive and the ambiguous alike; it is not a sort of a meaning of the word; it is a

real fact that is too sublime for words; Allah has dressed it with words so as to bring it a bit nearer to our minds; in this respect they (these truths) are like proverbs that are used to create a picture in the mind, and thus help the hearer to clearly grasp the intended idea. That is why Allah has said: (I swear) *by the Book that makes manifest* (the truth); *surely We have made it an Arabic Qur'an, so that you may understand. And surely it is in the original of the Book with Us, truly elevated, full of wisdom* (43:2-4). And this matter has been explicitly and implicitly mentioned in several Qur'anic verses. [20]

NOTES

[1] Ibn al-Fārs, *Mu'jam Muqāyīs al-Lūgha,* p. 90.
[2] Ibn al-Manṣūr, *Lisān al-'Arab,* vol. 13, p. 503.
[3] *'Ulūm-e -Quranī,* p. 272.
[4] Ibid., p. 274.
[5] Ṭūsī, *Al-Tibyān,* vol. 3, p. 394.
[6] *Al-Mīzān,* vol. 3, pp. 31-42.
[7] Ibid., p. 36.
[8] Al-Rāḍī, *Tafsīr al-Kabīr,* exegesis of the verse 6/103.
[9] *Al-Mīzān,* vol. 3, pp 33-36.
[10] Ibid., p. 119.
[11] *'Ulūm al-Qur'an 'inda al-Mufassirūn,* quoting Ṭūsī, vol. 3, p.114.
[12] Ibid.
[13] Āmulī, *Qur'an dar Qur'an,* vol. 1, p. 417.
[14] Hādī Ma'rifat, *Tafsīr wa Mufassirān,* vol.1, p. 23.
[15] Ibid.
[16] *Majma' al-Bayān.*
[17] *Tafsīr wa Mufassirān,* vol.1, p.24.
[18] Ibn Abī al-Ḥadīd, *Sharḥ Nahj al-Balāgha,* vol. 6, p. 404.
[19] For further examples of verses that restrict the knowledge of the unseen to God, see Yūnus, 10/20 and Al-An'ām, 6/59.
[20] *Al-Mīzān,* vol. 3, p. 62.